Ichbunde Musikfreund
30 Chrypte 1999

Warrant for
GENOCIDE

Vahakn N. Dadrian

Warrant for
GENOCIDE

Key Elements of
Turko-Armenian
Conflict

Transaction Publishers
New Brunswick (U.S.A.) and London (U.K.)

Library of Congress Catalog Number: 98-46214
ISBN: 1-56000-389-8
Printed in the United States of America

Library of Congress Cataloging-in-Publication Data

Dadrian, Vahakn N.
Warrant for genocide : key elements of Turko-Armenian conflict / Vahakn N. Dadrian.
p. cm.
Includes bibliographical references (p.   ) and index.
ISBN 1-56000-389-8 (alk. paper)
1. Armenian massacres, 1915–1923. I. Title.
DS195.5.D337   1998
956.6'2015—dc21   98-46214
                                                                          CIP

As you know the [Armenian] deportations were an event that triggered a worldwide outcry and caused us to be regarded as murderers. Before embarking upon it we knew that the Christian world would not indulge us and would direct its full wrath and deep-seated enmity against us on account of it. Why have we then [opted for] appending to ourselves the label of murderers (*Neden katillik unvanını nefsimize izafe ettik*)? Why have we involved ourselves in such a grave and difficult conflict? We acted thusly simply to ensure the future of our fatherland that we consider to be dearer and more sacred to us than our own lives.

—From a speech delivered by Deputy Hasan Fehmi (Ataç) during the 17 October 1920 secret sitting of the fledgling Kemalist Parliament in Ankara, presided over by Mustafa Kemal (Atatürk) himself. Subsequently Atatürk appointed him finance minister, a position in which Hasan Fehmi faithfully served in the 24 April 1922–2 January 1925 period.

Source: *T.B.M.M. Gizli Celse Zabıtları* (The proceedings of the secret sessions of the Grand National Assembly of Turkey), vol. 1 (Ankara, 1985), p. 177. For an examination of Fehmi's unabashed defense of the economic objectives of the governmental scheme of the wartime Armenian genocide and his parallel postwar economic policies which as finance minister he instituted against the scant survivors of that genocide see Vahakn N. Dadrain "Genocide as a Problem of National and International Law: The World War I Armenian Case and Its Contemporary Legal Ramifications," *Yale Journal of International Law*, vol. 14, no. 2 (summer 1989), pp. 270–1.

From the Interior Ministry to the Diyarbekir Province:

It has been reported to us that the Armenians of the province of Diyarbekir, along with other Christians, are being massacred, and that some 700 Armenians and other Christians, were recently slaughtered in Mardin like sheep after having been removed from the city through nightly operations. The number of people thus far slain through such massacres is estimated to be 2,000. It is feared that unless these acts are stopped definitely and swiftly the Muslim population of the region too may proceed to massacre the general Christian population. *The political and disciplinary measures (tedâbiri inzibatiye ve siyasiye) adopted against the Armenians are absolutely not to be extended to other Christians as such acts are likely to create a very bad impression upon public opinion* [italics added]. You are ordered to put an immediate end to these acts lest they threaten the lives of the other Christians indiscriminately (*alel-itlâk Hıristiyanların hayatını tehdid edecek*). Keep us informed of the true state of the matter.

—[Interior] Minister [Talât], 29 June 1915

Source: T.C. Başbakanlık Devlet Genel Müdürlüğü. Osmanlı Arşivi Daire Başkanlığı (General Directorate of the State Archives. Prime Ministry of the Turkish Republic), *Osmanlı Belgelerinde Ermeniler, 1915–1920* (The Armenians in Ottoman Documents 1915–1920), (Ankara, 1994), doc. no. 71, p. 69.

Contents

Abbreviations

AA = *Auswärtiges Amt*. German Foreign Office Archives. Political Department 1A (Berlin: presently Bonn)

BA/MA = *Bundesarchiv/Militärarchiv*. The military archives of the German Federal Republic, Freiburg im Breisgau

Cong. Rec. = Congressional Record

DAA = Diplomatic Archives of Austria, nineteenth century

DAF = Diplomatic Archives of France, nineteenth century

DAG = Diplomatic Archives of Germany, nineteenth century

Doc. = Document

DZA = Deutsches Zentralarchiv: The archives of the former German Democratic Republic (East Germany), Potsdam

FO = British Foreign Office Archives

K = Botschaft Konstantinopel (German Consular Files)

N.S. = *Nouvelle Série*. French Foreign Ministry Archives (AMAE), Departments Turquie (Arménie) and Jeunes Turcs. Guerre: volumes 887–9, covering events relating to Armenia from August 1914 to May 1918 under the heading Turquie.

RG= *Record Group*, U.S. National archives, Papers Relating to the Foreign Relations of the U.S. 1915 Supplement. World War I

T.V. = *Takvimi Vekâyi*. Official gazette of the Ottoman government, whose special supplements covering the proceedings of the Extraordinary Turkish Military Tribunal served as a judicial gazette.

A note on the use of dual-track dates:

Because of the prevalence in the respective periods of the twentieth century of the thirteen-day differential (twelve-day for the nineteenth century) between the Ottoman calendar, otherwise called *rumi*, Julian , or old style (o.s.), and the European-Western calendar, otherwise called *miladi*, Gregorian, or new style (n.s.), both variants have been adduced in connection with the narration of certain specific events for which purpose parentheses have been used.

Introduction

The Proceedings of the 1919–20 Turkish Courts Martial were replete with indications that the World War I destruction of the Armenian people in the Ottoman Empire was neither an accident nor an aberration. The essence of a plan for large-scale deportations and massacres, developed by the leaders of the reigning Young Turk Ittihadist regime, was evident in the ensemble of documents marshaled by the Military Tribunal. The Tribunal's Key Indictment and Key Verdict served to highlight the components of that lethal plan; as part of the legal evidence both documents were published in the Ottoman government's gazette, the *Takvimi Vekâyi*, numbers 3540 and 3604, respectively. It needs to be emphasized here that all the verdicts of this Military Tribunal were, just like in the case of the Nuremberg Tribunal, nearly entirely predicated upon official Turkish documents. The authenticity of each one of these was certified by competent Interior Ministry officials with the notation "it conforms to the original." This fact is of paramount significance for the proper assessment of the value of the findings of this Court. One may discern four essential features in the conception, design, and implementation of that plan: (1) a xenophobic nationalism, nurtured by atavistic impulses of Turkism aiming at the elimination of the Armenians as a non-Turkic and discordant minority; (2) the resort to violence through the use of arms to achieve that end; (3) reliance on the potential of Islam to incite the masses against the targeted Christian Armenians, (despite the irreligious stance of most of the Ittihadist leaders); (4) the maintenance of the utmost secrecy of the scheme, to be safeguarded by camouflage and deflection. In other words, the leadership of Ittihad is revealed here as having engaged in careful deliberations leading to the adoption of a radical policy for the resolution of a historically lingering nationality conflict.

In their embryonic form the respective decisions and resolutions about this plan were framed unofficially, covertly, and outside the purview of the formal sessions of the 31 October–13 November 1910 Ittihad annual convention in Saloniki. They were prefigured, in broad outline, in a speech which the then Interior Minister Talât delivered at a secret

1

conclave of Ittihad leaders meeting in the same city on 6 August 1910. In this speech Talât is reported to have pronounced as no longer applicable the principle of equality for the subject non-Muslim nationalities of the Ottoman Empire, declaring it anathema to Islam.

This was a drastic departure by Ittihad from its publicly proclaimed posture of egalitarianism heralding the dawn of a new era of multiethnic harmony and accord in the decaying empire. Concomitantly, the radical wing of the party began to agitate for a shift from Ottomanism to Turkism. Led by such influential individuals as Ziya Gökalp and physician-politicians Nazım and Şakir, for example, the supreme directorate of the party, comprising select members of the General Assembly and the Central Committee, proceeded to adopt a new orientation regarding the treatment of the issue of nationalities; this meant recasting the Ottoman policy of nationalities. The ideal of Ottomanism was eventually declared bankrupt and ultimately discarded. With this *volte-face*, the ideals of brotherhood and equality for all Ottoman citizens, with which Ittihad had appeared on the political scene as a new revolutionary movement and in July 1908 had overthrown the Abdul Hamit regime with minimum bloodshed, were abruptly jettisoned. The advent of a new ideology of Turkism, which was basically exclusionary and had elements of territorial expansionism by virtue of its organic links to pan-Turkism and pan-Turanism, served to rekindle the enmities between dominant Turks and the subject minorities. For decades these enmities had afflicted the Ottoman Empire, especially in the era of Sultan Abdul Hamit. As a result, the Ottoman Empire's notorious nationalities problem began to deteriorate and assume once more the general character of chronic nationality conflicts. The 1912 Balkan war was the climax of a series of disasters that ensued and further aggravated the woes of the empire. The human, territorial, and material losses, not to speak of the attendant massive trauma engulfing the Turkish nation and its Ittihadist rulers, were phenomena that still haunt the memories of many Turks. Paradoxically, however, instead of undertaking policy modifications regarding the cumulative grievances of the residual nationalities and minorities of the truncated empire, the Ittihadist rulers became even more hardened in this respect. Now in complete control of the Central Committee of the party, the radical wing in 1913 initiated measures which led to a quasi party dictatorship. The opposition for all practical purposes was either neutralized or eliminated, and the ground was paved to introduce and implement a new and radical nationality policy, the primary target of which were the Armenians.

Thus, the lingering Turko-Armenian conflict was reactivated through the convergence of a series of events. In this development the 1912–13 Armenian efforts to renegotiate the issue of provincial reforms proved a catalyst for the emerging resolve of the Ittihadist leadership to punish the Armenians drastically so as to preclude any future troubles in this regard. That resolve for punishment was coterminous with a resolve for genocide. The act of genocide appears here as a draconian method of resolving a lingering conflict. Accordingly, it may be proposed that no analysis of the Armenian genocide can be adequate without grasping the origin, elements, evolution, and escalation of the Turko-Armenian conflict. In the final analysis the Armenian genocide is but a cataclysmic by-product of this very conflict.

What follows is a dissection and examination of the components of this conflict whose results are summarized, conceptualized and redefined in chapter 12.

Finally the interjection of two clarifications may be called for. First, the meaning of the term conflict that dominates the entire organization of this study is more or less clear. It usually denotes the idea of a clash of interests, goals or ambitions animating those locked in hostile opposition. But when applied to the arena of international relations its connotations may become subject to misinterpretations with regard to the respective roles of the opponents in the precipitation of the conflict. The Turko-Armenian conflict did not involve a parity of strengths. Broadly speaking, the distinctly weak, if not impotent, Armenians could neither dare nor afford mounting a challenge to the dominant Turks who for centuries had been enjoying an absolute monopoly of power of every kind in the Ottoman state system. The conflict unfolded because the abuses of that monopoly were assuming a degree of insufferable severity, as argued by the Armenians. Therefore, the conflict is seen here as a fatal by-product of counteractive Armenian efforts to obviate a peril considered to be existential. In this sense the conflict may be viewed as an instrument imposed by a powerful dominant group upon a resistant but highly vulnerable minority group targeted for eradication.

Secondly, the words "Ottoman" and "Turk" throughout this study have been used alternately—in keeping with the prevalent contemporary practice among many historians and diplomats, including those from Germany and Austro-Hungary, Ottoman Empire's wartime allies. A separation of the meaning of these two terms for present purposes is considered to be more of an etymological rather than a historical issue. The countless quotations originating from these authors and incorporated in this study do require the adoption of this method of alternation.

1

The Liabilities of Islam in a Multiethnic State Organization

Islamic Sacred Law and Ottoman Patterns of Domination

In a socio-legal perspective, one has to single out the theocratic origins and bearings of the Ottoman system as a principal matrix of the Turko-Armenian conflict. Central to that theocracy was the Islamic Sacred Law, and its implications for non-Muslims. In principle, that Law was held to be Allah's law, not to be tampered with by human intelligence trying to probe into it, but to be accepted without criticism. That law also mandated that one disregard its obvious inconsistencies and other inadequacies, for that law embodied a kind of wisdom which defies human logic and, except for minor questioning, inquiry. Labeled as *Şeriat*, "Revelation" (of the laws of God), it incorporates fixed doctrines of infallibility, prescribing duties relative to not only the religious, but the social, political, and private lives of the faithful; certain other prescriptions extend also to the lives of those not professing but ruled by Islam, provided that Islam is not thereby compromised. This Sacred Law is spelled out in *fikh*, the Islamic version of jurisprudence, comprising the text of the maxims of the Revelation, that is, *Koran,* of the Prophetic Traditions, *hadis*, including the authentic or alleged words (*ehadisin ebeviye*) and acts of the Prophet Mohammed (*fiili Peygamberi*), and the evolving Commentaries on meanings incorporated in the pertinent formulation of the *fikh* books (*kiyasi fukeha*).

The Sacred Law is devoid of strictly legal formulas or formal codes, in line with the axiom that such codification is beyond human competence. It therefore emerges as a type of juristic philosophy without a body of statute laws; an ethical rather than a legal compendium of norms. Notwithstanding its elements of inconsistency, vagueness, and occasional incomprehensibility, endemic to the other monotheistic religions

5

as well, (including Christianity), the Koran—the centerpiece of Islamic Sacred Law—is an edifice of canons intended to promote such individual virtues as piousness, charity, fidelity, and magnanimity, among others.

But, in two respects it proved disastrous for the Ottoman Empire, and especially for the subject minorities. In one respect its ethos was divisive and exclusionary, by virtue of which mankind was reduced largely to two antithetical categories, i.e., the Muslim believers, the adherents of "the true religion," *hak din*, and the rest of the world, mostly consisting of "infidels," i.e., people who betrayed God, meaning essentially Christians and Jews, but excluding or discounting "the idolaters." This dogma is explicitly stated in the Koran on a number of occasions (chapter 2, verse 3 and chapter 3, verse 17). Elsewhere it goes one step further to proclaim Islam "superior" to all other religions (chapter 9, verse 33). Indeed, reaching a high point in his claim of superiority, the Prophet declared in his address to the faithful: "Ye are the best nation that hath been raised up into mankind" (chapter 3, verse 106).

In itself this claim of "true"ness and "superiority," and its corollary, a missionary zeal, is not alien to the two other branches of monotheism. Combined with and reinforced by another element, however, Islam, as practiced in the multiethnic Ottoman Empire, became a caldron of disastrous conflicts and clashes, domestically as well as internationally. The reference is to the inexorably martial penchant of Islam that viewed the area's "infidel" nations as targets of conquest, destruction, and plunder, as expressed in the injunction: "O true believers wage war against such of the infidels as are near you; and let them find severity in you" (chapter 9, verse 124). The Koran has over 200 injunctions in this respect beckoning the faithful to sanguinary forays, *istila*, to be executed in the spirit of "holy war" *cihad*, and "by way of 'massacres'" *kıtal*, rarely without the argument that the targeted victims were guilty of one kind of "transgression" or another, and, therefore, deserving of punishment. On one occasion, the Prophet even contended that the destruction of the infidels was enacted with "God's permission" (chapter 3, verse 145). Though at one point he directed his main wrath against "the Jews and the idolaters" as "the most violent of all men in enmity against the believers," (chapter 5, verse 85), he repeatedly asserted that there was no difference "between any of them," meaning all non-Muslims (chapter 3, verse 78; chapter 5, verse 62). In the field of secular matters reaching beyond the boundaries of the Şeriat, non-Muslims were subject to "the will" of the Sovereign, who was also a Muslim Caliph, that is, successor to Mohammed, and a vicar of supreme authority. As such, he had spiritual supremacy and his enactment of edicts, the *kanuns*, precluded any idea of equality between Muslims and non-Muslims, as in the case of Süleyman I's *kanuni raia*.

It has been argued that some of the Prophet's injunctions were nevertheless such as to prohibit violence. However, many of them were subsequently canceled (*mensuh*). His command: "Let there be no compulsion in religion," *lia ikrahe fiddin* (chapter 2, verse 257) belongs to this category of injunctions. With changing times and changing circumstances the Prophet's posture changed as well with respect to the treatment of "the unbelievers." His bellicosity increased in proportion to his successes in the field of military operations against his enemies; toleration gave way to militancy that was as lethal as inexorable.

The Islamic Legal Pact and the Ottoman Deviation from It

From the very outset it is necessary to characterize as distinct, almost unique, the Ottoman-Turkish perception and application of Islam, particularly as it relates to the treatment of subject peoples. Despite the effort of Mahmud II (1808–39) to modify the practice of inequality by introducing the concept of secular justice, *adalet*, Ottoman regimes persisted in mishandling non-Muslim nationalities to a degree not indulged in by any other Islamic state in the last five centuries. The incidence of a select number of individual non-Muslims having been favored—one might add, in default, i.e., for lack of better alternatives—by these regimes in a variety of ways, including high level appointments in the royal household and the Civil List, was but an incidence that is best characterized as an aberration, born out of considerations of convenience and expedience.

This bent for persecution stemmed from a specific deviation from the norms of the Islamic Legal Pact, *Akdı Zimmet*, stipulating a host of "safeguards," *ismet*, for those "infidel" communities whose territories would become incorporated into the domain of the Islamic Sultan-Caliph. As a form of contract with the Ottoman sovereign ruler the pact is a reflection of a Koranic tenet guaranteeing a measure of security to the subjects who thereby are "entering into a treaty" with their new ruler, which actually meant submission and payment of tribute (chapter 9, verse 29), mainly in the form of a poll-tax (also called by some "humiliation tax,") and of a land tax (chapter 3, verse 108). This arrangement of linking protection with special taxation can be traced to

Selim I, the Grim (1512–1520), whose ulemas, the Muslim doctors of law, and their head, Şeyhulislam Cemali, prevented him from either destroying, or forcibly converting the multitudes of Christians falling under his domain following his 1514 victory at Çaldıran against the Persians. This, in spite of the fact that Selim is said to have destroyed tens of thousands of Shiite Muslims considered to be heretics by the Ottoman Sunnis, who regarded themselves as orthodox Muslims.

The tax arrangement was attributed to "an enormous amount of human cunning" by a historian who went on to explain: "If Greeks, Armenians, Christians, Syrians, and the numerous Jews had become Moslem they would have ceased to be subject to many forms of taxation and their conversion would have produced a crisis in the treasury."[1] This arrangement is highlighted by C. Max Kortepeter, who, in his analysis of Ottoman Imperialism illustrates that imperialism by reference to an Ottoman imperial symbol adduced in appendix 8 of his book. There it is stated in the format of a syllogism that: "1. The ruler cannot govern without troops; 2. He cannot muster troops without wealth; 3. It is the Ra'iyah (subjects) who produce the wealth."[2] Perhaps the most explicit proponent of the idea of utilizing the non-Muslims as a fiscal resource and, therefore, as a source of the empire's economic strength, was Sultan Murad IV (1623–40). He was firmly convinced that the *raias*, the non-Muslim subjects of the empire, should be cared for and nurtured (*raia-perverliği*). In a speech in 1632 he posed the question as to "how can we obtain the revenues of our Treasury if there are no *raias?*...We can, therefore, ill-afford to plunder and disperse them."[3] Yet, the principle of mutual economic benefit as part of a symbiotic relationship between dominant Muslims and non-Muslim subjects gradually eroded as the latter increasingly became objects of economic exploitation; the unrelenting character of that exploitation resulted in large scale emigrations on the part of the victim populations. The exactions of the poll-tax, for example, were, according to Hamilton Gibb, "the most striking, if not necessarily the most onerous, disability of the non-Muslims." The crippling effects of its several features were gradual and were exceeded only by the violent methods of exaction. Compounded by the ravages of incessant wars, these abuses led, as described below, to large-scale dislocations, and ultimately to cycles of emigration threatening to denude "the Armenian home-lands"[4] of their indigenous population. Government functionaries not only denied protection, especially in the era of Abdul Hamit, but on the contrary, they virtually granted a license to marauding, seminomadic Kurdish tribes whose feudal chieftains held Armenian as well as non-Armenian but Muslim peasants in bondage, and, in certain areas, in abject slavery. For the Armenians, however, the problem was accentuated by the denial to them of the right to carry arms in a land full of outlaws armed to the teeth. In brief, the Armenians were not only deprived of their right of governmental protection mandated by the Islamic Pact, but were deprived of the auxiliary right of self-protection in settings in which Muslims could and did arm themselves as a matter of normal practice. It is precisely for this reason that the plight of the Muslim peasants, whether Turkish, Kurdish, Circassian, or Turkomen, cannot be reasonably compared to that of the permanently unarmed or disarmed Armenians, as some contemporary Ottomanists are wont to do.

Revolt against Oppressive Taxation and the Ottoman Practice of Charging "Sedition"

In a detailed analysis of the principal and subsidiary taxes levied against the Armenians, two European experts underscored the extortionate and instigative nature of these taxes. A German author suggested that they were pivotal in the rise and escalation of the Turko-Armenian conflict insofar as these taxes affected the bulk of the Armenian people which he called "an eminently agricultural people," adding: "without exaggeration one can assert that 85–90 percent of that population is engaged in agriculture and horticulture." His description of the plight of that Armenian peasantry, in terms of exorbitant taxation on them, is graphic and emphatic. He lamented that plight thus: "Poor people! Pay for building your houses; pay for your chief; pay for being born; pay for being alive, for breathing air; pay for your family; pay for the fruits of your labor; pay to the state; pay to the Kurds; pay to the usurers; pay, pay, pay without an end. Were it the sea, it would have dried up, were it a river, it would have stopped flowing."[5] A French fiscal expert of Turkish finances, on the other hand, went so far as to claim that the Armenian "uprising" of Sassoun (August 1894), producing the first link in the chain of Abdul Hamit massacres (1894–96), was due to the oppressive tithe (*aşar*), the farm-product tax.[6] These views are corroborated by a Turkish author who observed: "The Sassoun Armenians refused to submit to double taxation...The ignorant and obstinate governor began to incite the local Muslims against the Armenians..."[7] It is a fact that at the time of its occurrence, the Sassoun uprising was labeled sedition and continues to be treated as such in most Turkish history books. Yet, a longtime observer of Turkish conduct vis-à-vis subject nationalities offered a different perspective. After asserting that "the idea of revolution" is not entertained "by the peasants," Britain's Erzerum Consul Clifford Lloyd, a former magistrate in Ireland during the Land League troubles, wrote: "Discontent, or any description of protest, is regarded by the Turkish Local Government as seditious."[8]

Sedition, however, is the supreme violation of the Islamic Legal Pact described above, entitling the Sovereign to the right to invoke the retaliatory provisions of the Koran. In one passage of the Koran it is clearly stipulated that however hated the infidels may be, they can be inflicted upon only in the form of retribution, not of preemptive strikes: "Transgress not by attacking them first" (chapter 2, verse 186). But, the right to identify and define any act as "transgression," and the right to transpose any dispute to a level of real or imaginary provocation belonged only to the Turkish overlord. This type of definitional distortion, if not perversion, of a basically economic grievance into a political challenge from a subject minority to the ruling Turkish overlords was the context in which conflicts not only became ill defined and ill understood, but they also became unamenable to solutions as they tended to intensify and escalate as a result of a reliance on and misuse of that mechanism of distortion.

On the Cattle Status of the Non-Muslim Subjects

Within the framework of his challenge-and-response theory, historian Arnold J. Toynbee provides a clue to the mentality allowing such definitional vagaries. "The challenge to which the Ottoman system was a response...was treating their new subjects as human flocks and herds, evolving human equivalents of the sheep-dogs of the Nomad..."[9] With or without the benefit of such allegorical wisdom, it has to be pointed out, however, that the existence of the flocks and herds has but one purpose: the creatures involved are maintained for the sole benefit of their owners. There is no reason for their existence on any other grounds, much less any justification for them to disobey or dare to resist their masters. And to be even literal, such creatures are meant to be eventually slaughtered, notwithstanding the imputation by some students of the Ottoman Empire of affective sentiments to the Ottoman overlords who supposedly were fond of their *raias*. Based on cumulative experience, however, to the Armenian *raias* the term denoted the converse. That denotation was clearly articulated by an Armenian publicist in an editorial at the turn of the century. "To a Muslim, the Armenian is nothing but an animal, a beast of prey, to be used for his needs. For this purpose he is allowed to merely subsist in such numbers as needed. No one keeps animals that are useless. This policy has been maintained since the inception of the Ottoman system."[10] Decrying the troubles for which "the obstinate infidels" were blamed, the Koran called them indeed "the worst cattle in the sight of God" (chapter 8, verse 57). In the absence of acute troubles, however, the infidels were subjected to "contemptuous half-toleration" by Ottoman rulers who insisted on the latter's permanent status of "inferiority."[11] The contempt issued from "an innate attitude of superiority" vis-à-vis "the infidel *gâvours*," permanently relegated to a status of "inferiority," and was animated by "an intense Muslim feeling," capable of erupting in "open fanaticism."[12] Such "fanaticism" is endemic in acute conflicts for the consummation of which the Koran prescribes merciless massacres (particularly in chapter 2, verse 211; chapter 3, verses 10, 13, 14, and 135; chapter 8, verse 12; and chapter 9, verses 29, 38, and 41). All that is summed up in the paramount command of the Prophet: "When ye encounter the unbelievers, strike off their heads until ye have made a great slaughter among them" (chapter 47, verse 4). Whether in conditions of acute conflict or otherwise, the Ottoman treatment of Christian nationalities in general appears to have been animated by a proclivity for persecution that was considered to be preordained. A British lawyer with the benefit of experience gathered in forty-two years of residence, and of attendant legal practice in the Ottoman capital, who chronicled three rather large volumes on the modern history of the Ottoman Empire, especially on the Abdul Hamit era (1876–1908), described that persecution unequivocally:

> I assert that...the whole course of Turkey's history—say five hundred years—until the opening of last century was a period of Mahometan fanaticism during which tens of thousands of Christians died for their faith. I grant that it would be difficult to find records of such wholesale slaughter as occurred in Armenia in 1895–97, when at least a hundred thousand Christians were killed; the explanation being that the persecution under which the Christians suffered after the capture of Constantinople in 1453 was so continuous and so grinding as to strike terror in the sufferers and prevent them making any attempt to free themselves from it.[13]

Nearly half a century earlier, another British observer singled out the religious factor again to explain and confirm Ottoman tyranny vis-à-vis non-Muslim subjects. Following an extensive tour of the provinces in the summer and autumn of 1868, and based on experiences of six years of residence in that country, which he traversed "on horseback in every direction," England's Erzerum Consul J. G. Taylor made the following observation at the end of a long report to his foreign minister, the Earl of Clarendon. Speaking of the prevalence of a new brand of Islam, he denounced it as "Not one based on the practice of the precepts of a purer religion in accordance with those of the early Moslem period; but one unhappily, on the forms, oppression, persecution, and exclusion, *characteristic of a later Turkish date*, that primarily indeed contributed by their consequences so much to the decadence of the Empire."[14] This proclivity to subvert Islam and to reduce it to a convenient instrument of oppression and repression was even more pronounced in the era of Sultan Abdul Hamit (1876–1908). As one contemporary Turkish historian conceded, in order to justify his tyranny Abdul Hamit resorted to "a reinterpretation and perversion of Ottoman Islamic political theory."[15] All these arguments are summarized in the Annual Report for Turkey 1908, prepared by the British Foreign Office. In it is stated that "The stubborn and unyielding principle of Moslem religion…is more fixed and unrelenting in Turkey than in any other Mahommedan country."[16]

In order to gauge the nature of this perversion one may turn to the teachings of Islamic scholars not identified with Ottoman and Turkish political interests. Foremost among these are Korafy and Itazm, whose interpretations of the provisions of the Sacred Law of Islam are such as to elevate them to the position of foremost commentators of "the teachings of the Prophet." Here is an excerpt from their writings:

> The protection which we owe to non-Mussulmans under our authority necessarily carries with it the duty for us to hear their complaints and to pay attention to every matter that concerns their interests…. The protection which we accord imposes upon us certain duties towards those to whom we have accorded it, because they are placed under the Faith of God, of his Prophet and of Islam. If the enemies who invade our territory attack our non-Mussulman subjects, we must run to their assistance, and die in their defence, in order to maintain the faith, which is due to those we protect. To neglect their defence would be a violation of the pact of God. We must treat with humanity their weak, succour their poor, nourish their hungry, clothe their naked, speak to them mildly and with affability, support the inconvenience arising from their presence amongst us, not from fear, but out of generosity, aid them with our advice on all occasions, guard and defend their families, their property, and their honour, all their rights and interests, and, in short, to act in our relations with them as generous protectors towards the protected.[17]

In a recent publication Taner Akçam, a maverick contemporary Turkish author, for his part singles out and enumerates those injunctions of the Koran that paradoxically proffer the ideal of "equality for all God's creatures." They are reinforced, he argues, by the *hadis*, the sayings and acts of the Prophet handed down by his cohorts, and which avowedly are part of the Islamic tradition. Akçam likewise draws from what he believes to be the Prophet's doctrine of "human rights" as derived from the latter's espousal of the ideals of "equality and justice."[18]

It is clear that one has to account for that aspect of Ottoman history in which the Prophetic doctrine of fire and sword is seen conveniently singled out and exploited by wielders of power pursuing conquest and dominance. More particularly, the exploitation involves the Ottoman-Turkish tradition of gravitating to religiously sanctioned violence as a method of conflict resolution vis-à-vis an array of discordant nationalities and minorities. *No comparable Islamic regime has been burdened with a similar legacy of sustained oppressiveness highlighted by a long catalogue of massacres.* For this reason the patterns of Ottoman belligerence, and the determinants of Ottoman social structure merit a brief consideration here. The findings of the Military Tribunal bear out this observation; they unmistakably point to the final spasms of a disintegrating empire as being the violent climax of this pattern of conflict resolution.

Notes

1. William S. Davis, *A Short History of the Near East* (New York: Macmillan, 1923), p. 235.
2. C. Max Kortepeter, *Ottoman Imperialism during the Reformation: Europe and the Caucasus* (New York: New York University Press, 1972), p. 254.
3. Kemal Beydilli, "1828–1829 Osmanlı-Rus Savaşında Doğu Anadolu'dan Rusya'ya Göçürülen Ermeniler" (On the Armenians who were resettled in Russia during the 1828–1829 Russo-Turkish War), *Belgeler* (Documents), vol. 13, no. 17 (Ankara: Turkish Historical Society Publication, 1988), p. 403.
4. H. A. R. Gibb and Harold Bowen, *Islamic Society and the West*, I, part 2 (New York: Oxford University Press, 1962), pp. 223, 233, 251, 226.
5. La Barbe, "Die Steuern im türkischen Armenien und die Ursachen der armenischen Bewegung" (Taxes in Turkish Armenia and the causes of the Armenian movement), *Neue Zeit* 16 (1897), pp. 41, 46.
6. Du Velay, *Essai sur l'histoire financière de la Turquie* (Essay on the fiscal history of Turkey) (Paris: Rousseau, 1903), p. 668.
7. Mithat Sertoğlu, "Türkiyede Ermeni Meselesi" (The Armenian question in Turkey), *Belgelerle Türk Tarih Dergisi* 2 (November 1967), p. 48.
8. 2 October 1890, report in *Blue Book*, Turkey no. 1 (1890), pp. 80–2. Ten years earlier when the *Levant Herald*, which was run by a British editor, and the editors of two Armenian papers, pressed for "justice, protection, and better government in the provinces," the Censor of the Press suppressed all three men for being "seditious," *British Foreign Office Archives* (Kew, London). FO 424/106, folio 360A, Layard to Salisbury (26 April 1880).

9. Arnold J. Toynbee, *A Study of History* (abridgment of volumes 7–10), (New York: Oxford University Press, 1957), p. 362.

10. *Nor Giank* (bimonthly organ of the Huntchak Party in London), 3, no. 17 (1 September 1900), p. 257.

11. Gibb and Bowen, *Islamic Society* [n. 2], pp. 233, 258.

12. Roderic H. Davison, "Turkish Attitudes Concerning Christian-Muslim Equality in the Nineteenth Century," *American Historical Review* 59 (July 1954), p. 855.

13. Sir Edwin Pears, "Christians and Islam in Turkey," *Century* 58 (February 1913), p. 278.

14. *Blue Book*, Turkey, no. 16 (1877), enclosure to no. 35 (3 October 1872), p. 76.

15. Kemal H. Karpat, "The Transformation of the Ottoman State, 1789–1908," *International Journal of Middle East Studies* 3 (1972), p. 271.

16. *British Documents on the Origins of the War 1898–1914.* vol. 5: *The Near East*, G.P. Gooch and H.V. Temperley, eds., p. 258.

17. Quoted by veteran British diplomatist Richard Wood in a 27 November 1877 extensive report to British Foreign Secretary Earl of Derby. *British Foreign Office Archives.* FO 424/63, Doc. no. 25, enclosure pp. 16–7 of the pp. 12–27 report.

18. Taner Akçam, *Islam'da Hoşgörü ve Sınırı* (Tolerance and its limits in Islam) (Ankara: Başak Publications, 1994), pp. 74–8.

2

The Clash between Democratic Norms and Theocratic Dogmas

The Caldron of Legal Disabilities

One of the foremost factors affording persecution in a sociopolitical system is the set of legal disabilities denying a minority institutional protection and redress in the event of actual victimization. Such disabilities were an integral feature of Ottoman social structure and included two basic components.

1. The denial of the right to carry arms, as mentioned earlier. The import of this denial is measured by the chronic state of lawlessness and anomie that prevailed in the empire's distant provinces with large concentrations of Armenians. Many of these zones and enclaves were teeming with brigands and outlaws who were armed to the teeth, as were practically all Muslims in the countryside. The effects of this kind of subjugation proved most debilitating for the Armenian psyche.

On 13 May 1876, Germany, Austria, and Russia, and France and Italy who joined later, issued the Berlin Memorandum. The delivery of it was, however, deferred first, and then altogether dispensed with because of a change of occupancy of the Sultan's throne (from Aziz to Murad V), and because of the heralding of a new policy. Through that Memorandum the signatories had proposed, among other things, that the Christians be permitted to possess arms as part of the Sultan's 1856 Treaty engagements; England's Disraeli and his cabinet refused to join, mainly because England had not been consulted beforehand. The Ottoman-Turkish rejection came during one of the 1876 December sittings of the Constantinople Conference. After summoning and consulting the Ulema, the Islamic doctors of law, the Şeyhulislam, their head, issued a *Fetva*, the preemptory final opinion declaring such possession of arms by non-Muslim subjects a violation of the Islamic Sacred Law.

The consequence was assessed by a British author who in 1880 noted that as a result of this deliberate denial of the right to bear arms and to be trained militarily in the armed forces as citizens of the Ottoman state, the Armenians became "cowardly and wretched," and inept to resist or to mount countermeasures against the Kurds.[1] Lynch, however, has only negatively confirmed this conclusion, as he observed that once Armenian "freedom fighters" did finally arm themselves, they demonstrated martial aptitudes in contesting despotic local officials as well as marauding tribal bands and predators. Lynch stated that: "when given the chance, they [the Armenians] have not been slow to display martial qualities both in the domain of the highest strategy and in that of personal prowess."[2]

The Prussian military officer Helmuth von Moltke a few decades earlier had already recognized the profitability for the Ottoman state of a plan to enlist the Armenians in particular in the Ottoman army, which was exhausting the supply of the male population by excluding non-Muslims, he argued. He not only considered the Armenians quite fit for military service, but regarded them "more loyal and dedicated to the Ottoman state than the Muslim Kurds or Arabs (*treu, ergeben*)." Opposing the stance of Minister of War Hafız Paşa, the destroyer of the Yeniçeri Corps, who wanted to incorporate individual Armenians in combat squads by a ratio of one Armenian to twenty Muslims, Moltke proposed instead the formation of Armenian battalions, each of which was to be attached to each existing regiment comprising three Muslim battalions. This way an Armenian could be afforded the chance to advance to the rank of a major, he said. Otherwise, he may be abused as usual as a contemptible *raia* underling dragged into the Turkish army, he added. Moltke believed that such an arrangement could lead to competition between Muslim and Christian-Armenian battalions, a competition that "could only benefit both camps, reduce suspicions, augment the size of the army and bring about great relief to the country as a whole."[3]

2. The second component involved legal issues, in particular the inadmissibility of Christian evidence against that of Muslims in religiously administered courts. Even after the introduction of the 1839 and 1856 Tanzimat reforms, which were intended to equalize justice in civil courts, the old practice remained intact with one British Consul characterizing the respective reforms as "nominal." The following report in 1864 by a British vice-consul epitomizes the situation:

The great test of the equality of Christian and Mussulman before the law, the admission of Christian evidence, signally fails before the experience of the last ten years. Christian evidence is utterly rejected in the lower criminal courts, and only received in the higher when corroborated by a Mussulman...A Mussulman's simple allegation, unbacked by evidence, will upset the best founded and most incontrovertible claim.[4]

British statesman Lord Salisbury is said to have described these dual disenfranchisements as "abject slavery." It was slavery of a special kind that involved the recourse to torture as a standard means of extracting confessions from non-Muslims appearing in court on charges levelled against them by Muslims. The significance of this type of treatment issues from the fact that it was inflicted only on non-Muslims, while Muslims facing similar charges were routinely exempt from it. The following account, narrated by British Consul Robert Curzon, illustrates this practice as observed in Erzurum in 1843.

A Turkish merchant brought his merchandise to an inn where he spent the night. Two Turkish soldiers slept near him. In the morning his goods had disappeared. He accused the soldiers, who were the only people near him, of the robbery. Upon their denial, however, the two soldiers were promptly set free by the judge of the court to which they had been taken. A Turkish woman had witnessed their burying something and informed the merchant about the location where he might find his goods buried. The merchant went there but found only half the goods. The soldiers confessed to the theft, but accused the Armenian in charge of the rooms of the inn of possessing the other half of the goods. When the Armenian denied any part in the theft before the Tribunal, the judge "ordered him to be tortured...A metal drinking-cup of hot brass was put upon his head; afterwards a cord was tied round his head, two sheep's knuckle bones were placed upon his temples, and the cord tightened till his eyes nearly came out. As he would not confess, his front teeth were then drawn one at a time; pieces of cane were run up under his toe-nails and his finger-nails. Various tortures have been inflicted on him in this way for the last twelve days, and he is now hung up by the hands, in the prison of the Seraskier (War Minister), where he will be kept and tormented till he confesses or dies. "This is the deposition of his wife, Mariam, who begs me to interpose to save her husband, who, she declares, slept at home and not in the inn, on the night when the robbery took place." When a protest was lodged with the governor, Kâmil Paşa, the latter categorically denied that the Armenian was tortured. But Curzon's servant, Paolo Cadelli, an Italian, had personally visited the prison and saw the wretched victim there. As he related, "They had martyred him, they had drawn his teeth, his finger-ends and toes were black, by reason of the canes they had run into them; his thighs had been torn by pincers; he was half dead. He said to the people... 'I am innocent; kill me; but I cannot restore goods which I have not got.' Ah! he is a Christian...an Armenian. That is what these Turks do. They have not tortured the soldiers who are guilty...this man has been tortured because he is an Armenian. They are Turks, my master (*padrone*)...They are all Turks; that is what they do...." Despite the incidence of inaccuracy of a few minor details, the overwhelming evidence supplied by Curzon is substantiated. Speaking of the modalities of justice prevalent in Ottoman Turkey at the time, Curzon declared at the end of his account that "according to some doctors of the law, pashas, vizirs (ministers) might cut off a few heads every day, for no given reason, but just for amusement."[5]

The deeply entrenched cultural roots of this propensity for torture as a method of administering justice for non-Muslims are unmistakably identified with the precepts and dogmas of Islam as practiced in the social system of Ottoman theocracy. In fact the large majority of these administrators of justice in the provinces of the Ottoman Empire were the *kadis*, Muslim judges. They were bound to the obligatory tenets of the *Şeriat*, the canon law of Islam, and as such operated as the guardians of law and order, magistrates who represented "by far the most important category in the Turkish system."[6]

In a massive volume, Turkish author Taner Akçam examined the religious-cultural context within which the propensity for cruelty and torture crystallized as an integral part of the Turkish justice system in general, and justice with respect to non-Muslims, especially the Armenians. His conclusion is that this propensity was harnessed to political ends in the handling of the protracted nationality conflicts which punctuated the latter stages of the decline of the Ottoman Empire.[7] For his part, an Armenian academician, A.N. Der Ghevontian, focused on the historical antecedents of the discriminatory ill-treatment of the Armenian population of the Ottoman Empire, especially in the period stretching from the fourteenth to the eighteenth century. According to him the natural growth and development of the Armenian people was impeded as result of their treatment.[8]

The interconnections of the religious and the legal in Ottoman society stemmed from concepts of jurisprudence in which the sources of civil, administrative, and religious law were held to be the same. Until well into World War I, the guardians of the Ottoman body politic saw fit to combine the two domains in a single Ministry of Justice and Religions, that was vested with powers of supervision and control over the ecclesiastical authorities of the subject nationalities.

Admission of Turkey to the Public Law of Europe and the Rudiments of Formal Reform

Many students of Ottoman history seem to accept the view that the Ottoman regime was not only tolerant of the religions of its non-Muslim subjects, but in a certain sense appreciative as well. As evidence of this stance these historians cite, among others, the 1876 Constitution which is perceived and portrayed as the culmination of the liberal Ottoman spirit avowedly manifested by Sultan Mohammed II in the wake of his capture of Istanbul in 1453. It is argued in the same vein that this spirit was further advanced by Mahmud II in the period 1808–39, and loosely spelled out, purportedly in accord with Western democratic principles, in the 1839 and 1856 Tanzimat reform acts. On a terminological level at least the initiative of the nineteenth century reforms calls into question the validity of this claim of liberalism. For the word *tanzimat* denotes the idea of a *new order* thereby connoting the corollary idea that all was not well with the subject nationalities insofar as their civil rights were concerned and the institution of which was one of the central objectives of these reform acts. England and France, supported by Austrian diplomatic pressures, fought the Crimean War to deny Russia a victory against the Turks who "enthusiastically" had declared war against the latter in October 1853, but subsequently were facing the peril of defeat, and all that was implied by it. As the Allies managed to subdue Russia, they wrested from the Turks the February 1856 Reform Edict, repeating the 1839 guarantees to Christian subjects of "security of life, honor and property" for the sake of which Tsarist Russia professed to be contesting the Turks for so long. In the ensuing 1856 Treaty of Paris, the provisions of Articles 9 and 12 dealt one way or another with the lot of the non-Muslims of the Empire; by virtue of these provisions the Powers promised to respect the independence and integrity of the Empire. Superseding in importance all these arrangements, however, was the fact that Turkey, the first non-Christian state, was admitted "to participate in the public law and concert of Europe."[9]

The reform edicts of 1839 and 1856 had signal references to subject nationalities, with that of 1839 containing "the most novel aspect, [namely] its official declaration of equality," and with that of 1856 containing "an interesting antidefamation clause forbidding" derogatory and discriminatory practices against these nationalities. In his inaugural speech to the Council of State in 1868, Abdul Aziz, the successor of Sultan Mecid who had enacted the two Reform edicts cited above, vowed to protect and defend the members of all nationalities as "children of the same fatherland." Yet, in spite of all these professions and assurances, intermittently reasserted up to the 1876 Constitution and beyond, "No genuine equality was ever attained."[10] The reason was evident. The reforms were a repudiation of fundamental socio-religious traditions deeply enmeshed in the Turkish psyche, and institutionalized throughout the Empire. When the 1856 edict was proclaimed:

> Many Moslems began to grumble: "Today we lost our sacred national rights which our ancestors gained with their blood. While the Islamic nation used to be the ruling nation, it is now bereft of this sacred right. This is a day of tears and mourning for the Moslem brethren."[11]

Within a few years (1859), these reactions culminated in what is known as the Kuleli revolt in the capital. Army officers joined hands with Muslim clergymen and teachers in an attempt to overthrow the regime in protest against what they considered to be submissiveness to foreign powers, and the illegitimacy of the act of granting equal rights to the Christians.

The decision of the Christian Powers of Europe to embrace Turkey was an anomaly as European public law, the bastion of European legalism, was intrinsically on a collision course with the Ottoman theocratic system and its religious dogmas. The Concert of Europe already in 1648 in Westphalia had laid the foundation of the doctrine of the separation of church and state and thus, in a rudimentary form, had already decided to subordinate religious dogmas to legal principle, the rule of law; it thus consecrated secularism as the cornerstone of the system of the family of nations. But the Ottoman Empire, for most of its history, was and remained a theocracy which, by definition and fact, cannot be secularized; laws that are predicated upon permanently fixed and intractable religious precepts cannot be modified, much less reformed.

The Pattern of Reform Acts as Palliatives against Nationality Crises

The protests against the legal disabilities, which entailed the permanent subjugation of non-Muslim nationalities threatening to provoke

European, especially Russian, intervention, had impelled the Ottoman regime to introduce the twin Tanzimat reform edicts, as noted above. The proclamation of the 1876 Constitution took place in an almost identical setting of nationality upheavals, including the 1876 massacre against the Bulgarians, and the Russian threat of war. The Concert Powers, recognizing the futility of entrusting the Ottoman government with the critical task of reforms, insisted on some sort of control and supervision in the December 1876 Istanbul Conference. While arguing back and forth on the issue of whether European control would amount to a violation of Articles 9 and 12 of the Paris Treaty, which guaranteed the sovereignty and independence of the Ottoman state, the Turks obdurately resisted, and the conference failed. As the first Ottoman constitution was promulgated, which was deliberately synchronized to coincide with that moribund conference, some skeptics viewed it essentially as a mere palliative to mollify the European Powers and public opinion. Nevertheless, within months thereafter Russia, in response to Turkish intransigence, declared war, defeating the Ottoman armies in the East and in the Balkan peninsula, and forcing Turkey to sue for peace. Thwarted once more by England, which denied her the fuller fruits of her victory, Russia again had to acquiesce to the pressure of the other Powers to rely merely on the good will of the Ottoman government. This government offered to exercise such good will in accordance with the clauses of the 1876 Constitution. Accordingly, the two cardinal numbers of Article 16 of the San Stefano Treaty, which pertained to Armenian reforms, were inverted, and Article 16 was thus converted into Article 61; it was then incorporated in the July 1876 Berlin Treaty supplanting that of San Stefano. The latter had "muscular strength" insofar as it made the withdrawal of Russian forces from the occupied "Armenian provinces" in the East contingent upon the actual implementation of Article 16 of the Treaty. Article 61, on the other hand, prescribed the immediate withdrawal of the Russian army, while making it incumbent upon Turkey only to live up to her promise and to periodically report on the progress of the promised reforms, without attaching any specific conditions of supervision or control.

Social Disabilities versus the Claim of Nationality Privileges

The development of a string of social disabilities was a natural, if not logical, extension of the legal ones. Like the latter, the former originated from the verse of the Koran setting forth the principle of the

Islamic Legal Pact. After guaranteeing the protection, by way of clemency to the subjugated *zimmis*[12] willing to pay tributes, that verse goes on to command that : "they be reduced low" (chapter 9, verse 29). This command has been held to be the traditional matrix of social degradations to be applied through debarments and exclusions, the specifics of which are supplied through the following brief list of examples by two renowned Islamic scholars. The zimmis are expected to wear distinctive clothes so that they may be differentiated from the Muslims, the "true believers." They are forbidden to ride horses or to bear arms. Their churches may be converted into mosques and they are not allowed to build new ones. At best they may be permitted to undertake repairs of those churches that have fallen into disrepair. A zimmi may not marry a Muslim woman but conversely, a Muslim man may marry a zimmi woman. A Muslim murderer of a zimmi is exempt from the death penalty.[13] A Turkish regional historian provides a telling example of this type of disability practised in the nineteenth century. When passing through Tokad, Kör Yusuf Ziya Paşa, who was officiating as Grand Vizier in a second term, learned that Muslim landlords were keeping Christian tenants in their houses. Arguing that such a practice was against the principles of Şeriat, the Muslim Sacred Law, on 28 March 1809 he issued an order to the effect that Christians altogether be removed from Muslim wards and neighborhoods.[14]

The sustained character of the imposition of these restrictions and disabilities were bound to adversely condition the psyches of the affected populations. James Creagh, a former captain of the First Royals, provides additional and very specific examples of their impact. For example, the non-Muslims of the Ottoman Empire had to wear "a very peculiar costume, resembling that of females." Since they were not permitted to ride horses, they were "forced to ride about on mules or donkeys, which they were even compelled to mount in the attitude of women." They were not allowed to use bells. "The size of their houses or churches was regulated by law to a diminutive standard." They were forced to "treat the poorest or meanest Mussulman whom they might chance to meet, with every demonstration of deference and respect." The net result of this kind of treatment involved a level of coerciveness that "soon made the Christians servile, cowardly, deceitful, contemptible and even ridiculous."[15]

A close scrutiny of the relevant parts of the Ottoman constitution will confirm the view that, despite claims of toleration and religious liberalism, that document was meant to foster exclusivism and segregation, while purporting to extend and certify "privileges" to the subject minorities. The reference is to Article 11 proclaiming Islam as the state religion at the same time allowing religious "separateness" for minorities. This allowance has been interpreted as an act of granting privileges to the latter, except by the high priest of Turkish nationalism, Tekin Alp (Moise Cohen),[16] who saw in such provisions "the high separation wall" (*eine hohe Scheidewand*), and by such legists and experts of international law as Rolin-Jaquemeyns[17] and E. Engelhardt,[18] both of whom underscored the exclusionary bent of that constitutional article. The Ottoman term "*imtiyaz*" inserted in Article 11 has twin meanings. Colloquially it does mean privilege and concession, but in a more learned usage it means "separateness" or "distinctness." To be more specific, the religious-administrative "privileges" accorded to the religious chiefs of minority communities included the authority to regulate and manage matters pertaining to church and synagogue, marriage (there was no secular marriage in Turkey until 1917), inheritance, bequests to education and charity, and in a limited sense, pious foundations. All of these "privileges," and more, were fully granted, however, to the Muslims themselves via the offices of the Şeyhulislam, the ultimate authority and spokesman of the Sacred Law, and via the pious foundations, called *Vakıf*. As commonly understood, however, "privilege" denotes the idea of such benefits and advantages as they are meant to benefit only certain people, but not any other people. It also connotes some kind of exemption from, or favors beyond, the pale of prevailing laws. None of these advantages were extended to the Armenians, save the exemption from military service, from which a host of categories of Muslims were likewise exempt, including the citizens of the Ottoman capital. Moreover, thousands of *softas*, young theology students, went out of their way to enroll in schools of theology to evade military service. As Turkish army commander Mahmud Muhtar Paşa relates in his memoirs, "During the reign of Sultan Abdul Hamit the number of these draft dodgers had increased considerably. The main body of the reservists stationed in the provinces adjacent to Istanbul comprised people of this type of attitude."[19]

Though the nationalities at one level benefited from some kind of limited autonomy by pushing forward in the areas of education and cultural growth through a burgeoning network of churches, schools, and civic organizations, at another level they became trapped in a degraded quasi-caste system, organized around the principles of exclusion, segregation, and scornful subordination.[20] The manner in which the benefits of such an autonomy were severely undermined was evident by the disdain with which "the spiritual Chiefs" of these nationalities were "treated." Despite the conferral upon them of "both ecclesiastical and civil power over their respective communities" by the ruling sultans, these religious chiefs were stymied in the discharge of their duties and exercise of their authority. The obstacles came from a system of civilian and political administration that continued to discount all statutory arrangements formally instituted in the Ottoman capital by authorities. The sway of deeply entrenched traditions anchored on Ottoman theocracy almost mandated such discounting. Consequently, these religious chiefs "could not effectually exercise [their power] without meeting with opposition from all classes of the Mussulman population."[21] Turkish historian Taner Akçam, in his chapter on the institutionalized restrictions of the civil rights of non-Muslim Ottoman subjects and the limitations of the norm of tolerating them as "infidels," spells out some specifics in this respect.[22] Perhaps the most telling work in this respect is Ali Yıldırım's recently published book in which the Ottoman state system is portrayed as an "inquisitorial" system. The role of the Catholic tormentors is supplanted in this system by that of *Ulemas,* the doctors of Muslim theology who through the medium of *fermans* or *irades* (imperial edicts) and *fetvas* (the juridical decision of a *mufti*—a type of supreme court justice—dispensing a formal, legal opinion) authorized the persecution, including the torture and murder, of the untold multitudes of the victims of the state.[23] In the more ghastly episodes of the Abdul Hamit era and 1909 Adana massacres, for example, (barring few exceptions), the *muftis* in general played a decisive role by formally sanctioning the regional and local mass murders by declaring them permissible by the canons of Muslim law.[24] In presenting his central thesis Yıldırım goes out of his way to expose what he considers to be the falsehoods and cover-ups of most of Turkish historians identified with or controlled by the guidelines and directives of "officially [mandated] history" (*resmi tarih*).[25]

The norms prescribing the degradation of non-Muslim subjects were reinforced by the companion norms proscribing social intercourse with the infidel subjects. In one particular passage of the Koran, the Prophet strictly forbade the faithful to cultivate friendship with the latter through the call: "O true believers, contract not an intimate friendship with any besides yourself; they will not fail to corrupt you" (chapter 3, verse 114). This injunction was taken seriously enough by Sheik Abdul Hakk, "one of the most influential members of the Committee of Union and

Progress (Ittihad), a civilized Young Turk," to inveigh against the Christians in general with these words of unqualified decrial: "...to speak to [a Christian] would be a humiliation for our intelligence and an insult to the grandeur of the Master of the Universe. The presence of such miscreants among us is the bane of our existence; their doctrine is a direct insult to the purity of our faith; contact with them is a defilement of our bodies; any relation with them a torture to our souls."[26] Wartime American Ambassador to Turkey, Henry Morgenthau, offered the following confirmatory observation in this regard. The so-called privileges were not due to "a spirit of tolerance, but merely because they [the Ottomans] looked upon the Christian nations as unclean and, therefore, unfit to have any contact...the '*millets*' [were] regarded as vermin and therefore disqualified for membership in the Ottoman state."[27]

The practice of social distancing that Ottoman theocracy prescribed for Muslims in relation to the non-Muslim nationalities had a special ingredient that charged this practice with a lethal animus: scorn blended with latent hatred. Prolonged coexistence with those they considered "infidels" had made many a Muslim Turk unsure or insecure about the "trueness" of his own faith. Under certain conditions such "cognitive dissonance" can not only lead to frustration but also to aggression.[28] The opposing belief system of the Armenians was a major factor in the exacerbation of the Turko-Armenian conflict, in view of the fact that the Armenians were perceived by many dominant Muslims as prospering—despite, and perhaps because of, their being subjected to social distancing. The resort to lethal violence as a means of resolving a conflict is not only a function of overwhelming power but also a by-product of cumulative frustrations pressing for relief under opportune circumstances. The transition from the frustration-aggression cycle to a cycle of massacres is cogently described by British ethnographer William M. Ramsay. Of all the scholars who have hitherto dealt with the Armenian massacres of the era of Abdul Hamit, Ramsay stands out for his incisiveness. He had spent more than a decade intermittently conducting research in Turkey in a period covering the last two decades of the nineteenth century. Sufficiently fluent in Turkish, he was able to mingle with Turks and interact with them.

Turkish rule...meant unutterable contempt.... The Armenians (and the Greek) were dogs and pigs...to be spat upon, if their shadow darkened a Turk, to be outraged, to be the mats on which he wiped the mud from his feet. Conceive the inevitable result of centuries of slavery, of subjection to insult and scorn, centuries in which nothing that belonged to the Armenian, neither his property, his house, his life, his person, nor his family, was sacred or safe from violence—capricious, unprovoked violence—to resist which by violence meant death! I do not mean that every Armenian suffered so; but that every one lived in conscious danger from any chance disturbance or riot.[29]

In consideration of all these facts the conclusion becomes inescapable that the proclamation of the adoption by the Sultan of the Ottoman Constitution in December 1876 was more of an expedient move to mollify the Great Powers. The latter's representatives had gathered at Constantinople to induce Sultan Abdul Hamit to embrace their proposal of reforms in the administration of the provinces of the empire and to agree to their stipulation of establishing a mechanism of European control in the implementation of such reforms. As the outbreak of the subsequent Russo-Turkish war demonstrated, however, neither the apparent spirit of adaptability to Western ideas of equality, democracy and constitutionalism, nor the 101 booming canon salvos announcing the adoption of these ideas through the proclamation of the Constitution impressed the Powers; without exception all of them left the Ottoman capital in a spirit of exasperation and gloom.

While practically all Ottoman Armenians were exuberant about the advent of constitutionalism, viewing it as a good omen, full of promises for the Armenian community, a lone voice in the distant Van province in that very same year of 1876 not only dismissed the act as "a deceptive gimmick" but went on to prophetically forecast "the extermination of the Armenian population of the Ottoman Empire as soon as the Young Turks become masters of the situation."[30]

Notes

1. James Creagh, *Armenians, Koords, and Turks*, vol. 2, (London: S. Tinsley, 1880), p. 178.

2. H.F.B. Lynch, *Armenia: Travels and Studies*, vol. 1 (Beirut: Khayats, 1965; reissue of the 1901 edition), p. 465.

3. Helmuth von Moltke, *Briefe über Zustände und Begebenheiten in der Türkei aus den Jahren 1835 bis 1839* (Letters on conditions and events in Turkey in the years 1835–1839), 4th ed. (Berlin: E. S. Mittler und Sohn, 1882), pp. 354–5. Moltke entered Turkish service as an adviser to the Ottoman-Turkish army in 1835. He was then a staff lieutenant of the Prussian army and was thirty-five years old. He rose through the ranks, becoming chief of the Prussian General Staff in 1858. The German military victories in the Danish war of 1864, the Austro-Prussian War of 1866, and the Franco-Prussian War of 1870–71 were largely due to his blueprint of tactics and organizational skills. He was rewarded with the title of count by Emperor Wilhelm I and when he resigned from the military he had the rank of general field marshal.

4. *Reports from Her Majesty's Consuls Relating to the Condition of the Christians*

in Turkey, 1867 volume, pp. 5, 29. See also related other reports by various British consuls and vice-consuls, in ibid., vol. 1860, p. 58; vol. 1867, pp. 4, 5, 6, 14, 15; and vol. 1867, part 2, p. 3.

5. Robert Curzon, *Armenia: A Year at Erzeroum, and on the Frontiers of Russia, Turkey and Persia* (London: John Murray, 1854), pp. 84–6, 90–1, 93.

6. Niyazi Berkes, *The Development of Secularism in Turkey* (Montreal: McGill University Press, 1964), p. 15.

7. Taner Akçam, *Siyasi Kültürümüzde Zulüm ve Işkence* (Atrocity and torture in our political culture), (Istanbul: Iletişim Publications, 1992), pp. 90, 159, 163, 192.

8. A. N. Der Ghevontian, "Hai Zhoghovourtee Vidjagu Khalifayutian Deerabedoutyan Nerko" (The condition of the Armenian people under the domination of the caliphate), *Lraper* (publication of the State University of Yerevan, 4 April 1975), pp. 74–88.

9. Charles G. Fenwich, *International Law,* 2d ed. (New York: D. Appleton-Century, 1934), p. 83.

10. Roderic H. Davison, "Turkish Attitudes Concerning Christian-Muslim Equality in the Nineteenth Century," *American Historical Review* 59 (July 1954), p. 848.

11. Şerif Mardin, *The Genesis of Young Ottoman Thought* (Princeton, NJ: Princeton University Press, 1962), p. 18.

12. As explained in chapter 1, the relations of the non-Muslim subjects to the Sultan were governed by a contract, i.e., *zimma;* such a contract, as a rule, materialized in the wake of a conquest, and of the attendant incorporation of the vanquished country into the domain of that Islamic ruler.

13. H. A. R. Gibb and Harold Bowen, *Islamic Society and the West,* I, part 2 (London: Oxford University Press, 1962), pp. 208.

14. H. T. Cinlioglu, *Osmanlılar Zamanında Tokat* (Tokat in the Ottoman era), part 3, (Tokat, 1951), p. 55.

15. Creagh, *Armenians, Koords, and Turks,* [n. 1], vol. 1, p. 139.

16. Tekin Alp, *Türkismus und Pantürkismus,* (Turkism and pan-Turkism), (Weimar: Kiepenheuer, 1915), p. 89.

17. M. G. Rolin-Jaquemeyns, *Armenia, the Armenians, and the Treaties* (London: John Heywood, 1891), p. v.

18. E. Engelhardt, *La Turquie et le Tanzimat ou histoire des réformes dans l'Empire Ottoman,* vol. 2, (Paris: Cotillon, 1884), pp. 299–300.

19. Mahmud Muhtar Pascha, *Meine Führung im Balkankriege* (My leadership in the 1912 Balkan War) Imhoff Pascha, trans., 5th ed. (Berlin: E. S. Mittler und Sohn, 1913), p. 165. The author was directly involved in the conduct of the Balkan war, first as commander of the Third Army Corps and later of the Second Eastern Army. Prior to the war he was minister of marine in the Cabinet headed by Muhtar Paşa, his father, and a hero of the 1877–78 Russo-Turkish War. After the Balkan war he became ambassador to Germany.

20. W. M. Ramsay, *Impressions of Turkey during Twelve Years' Wanderings* (New York: Putnam's; London: Hodder and Stoughton, 1897), pp. 193, 203–4, 206, 210, 213–4.

21. *British Foreign Office Archives.* FO 424/63. Doc. no. 25, enclosure pp. 13–4 of the 12–27 pp. report of Richard Wood, who, on 27 November 1877, sent it to the British foreign secretary, Early Derby. Wood was a veteran Foreign Service officer with extensive diplomatic experience in various parts of the Ottoman Empire, including Asia Minor and "Kurdistan."

22. Taner Akçam, *Islam'da Hoşgörü ve Sınırı* (Tolerance and its limits in Islam) (Ankara: Başak Publications, 1994), pp. 69–74.

23. Ali Yıldırım, *Osmanlı Engizisyonu* (The Ottoman Inquisition) (Ankara: Emel, 1996).
24. For details of the role of Muslim clerics in the Abdul Hamit era massacres see Vahakn N. Dadrian *The History of the Armenian Genocide: Ethnic Conflict from the Balkans to Anatolia to the Causcasus*, 4th rev. ed. (Providence: Berghahn Books, 1997), ch. 8, pp. 147–51.
25. Yıldırım, *Osmanlı Engizisyonu* [n. 23], pp. 9–29.
26. André Servier, *Islam and the Psychology of the Mussulman*. A. S. Moss-Blundell, trans. (London: Chapman and Hall, 1924), pp. 241–2.
27. Henry Morgenthau, *Ambassador Morgenthau's Story* (Garden City, NY: Doubleday, Page, 1918), p. 280.
28. Vahakn N. Dadrian, "Factors of Anger and Aggression in Genocide," *Journal of Human Relations* vol. 19, no. 3 (1971), p. 400.
29. Ramsay, *Impressions of Turkey*, [n. 20], pp. 206–7.
30. The voice belonged to Dikran Amirjanian, a teacher at Van's Jesuit high school and an accomplished Armenologue in the fields of classic Armenian, contemporary literary Armenian, and Armenian liturgical music. He was elected chairman of Van province's Armenian Assembly consisting of forty-nine elected members. He had witnessed the plastering of his father's casket by Turkish youth with rocks and stones during the latter's funeral in March 1868. As a response to the protest the Armenians had lodged against this act of sacrilegious vandalism, the mob torched the Armenian Sourp Hagop school in Van. Hampartzoum Yeramian, *Houshartzan Van-Vaspourakanee* (Memorial for Van-Vaspourakan) (Alexandria, Egypt, n.p., 1929) vol. 1. pp. 61–3, 82, 92, 105, 106.

3

Massive Migrations, Demography, and the Kurdish Factor

The Unsettling Demographic Conditions

Interethnic and international conflicts of most kinds are capable of prolonged existence, without reaching a point of explosion. In the arena of dominant versus minority group relations, the possibility of such explosions is obviated by weak minorities learning the necessity to endure inequities by adaptive behavior. In any case, symbiotic relations are bound to develop, with the elements of conflict eventually being syncretized in one way or another. But, certain thresholds cannot be ignored. There are factors, for instance, that intrude into established states of symbiosis jeopardizing delicate threshold-balances. Critical demographic change is one such factor. Changes in population densities and in population ratios, and the dislocation of populations, which brings additional related pressures, become sources of new and dangerous tensions.

The Turko-Armenian conflict was aggravated throughout its stages of development by an ongoing series of Muslim mass migrations from the Caucasus, and to a lesser extent from the Balkan peninsula. Hundreds of thousands of Muslims were settled in areas adjacent to Armenian population centers. One German author estimated that about 300,000 Circassians and Abkhazians opted to emigrate to Turkey, in response to an 1864 Russian offer to allow them to exit following their defeat at the hands of the Russians, and subsequently established themselves in the Black Sea littoral around Trabzon. All the transport facilities, including the vessels, were provided by the Russian government.[1] This fact and figure are confirmed in a "confidential" report from the British ambassador at St. Petersburg, Lord Napier, to Lord Russell, secretary of state for foreign affairs, stressing the fact that the Russians had no desire to "exterminate" but to remove them; the latter had the options of war, emigration to Kouban, or emigration to Turkey, whose government had greatly encouraged it, but was now discouraging it.[2] Following the Russian victory in 1877, tens of thousands of Circassians, originally settled in the Balkans, resettled in Anatolia, especially in and near Adana.[3] According to an Armenian historian, altogether 30,000 Circassians resettled in the area of Cilicia.[4] Another area absorbing the influx of these refugees was the littoral of the Sea of Marmora involving the cities of Izmid and Adapazar, and their environs.[5] There were still other areas of settlement such as Konya, but especially Sivas.[6] Another ethnic group emigrating from the Russian Caucasus were the Lazes. This involved the settlement of 4500–5000 Laz families in Trabzon province despite the warning of local authorities that "there were no convenient spots."[7] These settlements were undertaken in spite of "intense" Armenian and Greek protests, for both the Armenian and Greek populations of these areas were already at that time experiencing growing depredations on the parts of these destitute migrants and refugees. The new settlements were, therefore, proving gravely unsettling to them.[8] It is most significant, however, that out of the destitution and the ensuing despair, 60,000 of these Lazes eventually returned to their country of origin.[9] Also, between 1878—the aftermath of the Russo-Turkish War—and 1884, over one million Muslims migrated to the Turkish provinces.[10] A Turkish student of the Ottoman Empire, on the other hand, estimated that "Between 1862 and 1870 close to two million Muslims altogether fled from the Caucasus into the Ottoman Empire and that this figure rose to 3 million by the first decade of the twentieth century."[11] Finally, according to the *Encyclopedia of Islam*, starting with 1861, a total of 1.5 million Circassians migrated to Turkey.[12] As a result of the inability of the Turkish government to assist these refugees in any significant way, poverty, destitution, and companion tendencies of lawlessness set in among many of them.

These ongoing migratory movements and the ensuing resettlement efforts ultimately proved to be destructive dislocations not only for the various communities immediately affected by their resettlement, but also for the refugee migrants themselves. Schweiger-Lerchenfeld describes the misery at Trabzon where Russian steamers kept unloading their human cargoes, the total unpreparedness of the Ottoman authorities for the bottlenecks developing, and the subsequent starvation of nearly one-third of them, i.e., 100,000 Circassians.[13] In this connection England's Consul at Sivas, Lieutenant-Colonel C.W. Wilson, decried the Ottoman government's "almost criminal action."[14] The "bitter" disappointment the Circassian refugees experienced evidently issued from the fact that they were neglected, abandoned, and at times even "plundered" by Turkish officials. Apparently, they were also exploited by the Turkish method of pitting race against race, particularly Muslim ones. It is not surprising, therefore, that these migrant-refugees resorted to robbery and lawlessness.[15] M. G. Rolin-Jaequemeyns, a Belgian scholar of international law, suspected an ulterior motive in this governmental negligence, namely "the abominable idea of ruining and decimating the Christian population by leaving the new arrivals without any resource save plunder."[16] When, on 6 December 1876, the Armenian patriarch lodged a protest against the European pressures to have the Circassian refugees transferred from the Balkan peninsula to Anatolia in the aftermath of the summer 1876 Bulgarian massacres, he was indulging in an exercise in futility.[17] A complacent explanation was provided to the British ambassador by the Ottoman foreign minister, to the effect that the Circassians have the choice of either robbery or starvation, "What can we do?"[18] Commenting on the devastating impact of these migratory cycles upon the Armenians in particular, one Armenian author described that impact in terms of the onset of violence and disturbances in the Zeitoun area.[19] Another Armenian historian focused on the resulting dislocations in the Erzurum area, calling them "an irremediable blow."[20]

The Kurdish Depredations:
"The Kernel of the Armenian Question"

The major demographic assault, however, came from the Kurds. Descending from the Taurus mountain ranges of south-central Turkey, and from Persia, they settled in those northeastern districts of Turkey that historically and geographically were identified as "Armenia." British Consul J.G. Taylor, following his inspection tour in "Koordistan" in 1868, declared: "The Koords, inhabiting the Erzerum districts, with the exception of the Hakkaree, *were originally immigrants from the vicinity of Diarbekir* [italics added] and there is only one tribe, the Mamakanlee, said to be descended from the Armenian Mamagonians, who are natives of the soil."[21] The combined feudal, tribal, and seminomadic elements of Kurdish culture posed serious threats to a subjugated, unarmed, and sedentary Armenian population through depredations, the chronic character of which began to destabilize and gradually erode the foundations of Armenian ethnic existence. Ottoman co-optation of the Kurds, professedly in the name and for the sake of Islam, aggravated the situation of large segments of the Armenian peasantry. Therefore, a brief review of the specifics may be warranted.

The assertion that the kernel of the Armenian Question involves the Kurdish depredations belongs to the British author H.F B. Lynch, according to whom that Question was formed by "the presence of this Kurdish population upon the Armenian plateau...their tribal organization...perpetual immunity from taxation...atrocious cruelty, [proving for] the Armenians disastrous in the extreme."[22] Another observer of the Kurds in the mid-nineteenth century focused on a special aspect of this disaster. Moritz Wagner drew specific attention to a particular type of depredation at which the Kurds were most adept: "The skill with which they steal loaded horses, and the speed with which they then plunder the horses, shirts, and pants of the Armenian losing them is incomparable (*unvergleichlich*)." Wagner believed that on account of the chaos and anarchy associated with "barbaric" Kurdish depredations Anatolia was doomed either to total disintegration or to falling into the hands of "the Nordic colossus,"[23] the reference being to Russia in the North.

Perhaps the most graphic descriptions of the Kurdish problem were provided by the Armenians themselves—specifically through an author articulating the intensity with which that problem was felt by many Armenian leaders. Through his Dashnak party organ in Geneva, this author—a party leader—in an editorial, branded the Kurds as predators who had become the nemesis of the Armenian people since the 1820s: "The Armenians suffered more than any other nation from this permanent enemy—day by day, month by month, year by year." Here is a detailed statement of his:

"He is armed, doesn't pay taxes, oppresses and persecutes the Armenian." This, in a nutshell is the description of the inferno that lasted several centuries. The Armenian problem was a problem of Kurdo-Armenian relations which came to international attention in the 1870s *de jure*, but as a *de facto* problem it existed for centuries. No other ethnic element, including the Turk, Tatar, and the Persian, has inflicted so much cultural and physical damage, so many blows and suffering, so many ruinous depredations and such pervasive oppression, perhaps not even reckless governments of tyranny, as the Kurd. In his centuries-old agonizing history, the Ottoman Armenian often could not even be aware of the presence of the Ottoman government, due to the latter's inability to extend its rule and control to the provinces far removed from its seat. But, he was forced to suffer the ubiquitous presence of another government, the Kurdish *derebeyi's* [feudal chieftains]. Every day, every minute in his existence, the Armenian has felt the crushing weight

of this adjunct yoke, of this savage, singular feudalism that for centuries has shack-
led his labor, ruined his economy through whimsical taxes and incessant brigandage, and as principal overlord of Armenia, has slaughtered, tortured, raped, and
desecrated all his institutions with impunity. A state within a state. A double and
formidable yoke, the like of which may well not be found in any part of the world,
in any page of human history. It is indeed difficult to ultimately compare this dual
enslavement and ascertain whether the Turkish or Kurdish aspect of it was more
consequential. Both have complemented each other by mutual support and sucked
the lifeblood of the small Armenian nation which for so many centuries struggled
to survive as a Christian oasis in a devouring sea of Mohammedanism.[24]

The two Islamic scholars, Gibb and Bowen, summed up the situation with respect to the Kurdish influx to "what had been Armenia," as
having been "in the long run deleterious to the Armenians since it added
to their disabilities as *Dimmis* a dominance by their mortal enemies,
the Kurds."[25]

The complaints and pleas of the Armenians for redress gradually
drove a weak, and in some respects, inept Ottoman government to a
decision to co-opt the Kurds. The rudiments of this policy were first
ushered in in the 1840s, or 1847, to be exact, by Commander Osman
Paşa, who, anticipating Abdul Hamit by four decades, instituted administrative measures in the regions of Van, Bitlis, Muş, Beyazid, and
Diyarbekir by virtue of which the Kurds were accorded license for brigandage, freedom from prosecution, and were offered supplies of arms
and ammunition. Referring to these sanctions for Kurdish depredations
an American observer stated: "Turkey's real sway in Armenia dates
from the year 1847."[26] These sanctions were institutionalized in 1891
by Abdul Hamit, who formed the Kurdish regiments of territorial cavalry consecrating them with his name as they were billed as "hamidiye
squadrons," or "regiments." The seriousness of this measure is reflected
in the preparatory work which preceded it. Hamit sent one of his high-
ranking military commanders, Sami Paşa, to the province of Van, the
heart of historical Armenia, where he arranged for outlaw Kurdish brigands to be legalized, lured and concentrated them around the area of
Van, and personally inspired them with praise and promises of rewards.
The official press in Constantinople, led by the newspaper *Tercümanı
Hakikat*, the quasi-spokesman of the sultan, proceeded to depict the
Kurds as patriots and national heroes, actual and potential.[27] Their chieftains were lavishly entertained at Yıldız palace, and some of them were
accorded high military titles, including that of Paşa. Even though these
newly formed units were not formally incorporated into the regular,
standing army, they nevertheless received ranks, uniforms, regimental

badges, and Martin rifles, served out to them from government stores. Their status was marginal, or paramilitary, of irregular standing, and, in the Ottoman context, akin to gendarmerie. According to Şakir Paşa, a member of the military commission at the palace, and later Imperial Commissioner for the Introduction of Reforms in the provinces, the idea was conceived first by Marshal Zeki Paşa, the Commander of the Fourth Army Corps stationed in Erzincan, and involved 40,000–50,000 horsemen.[28] By December 1892, the British military attaché in Constantinople estimated that these units involved thirty-three regiments, each consisting of five hundred men, with thirteen more being in the process of formation.[29] In 1899, however, the number of these regiments had grown to sixty-three.[30]

Notwithstanding the argument that the units were intended as a counterweight to the Cossack regiments of Russia, by all accounts the primary target of that plan were in fact the Armenians,[31] with Toynbee maintaining that the formation of the Hamidiye regiments was the culmination of a series of steps through which the Kurds were encouraged in their depredations against the Armenians since the Turko-Russian War of 1877.[32] Specifying the number of regiments as being thirty-six, each comprising 1,200 men, and in commenting on this plan, a Turkish sociologist recognized a sinister purpose behind it, aimed exclusively against the Armenians. According to him, Hamit exploited the Islamic religion to enlist the Kurds on the side of the Turks and "unleashed against the Armenians a campaign which seemed to have no end, and no abating…[he thereby] with [Kurdish] assistance averted the establishment of Armenia."[33]

The Insoluble Land Problem and the Aggravation of the Conflict with the Kurds and Turks

But the conflict with the Kurds, despite several Armenian attempts at conciliation with a view to forging a united front against the Ottoman rulers,[34] remained more or less persistent because of a host of other complex issues, many of which are dealt with in a monograph by Tessa Hoffmann and Gerayer Koutcharian;[35] some of these problems are also outlined in an article by a French author discussing the evolving Kurdo-Armenian relations.[36] One of the most fundamental and what proved to be consequential problems among all other problems was the land dispute that cast its shadow upon worsening Armeno-Kurd relations in eastern Turkey. During and in the wake of the 1894–96 Abdul Hamit

era massacres, huge tracts of agricultural lands and collateral posses-
sions of all kinds belonging to the Armenians were confiscated and
appropriated by countless Muslims from the respective localities; most
of these were Kurds. A British diplomatic report providing an appraisal
of the origin and dimensions of the Armeno-Kurdish conflict as an extension of the Turko-Armenian conflict, includes this observation:

> The Turkish Government, after the Treaty of Berlin, realising that a sense of nation-
> ality cannot easily live without a peasantry, and that if it succeeded in uprooting the
> Armenian peasantry from the soil and driving them into the towns or out of the
> country, it would in great part rid itself of the Armenians and the Armenian Ques-
> tion, condoned and encouraged Kurdish usurpation of Armenian lands. This retail
> process was repeated on a wholesale scale after the big massacres of 1895–96.[37]

A French military officer, Comte de Cholet, who had traveled in the
region in 1890, i.e., before the massacres, confirmed this pattern of
violent expropriation by the Kurds:

> The Kurds, who were once only a pastoral tribe living exclusively from the breed-
> ing and selling of their herds, aspired to become an agricultural people. In order
> to obtain this goal they simply stole the land surrounding the Armenians and be-
> came the legal owners of the land previously belonging to their neighbors, either
> by a fictitious sale or by flagrant infringements. They are not always satisfied
> with these illegal acquisitions and sometimes carry out their cruelty to such an
> extreme that they force those whose property they possess to work their heredi-
> tary fields, only as simple tenants, however, or even as day laborers.[38]

In order to appreciate the magnitude of this problem, it may be useful
to examine the litany of abuses of this type listed below. They are excerpted from the compilations of the provincial dioceses and the Armenian patriarchate in Istanbul and are reproduced in the booklet prepared
by Kegham Der Garabedian, the Armenian deputy from Muş district.

> In the districts of Khnus, Alashkert, Bayazid, Basen, Kemakh, Erzinga, Terian,
> Baberd, and others in the province of Karin [Erzerum], they occupied thousands
> of acres of land, meadows and pastures, houses and mills in 129 villages in vari-
> ous manners. For example, in Erzinga-Terjan it was more than 15,000 acres, 250–
> 350 buildings, as well as pasturages; in Baberd, Basen, and Alashkert 200–500
> fields and meadows; in Khnus more than 1000 fields and 400 buildings as well as
> 16,800 acres of land. In the entire vilayet of Karin [Erzerum] the figure totalled
> more than 100,000 acres. Of the 50 villages in the district of Akn, Arabkir, Malatia,
> and Dersim in the province of Kharberd more than 1,800 fields, 5,000 acres, and
> 203 buildings were destroyed; if we add to this the 40 villages of Charsanjak
> together with the fruit and vegetable gardens, it amounts to 200,000 acres.[39]

The advent of the Ittihadists in 1908 did not produce any remedies
sought by those Armenians who after the latter's revolution in that year

"in large numbers returned, especially from the Caucasus..." The Ittihadists "repeatedly promised" relief, but could not deliver.[40] The lands could neither be restituted, nor compensation for their loss could be secured. As is stated in the above-cited British document, this failure has become "the touchstone of Armeno-Turkish relations."[41] But Cemal Paşa, a member of the powerful Ittihad triumvirate, in his memoirs explains why Ittihadist promises could not be fulfilled. The Ottoman government had decided to send an Investigation Commission to the eastern provinces; of the five member group two were Armenians and the other two were Turks, one of whom was Cemal. The chairman, the fifth member, was Justice Minister Inspector Galip. But the Muslim deputies from Turkey's eastern provinces were implacable. They insistently and concertedly blocked all initiatives in the Ottoman Chamber of Deputies in this respect. These deputies claimed that the powers with which the Commission was to be vested were an infringement on the jurisdiction of the provincial governors.[42] The government did not pursue the matter energetically.

And so, the twin Armeno-Turk and Armeno-Kurd conflicts continued to fester.

Notes

1. Amand Freiherrn von Schweiger-Lerchenfeld, *Armenien*, (Jena: H. Constenoble, 1878), pp. 80–3.
2. *British Foreign Archives* (Kew, London). FO 97/424, Report no. 255 (17 May 1864). For a summary compilation on the facts of the influx of these refugees in the six provinces *see* England's chief military agent and Erzurum Consul major Henry Trotter's 7 October 1879 report in, *Blue Book*, Turkey, no. 4 (1880), p. 90; for subsequent migrations *see* in ibid, p. 27, and England's acting vice-consul at Trabzon, Marengo's report in ibid, no. 4 (1880), p. 55.
3. Vital Cuinet, *La Turquie d'Asie* (Asiatic Turkey), I, (Paris: Leroux, 1891), p. 6; *see* also *Blue Book*, Turkey (no. 6) 1881, p. 89, Ambassador Goschen's 30 August 1880 report.
4. Father Minas Nourikhan, *Badmoutiun Jhamanagagitz 1847–1867*, (Contemporary history 1847–1867), vol. 2 (Venice: St. Ghazare, 1896), p. 822.
5. *Blue Book*, Turkey, no. 6 (1881), Ambassador Goschen's 16 August and 13 September reports for Izmid, 7 August 1880 for Adapazar, and still another report on the same day on the general refugee question.
6. *Blue Book*, Turkey, no. 4 (1880), Lieutenant Colonel C.W. Wilson's 20 August 1879 report, p. 39.
7. Ibid, p. 26, Consul Bilotti's 20 April 1880 and 16 July 1880 reports.
8. FO 424/106 (20 April 1880), folio 360B.
9. A. B. Kuran, *Inkilâb Tarihimiz ve Ittihad ve Terakki* (Our history of revolution and Ittihad ve Terakki), (Istanbul: Tan, 1948), p. 225.
10. S. J. Shaw and E. K. Shaw, *History of the Ottoman Empire and Modern Turkey*, vol. 2 (New York: Cambridge University Press, 1977), pp. 238–9.

11. The 2 million figure is in Kemal H. Karpat, "Ottoman Population Records and the Census of 1881/2–1893," *International Journal of Middle Eastern Studies* 9 (May 1978), p. 246; the 3 million figure, on the other hand, is in idem., *Ottoman Population 1830–1914* (Madison, WI: University of Wisconsin Press, 1985), p. 27, left-hand column.

12. vol. 3, p. 384.

13. *Armenien* [n. 1], pp. 80–1.

14. *Blue Book*, Turkey, no. 4 (1880), 14 October 1879 report, p. 113.

15. W. H. Ramsay, *Impressions of Turkey* (New York: Putnam, 1897), pp. 94–5, 108, 110–4, 116.

16. M. G. Rolin-Jaquemeyns, *Armenia, the Armenians, and the Treaties* (London: John Heywood, 1891), p. 61.

17. See British Ambassador's 7 December 1876 report in FO 424/46, no. 336.

18. An Eastern Statesman, "Contemporary Life and Thought in Turkey," *Contemporary Review* 37 (February 1880), p. 342.

19. Nourikhan, *Badmoutiun* [n. 4], p. 822.

20. Father Hagop Kossian, *Partzur Haik* (Upper Armenia), I, (Vienna: Mechitarian Press, 1925), p. 99.

21. *Blue Book*, Turkey, no. 16 (1877), enclosure no. 13/1, 1 March 1869 report, p. 28. See also ibid., p. 66, Taylor to Ambassador Elliot, 16 October 1871, enclosure no. 27.

22. H.F.B. Lynch, *Armenia: Travels and Studies*, vol. 2 (Beirut: Khayats, [1901]1965), pp. 420–3. It should be observed that the nomadic Kurds were not entirely exempt from taxation as they were obliged to pay "sheep tax."

23. Moritz Wagner, *Reise nach Persien und dem Lande der Kurden* (Travel in Persia and the land of the Kurds), vol. 2 (Leipzig: Arnoldische, 1852), pp. 213, 236.

24. Quoted in Michayel Varantian, *Haigagan Sharzhman Nakhabadmoutiunu* (The history of the rudiments of the Armenian movement), vol. 2 (Geneva: Armenian Revolutionary Federation, 1913–4), pp. 96–8. The party organ mentioned in the text was *Droshag*, vol. 9, no. 4 (June 1901), p. 65. The author, Christapor Michaelian, was one of the arch leaders of the Dashnak party, a member of the triumvirate of the party leadership.

25. H.A.R. Gibb and Harold Bowen, *Islamic Society and the West* I, part 2 (London: Oxford University Press, 1962), p. 227.

26. Emile J. Dillon, "The Fiasco in Armenia," *Fortnightly Review*, no. 59 (1896), p. 379.

27. Leo [A. Babakhanian], *Tourkahay Heghapochoutian Kaghaparapanoutiunu* (The ideology of the Turkish-Armenian revolution), vol. 1 (Paris: Bahree, 1934), pp. 117–8.

28. Sidney Whitman, *Turkish Memories* (London: Scribner's, 1914), p. 73.

29. For the estimate of thirty-three regiments see A. O. Sarkissian, "Concert Diplomacy and the Armenians 1890–1897," in *Studies in Diplomatic History and Historiography* (London: Longmans, Green, 1961), p. 58.

30. Shaw and Shaw, *History of the Ottoman Empire* [n. 10], p. 246.

31. French Ambassador Cambon to his foreign minister, *Documents Diplomatiques*, vol. 11 (Paris, 1947), p. 72. Report of 28 February 1894.

32. Viscount Bryce (and Arnold J. Toynbee), *The Treatment of the Armenians in the Ottoman Empire 1915–16*, (Official publication of the British Foreign Office), Miscellaneous no. 31 (1916), p. 624.

33. Ismail Beşikci, *Doğu Anadolunun Düzeni: Sosyo-Ekonomik ve Etnik Temeller* (Eastern Anatolian policies: ethnic and socioeconomic foundations) (Erzurum: Sumer, 1969), pp. 89, 236, 343, 479, 239.

34. Garo Sasouni, *Kürd Azkayeen Zharjoumneru yev Hai-Kurdagan Haraper-*

outiunneru (The Kurdish national movements and Armeno-Kurd relations) (Beirut: Hamazkayeen, 1976), pp. 171–91; S.G. Boghossian, *Kurderu yev Haigagan Hartzu* (The Kurds and the Armenian Question) (Yerevan: Hayasdan, 1991), pp. 137–68.

35. Tessa Hoffmann and Gerayer Koutcharian, "The History of Armenian-Kurdish Relations in the Ottoman Empire," Dorothea Lam, trans. *The Armenian Review* 39, 4 (Winter 1986), pp. 1–45.

36. S. Zarzecki, "La question kurdo-arménienne," *Revue de Paris* (15 April 1914), pp. 873–94.

37. FO 40170/19208. no. 747. Ambassador Sir Charles Marling's "Very Confidential" 27 August 1913 report to Foreign Minister Sir Edward Grey. enclosure in no. 567. Memorandum by Fitzmaurice.

38. Comte de Chalet, *Arménie Kurdistan et Mésopotamie* (Lieutenant of the 76 Infantry Regiment) (Paris: Plon, Nourrit and Co., 1892), p. 171. The English translation transferred from Hoffmann and Koutcharian, "The History of Armeno-Kurdish Relations" [n. 35], pp. 18–9.

39. Sasouni, *Kurd Azkayeen* [n. 34], p. 199. The English translation is from Hoffmann and Koutcharian, ibid., p. 19. The title of the booklet is *Hoghayeen Hartzu* (The land problem).

40. FO [n. 37] (p. 513 in *British Documents on the Origins of the War*, vol. 21).

41. Ibid.

42. Cemal Paşa, *Hatıralar* (Memoirs), Behçet Cemal, ed. (Istanbul: Çağdaş, 1977), pp. 422–3.

4

The Abortiveness of Ottoman Reforms

The Period of Armenian Pleas and Petitions, 1850–76

When Khrimian became patriarch of the Armenians of Turkey in 1869, in his first visit to Grand Vizier Ali Paşa he not only detailed the sufferings of the Armenian population of the provinces, but underscored the fact that compared to the Muslims the Armenians were relatively lucky. As the *Vezir* looked at him astonished and perplexed, the patriarch went on to explain that whereas the Armenians had their dioceses and primates and their patriarch to complain and seek redress, the Muslims did not have anyone to seek relief from their wretched conditions. Moved by this display of even-handed concern for the Muslims, Ali Paşa instructed the Armenian patriarch to prepare an extensive report recording all the details, and to append to it concrete and practical propositions for remedy. Disillusioned and alienated, the patriarch resigned in less than four years, however, as two successive reports had failed to bring about any relief for the Armenians. The circumstances of this abortive effort merit a brief review.

In a period of twenty years, up to 1870, Armenian patriarchs, in their capacity as recognized heads of the Armenian *millet*, had submitted to the Ottoman government 537 memoranda (*takrir*) detailing the depredations in the provinces involving fraud by officials, abductions, forcible conversions, brigandage, murder, denial of religious practices, including funeral and burial rites, and confiscatory taxes. This aggregate effort culminated in a major report in the form of a Memorandum of Grievances that was prepared by an eight-member Special Commission of Inquiry in 1870. The Memorandum was debated in the very same Armenian National Assembly (22 October 1871) which, in compliance with Ali Paşa's request, had created that Commission during its twelfth session; it was intended to be sent to the sultan and his government. Before that report was compiled, however, Khrimian sent a circular (4 January 1871), along with a questionnaire to all the Dioceses in the provinces seeking specific data on depredations and governmental corruption, with the following key instruction: "Leave out anything and everything which is false or inaccurate. You are to report to us only those facts the certainty and authenticity of which you personally examined and have verified."[1]

22 October 1871, the day of the debate in the Armenian National Assembly, has been viewed by some Armenian authors as one of the most memorable occasions in the history of that Assembly where skills of oratory, debate, and eloquence were tested on a parliamentary battleground. Throughout that debate forces of conservatism, vested interest groups, and political timidity were contesting the forces of reform, national pride, and emancipation on behalf of the oppressed peasants in the provinces. Several deputies wanted, for example, to press for a right to serve in the Ottoman army and to be allowed to bear arms so as to generate a spirit of combativeness and self-respect to supplant despair and the national temper of helpless resignation to abuses. In countering the arguments of the conservatives that nothing should be proposed which may cause bloodshed, one deputy retorted: "Are we not bleeding enough already? If this is inevitable, why not shed blood by fighting for our honor and dignity?" The advocates of caution and circumspection had managed, for example, to substitute a reference to "Moslem fanatics" for one to "religious prejudice." Another deputy, Krikor Odian, who later became one of the architects of the 1876 Ottoman Constitution[2] (but remained behind the scenes, thus allowing the famous Midhat Paşa to assume the credit for it) declared: "We ought to tell the world that we too are men, and capable of courage."[3]

The Memorandum of Grievances that finally emerged had four parts and addressed such issues as: (1) tax abuses; (2) corruption of governmental officials; (3) the venality of the Judiciary, primarily arising out of the inadmissibility of Armenian testimony in courts; and (4) special types of depredations. The patriarchate, for two years, repeatedly tried to get the Porte (the seat of the Ottoman Government) to act upon the Memorandum, and when the Constantinople Conference of the Ambassadors of the Powers had convened in December 1876, still no action had been forthcoming. On 10(22) September 1876 the Armenian National Assembly elected a new Reform Commission which, by 17(29) September, i.e., in one week, had prepared and submitted to the Assembly a new report, which was but a continuation of the first in terms of complaints received from the provinces since April 1872.[4] On 24 August 1876 the new patriarch, Nercess Varjabedian, sent a special memorandum to the Porte focusing exclusively on large-scale expropriations of agricultural land tracts belonging to Armenian peasants who "comprise the overwhelming part of the Armenian people." Dismissing it as non-specific and vague, the Porte directed the patriarch to name names, places, and concrete facts. The ensuing statistical tables prompted the Porte to create a commission to inquire into the problem. Having done so, the commission submitted its report and disbanded itself without achieving any concrete results.[5] The rapid succession of Grand Viziers following the death in 1871 of Mehmed Ali Paşa Emin, (i.e., Mahmud Nedim, Ahmed Şefik, Midhat, Mehmed Rüşdü, Ahmed Essad, Hüsseyin Avni, and again Nedim, Rüşdü, and Midhat), certainly encumbered the attainment of such results. As will be seen below, however, more vital Ottoman and Turkish interests were involved in the Ottoman decision to shelve this aggregate volume of grievance memoranda.

With the installation of Midhat as Grand Vizier in July 1872, a major change was effected in the relationship of the Armenian patriarchate with the Ottoman government. Until then, it was customary to submit the memoranda (*takrir*) to the Foreign Ministry (*Hariciye*) as the Armenian *millet* was regarded as a community whose affairs were being overseen by the Powers. This treatment was somehow in conformity with diplomatic protocol. Midhat switched the jurisdiction to the Ministry of Religion and Justice (*Adliye*), whose reliance on the dictates of Islam and Sacred Islamic Law were brought to bear upon the new relationship. As a result the Armenian millet was no longer seen and treated as a nationality under the tutelage of the Christian Powers, and consequently it was no longer treated with any semblance of diplomatic protocol.

Alienation and Prerevolutionary Unrest

A number of clergymen, though inclined towards the status quo regarding Ottoman rule, began to raise their voices against the persistence in the provinces of governmental misrule that was threatening to erode the rural infrastructure of the Armenian Church. Typical of this type of clerical leadership emerging on the landscape of the Armenian peasant community in the Ottoman provinces was the above-mentioned Church leader Khrimian, who eventually became to be venerated by the Armenian people as "Papa," or in Armenian, *Hayrig*. Shortly after his elevation to the position of patriarch, with emotion he compared his role to that of "a captain entrusted with the task of steering the ship, the Armenian nation, in a turbulent sea." He alternately cajoled, chastised, and pleaded so as to prompt the uninformed, the timid, and the conservative elements of the Armenian National Assembly to embrace the cause of the disaffected and neglected masses in the provinces in the heartland of which, the region of Van, he had been born and raised and had officiated as a prince of the church. He repeatedly argued that unless the Armenian peasantry was rescued from the scourges of the unending depredations afflicting it, there was no future, nor any justification for the survival of the nation. His ardent efforts within the Assembly and outside it and his bold entreaties with the Ottoman government all proved abortive; as mentioned above, disappointed and broken, he resigned after four years of service as Armenian patriarch (in 1873). He was later to be elected Catholicos, the Supreme Patriarch of all Armenians, with residence in Etchmiadzin, the Armenian Holy See, located near Yerevan, then part of Tsarist Russia. He also played a major role in dramatizing in several European capitals the plight of the Armenians prior to his pleas to the representatives of the six Powers who had convened for the Congress of Berlin (1878). His personality, priorities, and simple but keen style of oration, combined to make a powerful impact upon his contemporaries, lay as well as clerical, within and without Turkish and Russian Armenia. In a way, he was the sublime embodiment of the deluge of the sorrows tearing his ancient nation asunder in the shadows of Mount Ararat, the landmark of that nation, and a silent witness to its gradual and violent atrophy.

Two features of his legacy warrant singling out as significant. First to be noted is his gradual transformation from a loyal and dedicated Ottoman subject to a foe of the Ottoman regime, highlighting a particular form of dynamics fueling international conflicts. When a nation experiences subjugation over a period of time, its identifying properties, its culture, and its forms of social organization are bound to change reflecting the deleterious consequences of the subjugation. These changes are best observed in the personalities of the leadership stratum trying to cope with the resulting turmoil. When domination becomes debilitating oppression, a minority group, through the rise of a crisis-oriented leadership, may abandon efforts at accommodation and may consider resorting to active antagonism, irrespective of risks and pitfalls. Throughout his career, Khrimian was an advocate of Ottoman-based Armenianism; he espoused neither political autonomy nor secession, nor Russian sovereignty. His chief concern was the introduction of administrative, internal reforms in order to improve not only the lot of the Armenians but, equally important, the overall Ottoman system, in the framework of which he hoped to secure for the woes of his people remedies that included amicable relations with the Kurds. In the end, however, he reluctantly abandoned this stance and drifted into one that actively supported revolutionary change through militancy. Thus it was that while serving as Catholicos, he enjoined Armenians in an encyclical to back the ranks of the revolutionaries. Here is the text of that injunction:

> I know, I know people of Armenia, thy soul is tormented, thy heart lacerated. But take notice and awake. If you fail to brandish your own sword against swords threatening you, and to grit your teeth defying those of the foe, you will be doomed to extinction. Come on, come on, people of Armenia, join the ranks of the new Armenian knighthood, aid and abet the revolutionary movement, for along with the handle of the plough and the cross, the sword of the knight is equally liberating.[6]

A more or less similar transformation affected Khrimian's successor, Patriarch Nercess Varjabedian, whose dedication to the Ottoman Ruling Institution had earned him the stigma of servility and lack of patriotism among Armenians, many of whom had openly denounced him as a traitor and had demanded his resignation. During the 1877 Russo-Turkish war, he went out of his way to encourage Armenians to fight and sacrifice themselves for the defense of the Ottoman fatherland, had his message read in all Armenian churches, and personally reassured the sultan of his loyalty and devotion. On his insistence, several thousand Armenian men volunteered in the war against Russia, and despite some opposition by certain lay and clerical leaders of the community, plans were made to meet quotas for a general draft—to establish co-equality with Muslims in conscription and military participation. The patriarch was decorated by Sultan Abdul Hamit with the *Osmaniye* Medal First Class for this support.[7] Yet, at the very same time, Ottoman Turks, soldiery, and Kurdish and Circassian brigands were devastating the heavily populated Armenian towns and villages in and around the theaters of military operations in the provinces. When the Congress of Berlin convened to consider reforms for these provinces, the patriarch sent a delegation to plead for the Armenian case. He boldly refused to comply with Sultan Abdul Hamit's request to recall it, arguing that only the Armenian National Assembly could do so. A second command from the sultan elicited a sharper retort to the latter's emissaries: "Go and tell the sultan that I myself sent these delegates to the Congress to secure remedies for the woes of my communities, and I will not recall them even if he means to hang me at the door of the patriarchate as the Greek patriarch was hanged half a century ago."[8]

Khrimian's call for armed resistance was anticipated by almost two decades by another clergyman, a celibate priest, whose clarion call for armed resistance in a journal published in the Ottoman capital was as unprecedented as it was daring and defiant. Here are some excerpts from that article:

> Why are the Armenians so oblivious to Armenia being reduced to a cemetery of the living...Alas, the Armenian nation is accustomed to subservience and slavery. All her hopes are centered on schools and education. But can such education equip the Armenian with means to smash the sword of the bloodthirsty Kurd? What will become of us...We may well disappear as a nation in short order...We must protect our national existence by any and all means, including bloodshed and revolution. Can we without shame claim that our existence is secure? Our affliction is lack of moral fortitude and stamina. What was the reward for our proverbial loyalty to the Ottoman State? Our churches have been desecrated; our virgins outraged; old and young, men and women without distinction have been cut down by swords...our homes have been emptied of furniture and money; our cellars, stables, sheepfolds have been cleared of their contents. Only famine is left to linger with us. Let Armenians continue to remain indifferent to the woes of their compatriots. He who cannot take care of himself, can he expect help from others? Can we preserve the fatherland? Can we stop our dispersal and concentrate in our homeland? Can we forge national unity? These are the conditions to be fulfilled towards the goal of earning a rightful place in the constellation of nations.[9]

Ottoman Resistance to Reforms

The substance of these Armenian complaints was corroborated by the contents of an extensive report in which the roots of the Turko-Armenian conflict were being diagnosed. In that report veteran French Ambassador Cambon wrote: "The Armenian masses merely wanted reforms and were dreaming only of a workable administration under Ottoman domination. The inaction of the Porte has undermined the goodwill of the Armenians."[10]

The voluminous debates and the associated literature relative to the enacted Ottoman reforms have not resolved the serious doubts surrounding the nature and intent of these reforms. In considering such doubts one has to separate problems of administrative incompetence and/or impotency from the more serious issue of willingness for reform; the absence of the latter reduces the significance of the former. And yet, there seems to be a third, more fundamental issue, superseding these. It concerns ideology and cultural feasibility. Without exaggeration, one may contend that the most central, the most quintessential challenge in matters of reform was the urgency, and the European pressures attached to it, of placing the non-Muslim subjects on an overall equal footing with the dominant Muslims. It is believed that the formidable impediments connected with this task contributed heavily to the obstruction successive Ottoman regimes indulged in to thwart these reforms and thereby aggravated the evolving Turko-Armenian conflict. A telling example in this respect is the case of Koca Mustafa Reşad, who in the period 1846–1858, with intervals, occupied the post of Grand Vizier six different times. In his Memorandum to Sultan Mecid in 1856 he reportedly cast aspersions on the ideas of "complete emancipation" and "total equality" to be granted to non-Muslim subjects; these terms were inserted in the very reforms he previously had helped formulate and enact, especially the 1839 Reform Act. With reference to the text of the 1856 Reform Edict, he is quoted as saying that it contained "misleading definitions of meanings," the purpose of which was "to fool" the Europeans (*iğfal için konulmuş*). Finally, the Grand Vizier is seen providing in the same Memorandum a clue to this deception by way of deprecating the non-Muslims as mere "subject nations" (*milleti mahkûme*) to be ruled by "the dominant nation" (*milleti hâkime*).[11]

Echoing the common European view of the farcical character of these reforms prevalent at the end of the 1894-96 Abdul Hamit era massacres, which he had defined as "the pre-meditated, systematic and sustained extermination of the Armenian race," a French Academician dismissed these reforms as "pseudo-reforms."[12] Similarly, a French state document confirms the Ottoman pattern of issuing formal edicts and laws but countermanding them in subsequent orders. Within days after Abdul Hamit was persuaded by the Powers to issue the 1895 October Reform Act, for example, Grand Vizier Kâmil Paşa is reported to have issued a circular to provincial prefects directing them to disregard the Act.[13] Nearly two decades later the then ex-Grand Vizier is reported to have repeated his aversion to reforms as proposed by the Powers.[14]

Notes

1. *Nor Giank* 3, no. 11 (1 June 1900), pp. 164–5. The five published installments on this subject are all authored by Arpiar Arpiarian.
2. Even Sultan Abdul Hamit is on record as acknowledging this leading role by Odian. See Ismail Hami Danişmend, *Izahlı Osmanlı Tarihi Kronolojisi* (Annotated chronology of Ottoman history), vol. 4, (Istanbul: Türkiye Publications,

1961), p. 293. Another Turkish author, who for a while served as adviser to Sultan Abdul Hamit during the period of the massacres of that era, confirms the role of Odian, who "particularly distinguished himself" in drafting the Ottoman constitution. *The Memoirs of Kemal Bey*, Summerville Story, ed., (London: Constable and Co., 1920), p. 254.

3. Michael Varantian, *Haigagan Sharzhman Nakhabadmoutiunu* (The history of the origins of the Armenian revolutionary movement) (Geneva: Armenian Revolutionary Federation, 1913–14), pp. 56, 57, 66.

4. *Nor Giank* 3, no. 11 (1 June 1900), pp. 164–9; 3, no. 14 (15 July 1900), pp. 215–8.

5. Ibid., vol. 3, no. 16 (15 August 1900), pp. 245–50. For the work of the Commission on Reforms see Lilian Etmekjian, "The Armenian National Assembly of Turkey," *Armenian Review* 29, no. 1-113 (Spring 1976), pp. 38-52.

6. The encyclical was issued in Etchmiadzin, the Holy See near Yerevan, on 20 September 1896; a variation of the same encyclical is in Vartouhie Nalbandian, "The Armenian Revolutionary Movement," *Armenian Review* 2, no. 4-8 (Winter 1949–50), pp. 65–6. By mistake the name of Vahan Cardashian is given as author there.

7. Etmekjian, "The Armenian National Assembly," [n. 5], p. 48.

8. Quoted in A. O. Sarkissian, "History of the Armenian Question to 1885," *University of Illinois Bulletin* 35, no. 80 (3 June 1938), p. 88.

9. Yeghishe Ayvazian, *Pountch* (29 April 1878).

10. 28 February 1894 report in *Livre Jaune: Affaires Arméniennes, Projets de Réformes, 1893–1894* (Paris, 1897), p. 11; also *Documents Diplomatiques* vol. 11 (Paris, 1947), p. 11.

11. N. Nercessian, "Gardjarod Tzoutzoumner" (Succinct pointers), *Tashink* (Izmir Armenian Daily) vol. 7, no. 1923 (24 April 1919), p. 1. This article was the sixth in a seven-part series written to refute an Armenian deputy of the Ottoman Chamber who had declared the Turkish nation innocent of the crime of genocide while blaming the government and its provincial agents. In his declaration the Armenian deputy had invoked the spirit of Islam as embodying the principle of "freedom of conscience" (*hürriyeti vicdan*). For a Turkish source see A. Cevdet Paşa, *Tezâkir* (Memoirs), vol. 1, C. Baysun, ed. (Ankara: Turkish Historical Society, 1953), p. 79.

12. Albert Vandal, *Les Arméniens et la Réforme de la Turquie*, (Paris: Plon, 1897), pp. 10, 22–3.

13. French Aleppo Consulate Chargé Barthélemy to Ambassador Cambon, 26 October 1895 in *Livre Jaune: Affaires Arméniennes, Supplément, 1895-1896*, (Paris, 1897), p. 52.

14. FO 195/2452, no. 2526, 27 May 1913 report of British Consul General Cumberbatch.

5

The Advent of the Abdul Hamit Era
and the Onset of New Crises

The Outbreak of the 1877–78 Russo-Turkish War
and the Issue of Armenian Support

When Russian armies on 24 April 1877 started the war against Turkey by crossing the frontiers in the east of Turkey and in the Balkans, Patriarch Nercess Varjabedian the religious head of Ottoman Armenians, dispatched an encyclical to the primates and preachers of all Armenian churches of the Ottoman Empire. In it he stressed the centuries-old and unshakable loyalty of the vast majority of the Armenian *millet* towards the Empire and the Throne. "Consistent with the spirit of our Lord Jesus Christ's sublime injunction to 'render to Caesar the things that are Caesar's, and the things to God that are God's' (Mark 12: 17), we shall continue to remain loyal with much sincerity and dedication…Let us assist the Empire materially and morally."[1] Shortly thereafter Sultan Abdul Hamit, who only about six months previously had ascended the throne, urged the Armenians to form volunteer units to fight against the Russians. In complying with this request the patriarch had his circular read in all Armenian churches, inviting young Armenians to enroll in such units so that "Muslims and Christians could jointly defend the common fatherland, thereby establishing equality and at the same time affording the Armenians a chance to learn to defend themselves."[2]

It took several months, however, before the sultan's request was formalized through an Imperial Decree, which was issued on 28 November 1877. It provided for the raising of a reserve army of 150,000 men and a new militia force (home, or civil guard), comprising many battalions, from among able-bodied men twenty to forty years of age. The Imperial Ordinance required that "all non-Mussulman subjects share in the service of the Civil Guard, and so contribute, on the same footing as their Mussulman fellow-countrymen, to the defense of their homes and to the maintenance of public order."[3] This request was repeated in the Imperial Speech on the occasion of the opening of the second session of the newly established Ottoman Parliament on 13 December 1877. In it the sultan expressed "the true satisfaction of our Government" at "the readiness with which our non-Mussulman subjects volunteer to take part in this patriotic duty....the Constitution...has conceded them equal rights, which consequently entail equal duties."[4] Two weeks later Abdul Hamit appointed five non-Muslims as his aides-de-camp from among the *millet* leaders who had enrolled in the Civil Guard; of these, two were Armenians, including Tchayian Ilias, director of the Archives in the Ottoman Foreign Affairs Ministry, and of the remaining three, two were Greek, the other a Jew.

The information on the actual formation and performance of these home guard military units is not only scant but also somewhat contradictory. On the one hand, the General Assembly of the Ottoman Armenian Community, consisting of 120 deputies, all of whom were present, on 7 December 1877 in an atmosphere, "the solemnity [of which] was imposing," unanimously decided to proceed with the organization of the home guard Armenian units. The decision declared that the idea of such units "fully met the often reiterated wishes of the Armenians." More than 5,000 constituents "were assembled round the Deputies" while the latter deliberated.[5] However, on 17 December,—barely ten days later—the Armenians by a majority vote reversed themselves, thereby embarrassing their own patriarch, who had relayed to the Porte the previous pledge of the Armenians to assist in the defense of the Ottoman fatherland. In communicating this news to London, British Ambassador A. H. Layard expressed his belief that the German ambassador to Turkey, Prince Heinrich Reuss, had intervened in the meantime and pressured the Armenians. "It is by no means improbable that his Highness's [the German ambassador] counsels and warnings have led the Armenian clergy to reverse the decision they had previously come to."[6] It should be noted in this connection that Prince Bismarck, at the time chancellor of Germany, was overtly and covertly trying to help the cause of Russia. He considered the prospect of the latter's defeat in the 1877–78 Russo-Turkish War to be a major blow to German interests because of the probability of Austria then becoming a dominant power in Central Europe and in the Balkans.

The Problems of Integrated Military Service

The handling of the problem of military conscription for the non-Muslim subjects of the empire proved always vexing for the central government, as well as for the subjects themselves. On both sides there prevailed ambivalent sentiments, prejudices, and views, and opinions were divided. Armenians of modest means mostly preferred to serve in the army instead of being forced to pay the exemption fee of more than forty Turkish pounds, which was a huge sum for most of them. Others objected on the grounds that there was very little incentive to assist in the defense of a country whose governments would not or could not protect their subjects from ongoing depredations in the provinces, and who were forbidden to bear arms to defend themselves against outlaws and marauders freely roaming in the provinces. To be sure, the participation of the Armenians in the home guard was to be voluntary rather than compulsory,[7] but one of the rationales advanced in the debates of the second session of the Armenian Assembly, during which the Armenians withdrew their previous pledge to serve militarily, was their lack of military experience. They argued that having been denied the benefits of military training for centuries, they could not possibly acquit themselves in this respect by simply being dragged into military service at the height of a war.[8]

The Ottoman-Turkish aversion to the whole idea of non-Muslims being trained for incorporation into the military establishment was based on multifaceted considerations. Religious dogmas and associated traditional beliefs and values underlay these considerations. The dilemma that sprang up in this connection concerned the question of whether or not the non-Muslims should be integrated with existing army units or be formed into separate companies, battalions, and regiments. Other questions related to the matter of the highest rank to which non-Muslim officers could be allowed to advance. A more troubling question was the matter of placing Muslims under the command of "infidel" officers; could they be expected to be obeyed, and if not, was there not a danger to discipline? As noted earlier (chapter 2, note 3), already in 1835–36 Prussian Major Moltke, who entered Turkish service to reform and reorganize the army, had pondered these issues and made his recommendations. The issue was revived in the aftermath of the 1853–56 Crimean War, when the terms of the 1856 Paris Peace Conference were being negotiated between the Great Powers and Turkey. One proposal advocated the development of an integrated army by steps and through incremental progression, as far as the proportion of non-Muslim conscripts to that of Muslims was concerned. The Powers urged Turkey to adopt the principle of integration rather than separation, believing as they did that only through such integration involving "mixed" army units could there be achieved a *"rapprochement des races,"* and that the army was *"le moyen le plus efficace de l'obtenir."*[9]

There was another reason why separate units based on religion were intrinsically problematic. The Armenian *millet* had three confessional subdivisions involving Gregorian, Protestant, and Catholic Armenians, with separate ecclesiastical and civilian administrative bodies. Moreover, the lack of accord and harmony among the representatives of the Greek, Armenian, and Jewish communities was a condition that extended to these subsidiary communities themselves. In other words, the cleavages were quite pervasive, not only between Muslims and non-Muslims, but also among non-Muslims as well.

Abdul Hamit's Conflict with Midhat Paşa Regarding Racial-National Integration

Given these obstacles, the problem of the military involvement of the non-Muslim subjects of the empire remained insoluble; final, formal decisions were put off repeatedly. This was the case in 1856, after the Crimean War, and in 1877–78, in connection with the Russo-Turkish War. (The law of 7 August 1909, promulgated during the Ittihadist regime, and reconfirmed through the Temporary Law on Conscription of 12 May 1914 (*mükellefiyeti askeriye kanun*), ended this state of governmental hesitation and uncertainty.) A closer scrutiny of the manner in which Sultan Abdul Hamit handled the matter is instructive of the covert designs and intentions of Ottoman authorities confronting the emerging Armenian Question. One becomes readily cognizant of the rudiments of the governmental tactic of publicly declaring a policy, which is then countermanded by secret orders.

During the monarchical crisis of 1876, which ended with the removal from the throne of Sultan Abdul Aziz, his subsequent "suicide," and the ensuing crowning of Murad V, the veteran reformer Midhat Paşa had carried out negotiations with heir-apparent Prince Abdul Hamit regarding the need for radically reforming the Ottoman state system. Murad V was at the time proving a liability on account of some alleged mental problems. Eager to replace his older brother on the throne, the thirty-four-year-old Prince Abdul Hamit agreed, at Musluoğlu, to implement the reforms proposed by Midhat; that agreement was a condition for the reformists, led by Midhat, to marshal their forces to engineer and railroad Abdul Hamit's accession to the throne. As related by Ali Haydar Midhat, Midhat Paşa's son, Abdul Hamit skillfully reneged on most of his promises of reform once he ascended the throne and firmly established himself as monarch. Midhat wanted to introduce a measure of accountability and responsibility in the affairs of the Ottoman government and restrict the powers of the monarch. Above all, he insisted on the effective promulgation of the principle of political and legal equality of all Ottoman subjects, irrespective of race and creed. He desired to make the new Ottoman constitution "a matter of international obligation."

In fact, Midhat Paşa believed in the eventual fusion of all Ottoman subjects into a single nation-state in spite of existing religious and nationality differences. He considered integration in the educational system an essential tool for the accomplishment of this goal. As his son declared, "Midhat attached the greatest importance to the question of mixed schools in the provinces where Christians and Mussulmans lived together." And the thrust of that question became a major bone of contention between Midhat and the new monarch. After emphasizing this point repeatedly, Midhat's son reveals how the dogged pursuit of "this most important reform" precipitated the downfall of Grand Vizier Midhat Paşa, his father. For the attainment of his objective "of welding together the different elements of the nation he desired to make a beginning by applying it to the military academies of the Empire."[10] The sequence of events demonstrates that Abdul Hamit not only objected to this proposal, but that he was vehemently opposed to it. When Midhat Paşa wrote the inaugural speech the sultan was to deliver on ascending the throne, the *Hattı Humayun*, on 9 September 1876, Abdul Hamit in a breach of faith "omitted the essential sentences," transforming its key element. In expressing his "cherished scheme" regarding "mixed schools in the provinces," for example, Midhat had written: "We decree the foundation of these schools, in which instruction and education shall be common to all." The monarch changed this sentence to: "We desire that all our subjects...shall be able to profit by the benefits of knowledge..." Noting that the sultan was equivocating and temporizing on the issue, Midhat confronted the monarch, who demurred, whereupon the Grand Vizier, in a terse memorandum berated the monarch for an act of duplicity. It develops that Abdul Hamit had issued for public consumption, in particular for the benefit of the European diplomats who had gathered for the Constantinople Conference, a decree authorizing the admission of Christians into the military schools of the empire. An Armenian source confirms the publication of this decree in the official gazette of the Ottoman government.[11] But Midhat's memorandum of 24 January 1878, addressed to the monarch, reveals that the decree, i.e., the Imperial Rescript, was subsequently countermanded secretly, thereby prohibiting the enrollment of Christians. Midhat's reaction, conveyed through this memorandum, is excerpted below.

> Now, such a prohibition is calculated seriously to compromise, from the very beginning, an important reform that the whole world expects from the Constitution, and it is natural that obstacles of this kind should discourage and paralyse the efforts that we are constantly making to serve our country with devotion. We therefore regret sincerely that of all the questions which are now placed on the order of the day to be studied by the Council, this important one alone remains in suspense, and we regret it all the more inasmuch as the explanations that we addressed to His Majesty on the subject yesterday morning have remained unanswered.[12]

Exasperated by the failure of the sultan to remedy the situation and by the disdain with which his appeals and counsels were being treated, Midhat, in a daring memorandum six days later, openly challenged his monarch thus.

> SIRE—The object of promulgating the constitution was to abolish Absolutism, to indicate Your Majesty's rights and duties, to define and establish those of Ministers; in a word, to secure to the nation complete and entire liberty, and thus by a common effort to raise the condition and position of the country.
>
> Contrary to what had occurred in the case of former *Hattı Humayuns* promulgated thirty years back, the new charter was to subsist and receive its full application after the present political crisis should be at an end; for our object in promulgating that Constitution was certainly not merely to find a solution of the so-called Eastern Question, nor to seek thereby to make a demonstration that should conciliate the sympathies of Europe which had been estranged from us.
>
> Allow me, Sire, to offer a few observations on this subject. In the first place, Your Majesty, who is responsible before the nation for your acts, is bound to be acquainted with your duties as well as with your rights and prerogatives. It is, moreover, indispensable that Ministers should have the certain conviction of being able to accomplish their tasks, and that we should be able to free ourselves from that habit of servile flattery which has debased our people and ruined the country during the last four centuries.
>
> I am animated by a profound respect for the person of Your Majesty. But basing my conduct on the ordinances of the Cheri [sacred law], I am bound to withhold obedience to the commands of Your Majesty whenever they are not in conformity with the interests of the nation; otherwise the weight of my responsibility would be too heavy for me to bear. The dictates of my conscience that command me to conform my acts to the salvation and prosperity of my country impose an imperative obligation on me; and the judgment of my country, which is what I respect and cherish most, forbids me to act otherwise.

It is now nine days, Sire, since you have abstained from giving a favourable answer to my petition. You thereby refuse to sanction laws indispensable to the welfare of the country, and without which our whole previous work will be rendered futile. Whilst Your Majesty's Ministers are engaged in endeavouring to restore the governmental edifice which has with much difficulty escaped total ruin, surely Your Majesty would not willingly add to the work of destruction.[13]

In the end, Grand Vizier Midhat was not only relieved of his post, but was banished into exile, only to meet there during his second exile a violent death perpetrated by the agents of the sultan. First, through deception, Midhat was lured into the palace within four days of sending the above-cited memorandum to the monarch. Without being granted the promised audience and the associated concessions Midhat had set forth in that memorandum, on 5 February 1878 he was forcibly put on board the Imperial yacht and promptly expelled from the country for an indefinite period. Afraid that Midhat could return, regain power, and avenge himself, Abdul Hamit lured him back to Istanbul under the pretense of a pardon, and after some temporary appointments to administrative posts, in April 1881 put him on trial on charges of complicity in "the murder" of Sultan Abdul Aziz, the monarch's uncle. Following his conviction, Midhat was exiled once more, which this time proved lethal, as in May 1884, after some three years of perilous banishment, he was strangled by the sultan's henchmen.

Three points call for discussion in this macabre drama that played out at the very start of Abdul Hamit's reign. These are points that have a critical bearing upon the dramas associated with the evolving stages of the Turko-Armenian conflict: (1) the prevailing Ottoman-Turkish aversion to the idea of integrating non-Muslims into mainstream national life, whether through public education or military training; (2) the concealment of this fact through the promulgation of formal edicts intending to mislead the European Powers pressing for reform; and, (3) early evidence of the practice of a system of dual-track communications, whereby official orders given for public consumption are countermanded by subsequent or concomitant secret orders in particular, in matters relating to the non-Muslim minorities.

The Ambivalence of Armenian Voices in the First Ottoman Parliament and in Other High Councils

Due to the unrelenting pressure of the Powers, the newly installed monarch, Abdul Hamit, undertook to appoint several non-Muslims to relatively high posts in the system of Ottoman provincial administration. From among the Armenians Gosdan Paşa was appointed to the post of *müsteşar*, undersecretary or councillor, of the province of Bosnia and Herzegovina, and Margos Ağapegian was appointed *müsteşar* of Van province. Furthermore, Hovannes Tchamitch became minister of commerce and agriculture and Hovannes Sakız *Müsteşar* in the Ministry of Public Education. In the general assembly of notables, which Grand Vizier Midhat had convened to respond to the final version of the demands for reform by the European representatives of the Constantinople Conference, about 50 of the total of 237 participants of this "Grand Council" were non-Muslims. Those demands were a diluted version of the original demands of the Powers who, through the leadership of British representative Lord Salisbury, did all they could to accommodate Turkish objections and thereby avert the ultimate failure of the conference.

The conference was convened to stop the insurrections and wars in the Balkans and to pacify the regions through the promulgation of reforms to be guaranteed by the Powers. During the debates in this Council Father Hovannes Mugurian, the Locum Tenens of the Armenian patriarchate, and Reverend Krikor Enfiyedjian raised their voices to declare the demands of the Powers unacceptable. Despite the warning of then-Grand Vizier Midhat Paşa, who himself was dead-set against the idea of foreign involvement in Ottoman internal affairs, but nevertheless was wary of the consequences of a rejection of the demands of the Powers, and despite the grave risks inherent in any rejection of these demands, including the threat of a war with Russia, about the probability of which Salisbury had warned the Turks, the Grand Council almost unanimously decided to reject the demands, i.e., the ultimatum of the Powers. Only one Turk, Halet Paşa, then minister of commerce, and one Armenian, Reverend Hagop Madteosian, the religious head of the Armenian Protestant community, dared to disagree, in the firm belief that the war, expected to break out following such rejection, would prove disastrous for Turkey. The latter's mastery of Ottoman Turkish enabled him to stir up the patriotism of the assembled notables through his eloquence. In a gesture of appreciation for the manifest support he received from the representatives of the *millets*, Grand Vizier Midhat departed from established custom and by a personal visit to the Armenian patriarch, as well as to the other two religious leaders, the Greek patriarch and the chief rabbi, expressed his thanks. The reception was enthusiastic. As flowers were thrown Midhat's way, he declared that he recognized no distinctions between Muslims and non-Muslims, as "they were all children of the same country."[14] The Armenian deputies of the first Ottoman Parliament were even more ardent in their display of Ottoman patriotism during the crisis of the Russo-Turkish War. Following the November 1876–January 1877 elections, ten of the eighty-six elected deputies were Armenian,[15] seventeen Greek, eight Slavs, and three Christian Arabs.

Even though evidence indicates that the Armenian Assembly, in a heated debate on 17 December 1877, rejected the proposal for the military conscription of non-Muslims after it had approved it previously, the speeches of several Armenian deputies in the Parliament nevertheless do refer to the actual formation of Armenian combat units engaged in battle in the ongoing war against the Russians. This is in spite of the fact that on 3 January 1878, the first items on the agenda of the Ottoman Chamber of Deputies was the matter of the military service of non-Muslims. Istanbul's Armenian deputy, Hagop Kazezian, had suggested at that sitting that the issue should be allowed to clarify itself in due course of time and should not be railroaded through the Chamber. In the same vein, he caustically observed that "if military service is an obligation for non-Muslims on the basis of the principle of equality with Muslims, the same principle of equality should be extended to their rights." Consequently, the Chamber decided to defer the matter until such time as a concrete draft bill materialized.[16] Notwithstanding, the formation of non-Muslim military units proceeded in some areas "and a battalion of Christian volunteers was raised at their own expense," and marched to the front, "where they distinguished themselves greatly...by their courage and devotion."[17] Moreover, the Armenians of Erzurum "had integrated for more than a year with their Muslim brethren in defense of the common fatherland."[18] Furthermore, when the Russians demanded the surrender from Muhtar Paşa of the city of Erzurum and its fortress—due to the untenable military situation of the Turks—the two Armenian deputies of Erzurum, Ballarian, and Kharadjian, spearheaded the movement to reject the Russian ultimatum. The governor-general of that province, in a telegram, informed the grand vizier that "the Armenian people of Erzurum is prepared to fight to the last drop of their blood for the defense of the rights of the Ottoman state with which the destiny of the Armenian people is inextricably interwoven." With words of thanks and congratulations, the Vizier forwarded the telegram to the Armenian patriarch.[19]

The tacit indictment of the Ottoman system and government regarding the matter of inequality alluded to above by the Armenian deputy

Kazezian was symptomatic of the frustration and bitterness of the Armenians in this respect. It had reference to the latter's plight despite the solemnly promised benefits associated with the promulgation of the twin Tanzimat reform acts of 1839 and 1856, and of the new and purportedly model liberal constitution of 1876. For the wary Armenians there was a subdued but pervasive sense that all the official proclamations and public gestures of esteem toward the Armenian people were convenient conjurations prompted by the critical exigencies of the ongoing war. The intensification of the tempo of wholesale plunders, rapes, abductions, and massacres by the Kurds in the eastern theaters of the war, that continued the process of dislocating and decimating the provincial Armenian population, was a source of grave concern. The authorities seemed to be relying on their aptitude to feign punishing these predators, but when it suited them, these authorities, led by Sultan Abdul Hamit himself, did not hesitate to openly woo and pamper the chieftains of these marauding tribes in the very capital of the empire. The chieftains included the emirs of certain Kurdish tribes and the notorious Sheikh Celaleddin; they were the guests of Hafız Paşa and the palace camarilla who decorated them.[20]

The gravity of Armenian concerns was brought into special relief by Bishop Narbey during the courtesy visit Grand Vizier Midhat granted the Armenian patriarch on 24 December 1876. Addressing Midhat, the bishop intoned: "Do hear our humble entreaty. Deliver us from the depredations of the *derebeyis* and the Kurds. The Armenian thus delivered shall demonstrate that he is the loyal servant of this mighty state bent on laboring with docile faithfulness."[21] That Armenian concerns were well founded is attested to by no lesser a figure than the sultan, himself. When, upon Imperial request, Patriarch Varjabedian appeared in the palace for an audience on August 10(22), 1877, the monarch expressed his satisfaction with the Armenian *millet* in the following words.

> I know that the Armenian people suffered a great deal in this war. But they should know that as compensation for these hardships very good times await them. They will reap all the benefits due them for their loyalty; good fortunes are in store for them. I am fond of all my subjects but especially the Armenian people who in these grave times have demonstrated the fruits of their centuries-old fidelity. For me there is no difference between Muslims and Christians; they are all Ottomans. Religion is a domain that pertains to God.

The sultan then decorated the patriarch with the bejeweled *Osmaniyye* medallion.[22]

As the monarch so spoke, once more displaying his gift for showering his guests with beguiling compliments to suit his momentary needs, the condition of the Armenian population in the war zones of the eastern provinces remained as perilous as Kurdish and Circassian outlaws were free to render it. As recounted by the correspondent of the *London Times*, and eyewitness to the atrocities, the Armenian population of the entire region situated between Kars and Köprüköy, near Erzurum, was the target of a frenzy of destruction. The correspondent of the German newspaper *National Zeitung* for his part observed: "It is clear that had the war continued in this fashion under these conditions, the Christian population of Turkish Armenia...would have been exterminated in less than a year."[23] One common atrocity was the burning alive of men who "were smeared with shoemaker's wax and naphtha and were set afire by way of torches in order to illuminate the orgy of these barbarians."[24] The correspondent of the "entirely Turkophile" *Daily Telegraph* felt constrained to report, on 12 June 1877, on an array of other Kurdish atrocities in the areas of Beyazid and Van. A Russian officer, Captain Stokvitch in his report described how "children and adults were being thrown into flames and the cries of these unhappy victims, especially women, were heartrending. The streets of Beyazid were strewn with decapitated and mutilated corpses."[25] It was in consideration of the horrors of these atrocities that former Patriarch Khrimian bitterly and sarcastically deplored the sultan's gesture of decorating his successor, Patriarch Nercess, with these words: "They fashioned a necklace out of the bones of the sheep and hung it on the neck of the shepherd."[26]

Despite a full measure of knowledge of these conditions, to which large segments of the provincial Armenian population were exposed, there was no consensus among the Armenian masses, nor among their diverse leaders, about the right political choice. Should they be able to choose, which regime might be preferable, the Tsarist Russian or the Ottoman Turkish? The Russo-Turkish War had accentuated the need for such a choice. Generally speaking, the lower strata of the provincial Armenian population, and even of the Ottoman capital, yearned for a Russian regime. The merchant classes, the higher echelons of the clergy and conservative Armenians preferred the Ottoman regime. The dual rationales thus dividing the Armenian *millet* had reference to more or less two antithetical, imageries. It was maintained, for example, that even though the Ottoman Turks were capable of barbaric behavior, they did not try to forcibly assimilate the Armenians who within certain bounds and restrictions were allowed to retain their ethnic identity. The Russians, on the other hand, it was believed were bent on absorbing the

Armenians within the Orthodox Church and mainstream Russian national life through methods of assimilation that bordered on coercion. In the end, it was argued, the Armenian nation may end up dissolving itself, whereas under Turkish dominion it may survive and even flourish as a distinct nation. In this sense the proponents of Ottoman orientation, apart from some selfish motives issuing from their socioeconomic advantages and privileged positions, were imbued with a spirit of Armenianism that placed a premium upon ethnicity, despite their Ottomanist loyalties.

Within days after the outbreak of the war with Russia, Armenian deputies in the Ottoman Parliament vociferously, and to the loud acclaim of their fellow Muslim colleagues, inveighed against Russia. In the 25 April 1877 session, for example, the Armenian deputy from Aleppo, Manouk Kharadjian (Karaca), was in the forefront of those repudiating Russian claims that they, the Russians, were coming as the protectors of the Christians. He categorically declared that the Armenians did not need Russian protection, as they were content with their lot. He added that the Armenians of his district were ready to make any sacrifice in defense of their Ottoman fatherland.[27] Istanbul's Armenian deputy, Sebuh Maksudian, subscribed to the view expressed by his Armenian colleague and proposed that the government come up with a project to maximize the ability of the Christians to serve the state. Edirne's Armenian deputy, Roupen, reiterated the point that the Armenians he represented could never accept Russian protection and were ready to make every sacrifice to repel the aggression of Russia.[28] In his speech, Erzurum's Armenian deputy, Hamazasb Ballarian, endorsed the views of his Armenian colleagues, adding: "Ever since they lost their independence, the Armenians for five hundred years have been able to preserve their religion, language, and nationhood under Ottoman rule." He was seconded in this view by Daniel Kharadjian, the other Armenian deputy from Erzurum, adding that "Armenian and Muslim brothers are armed together and that in order to serve as an example to my compatriots, I too enlisted as a simple soldier."[29]

The Muslim deputies, especially those from Erzurum (Mehmed), Hicaz (Arab Ülema), Syria (Nakaş), were elated. The proposal was made to translate the speeches in every language so that "the whole world becomes cognizant of the views of the Christians and accordingly assess the value of the Russian pretext." Finally, Interior Minister Cevdet Paşa came to the podium and expressed the appreciation of the Imperial Government for the sentiments of patriotism and accord displayed by Muslim and Christian deputies. His words were received with prolonged and energetic applause.[30]

It was the thrust of this type of Ottoman patriotism that emboldened some of these very Armenian deputies, however, to reverse themselves and some two months later assail what they considered to be the wicked and sinister aspects of the Ottoman regime affecting the provincial Armenian population. The issue was the ongoing depredations by the Kurds and the impunity accorded to them by the Ottoman authorities. By raising this issue the Armenian deputies imparted to the Armenian Question a formal, institutional character; it was introduced in the Ottoman Parliament for the first time as an urgent national issue requiring public debate, parliamentary deliberation and solution by the Executive. As such, this Armenian initiative served to openly formalize the Turko-Armenian conflict that, in its rudimentary stages of development—and some years earlier than the convening of the Berlin Congress—already acquired an official character. In commenting on the significance of this initiative by the Armenian deputies, *Massis*, the principal contemporary Armenian newspaper in the Ottoman capital, wrote the following words: "For the first time this important question was raised and a remedy was sought before a great assembly of the state."[31]

Several Armenian deputies, supported by Greek and even Turkish colleagues, directed attention to the fact that while the Armenian *millet* was demonstrating its will to defend the Ottoman fatherland, thousands of Armenians were being assaulted and killed in the border regions by marauding regular and irregular Ottoman troops, including Kurds.[32] Apart from this issue of war-related conflict, a more fundamental source of conflict came to the fore and on 4(16) June 1877, which fell on a Saturday, it dominated the debate in the fledgling Ottoman Parliament. It was an issue which, evolving gradually, came to be called Armenian Reforms and as such, it formed the core of the Armenian Question. The issues specifically involved (a) the depredations perpetrated against the unarmed Armenian population in the eastern provinces by fully armed Kurdish tribes (*aşirets*); (b) the impunity attending and following these depredations; and (c) the suspected complicity of the local as well as central authorities. For the first time in Ottoman history, representatives of the *raya*, subject peoples, ventured to publicly and officially raise their voices in protest against inequities endemic in the Ottoman provincial social system. The first speaker was the Greek deputy Soulides. He compared the plight of the Armenians to that of the Greeks and Bulgarians in the Balkans who, however, were able to sensitize Europe about their suffering and secure remedies. He then added, "Deprived of this vehicle of remedy, the Armenians silently endured their bitter hardships. But is it just that the Armenians, the most loyal and obedient subject of the state, be so plagued and persecuted, by of all people, the Kurds, who are rebels acting against our state?" He ended his interpellation by demanding "an immediate end to this unbearable state of affairs." He was followed on the podium by Erzurum's Armenian deputy Hamazasp Ballarian. After recounting the litany of abuses committed by a host of Kurdish tribes in Muş, Van, and certain other districts of Erzurum, the Armenian deputy detailed the prevailing procedures of dealing with the offenders who were caught by the authorities. Upon payment of a bribe, they would be released,

> only to resume their crimes with greater ferocity against their accusers. Many of the governors, *valis* and *mutesarrifs*, were the accomplices of these Kurds and whose names at present I would not care to reveal. Upon my question as to why these Kurds are not being punished when two battalions might be enough to deal with them, the answer which I received was that there lies in this matter high governmental wisdom, a hidden political dispensation [*hikmeti hükümet*]. Only later did I learn what this meant: the Kurds would be needed for the purpose of repressing the Armenians in the event they should rise up in Armenia [eastern provinces of Turkey].
>
> In addition, these Kurds were envisaged as potential volunteer corps to be engaged against Russia in the event of a war.... On what grounds did the Kurds manage to inspire such confidence, on the basis of what attributes or what usefulness?

The next speaker was Vasilaki, another Greek deputy, who concurred with the charges and suggestions made by the two previous deputies; he made a motion to authorize the Sublime Porte to initiate concrete steps for the immediate implementation of the remedies proposed. "All Muslim deputies voiced their agreement with the diagnosis of the problem and the proposals for a solution advanced by the three deputies."[33] The sultan not only ignored these recommendations but subsequently and finally prorogued the Parliament when military setbacks and continuous expressions of discontent against the rule of the sultan in the winter 1877–78 session by Muslim and non-Muslim deputies proved too unsettling for the monarch.

With this lapse into the traditional traps of the pre-parliamentary regime and this reversion to the preconstitutional autocracy of the Ottoman monarchs, the Turko-Armenian conflict entered a new phase of aggravation. The Armenian grievances and the attendant efforts to seek and obtain redress against incremental inequities were progressively castigated by the provincial as well as central authorities as signs of patent disloyalty and seditiousness. The advent on the scene of group-ings of Armenian revolutionaries and the transition from the govern-mental practices of oppression to those of repression were the catalysts for the steady escalation of the levels of the Turko-Armenian conflict. At the center of this sanguinary drama stood the personality and stan-dards of misrule of Sultan Abdul Hamit. Within a few years after dis-solving the Ottoman Parliament and suspending the constitution he emerged as a resourceful and agile, but lethal tyrant, acquiring the epi-thet "The Red Sultan." In brief, the general imagery of "the loyal *mil-let*," which Ottoman Turks held about the Armenians of the empire, was discarded and supplanted by a new image depicting the Armenians in general as the internal foe of an empire beleaguered by covetous external foes.

The Issue of Military Service Revisited

The significance of this issue in terms of its relationship to the pos-sibilities of obviating, if not resolving, the Turko-Armenian conflict cannot be overestimated. Military service, predicated on the principle of equality, i.e., equal rights and equal obligations, has always been viewed as an instrument of leveling basic differences in race, ethnicity, and above all, religion, in multiethnic state organizations. Through the dynamics of integral training, involving disciplined combativeness for the defense of a common fatherland rather than for Islam, for example, ethnocultural cleavages seem to be amenable to a process of transfor-mation whereby such cleavages may attenuate; under certain circum-stances they may even prove capable of disappearing in due course of time.

The first formal decree stipulating conscription in the Ottoman army for Muslims and non-Muslims alike was issued in connection with the second Tanzimat reform act (1856), in the wake of the Crimean War. At that time, when the head tax was abolished in compliance with the wishes of the Powers (1854), Sir Henry Bulwer, British Ambassador in Istanbul, was anxious to help save the Ottoman Empire from disinte-gration by promoting efforts to create a truly Ottoman fatherland and Ottoman people. For him the conditions of military training were best suited to encourage the decline of prejudices; he considered the cama-raderie of barrack life a potential fertile soil where the process of social merging and amalgamation could proceed with a degree of certainty. "Let the subjects of the Porte be made into real soldiers, and they will soon forget whether they be Mussulmans or Christians," he declared.[34] By the Imperial Firman of Reforms, issued by Sultan Abdul Aziz in December 1875, the first significant modification was undertaken in the regulation of the military exemption tax. When Sultan Mahmud II destroyed the troublesome and dangerous *Yeniçeris*, a kind of praetorian guard system, he established in their place the regular (*nizam*) army, thereby introducing the principle of universal conscription. By exempting the non-Muslims from it, he imposed upon the latter the exemption tax to be paid indiscriminately by all males of non-Muslim families. In the modification described above, the exemption tax was confined to those between the ages of twenty and forty.

The financial burdens resulting from this tax proved nevertheless exacting for most non-Muslims, including Armenians, of these age categories. It was largely the urge to obtain relief from these burdens that prompted multitudes of Armenians to welcome the Ottoman proposals for universal conscription "rather than from any military ardour to bear their share of the Empire's defence."[35] When, in 1909, the Young Turk Ittihadists finally decided to introduce legislation mandating military conscription—instead of voluntary enlistment—for non-Muslim citizens, the Armenians welcomed the act. But, given the resistance of some Turkish groups, they became nevertheless wary. This attitude was manifested in a mass meeting at which, through the leadership of Armenian deputy Krikor Zohrab, a resolution was passed, excerpts from which are adduced below.

Considering that:

1. Military service for the various elements of the nation is the fundamental condition of safeguarding civil equality under the Constitution;
2. It is the earnest wish of the Armenian people to serve the Motherland as citizen-soldiers;
3. The disastrous economic condition of the Armenian population renders it impossible for it to pay the onerous military tax;
4. By general agreement, all political parties in the country have accepted the principle of military service for Ottoman subjects of every race;
5. Above all, the Government has not only shelved the question of military service, but is also laying before Parliament a measure for the continued levy of the military tax;

it is hereby unanimously resolved:

to approach Parliament and all political parties, so as to claim the right of military service for Armenians, a claim based on the principle of equality under the Constitution for all Ottoman subjects, a right that can never be withdrawn; and to pray that Parliament shall reject such proposals of the Government and shall forthwith sanction the project of military service for Christians, since further to postpone the question might cause discontent in those elements of the Ottoman nation which rightly regard the fulfillment of this demand as a guarantee of the consolidation of the Constitution. The meeting also considers it right to add that the Armenian nation is starving and will never be able to pay this crushing tax, and that it will insist on its sacred right to serve the country with its life and not by a pecuniary compensation which is at once unfair and contrary to the principle of the Constitution. Only the granting of this right can ensure the sincere and fruitful union of Mohammedans and non-Mohammedans.[36]

But there was considerable temporizing in the Ottoman Parliament. When early in 1909 several young Armenians applied for training as officers in the military academy (*Harbiye*), they were turned down on the ground that the new draft bill on compulsory military service for non-Muslims had not yet become the law of the land. The applicants protested, and decried the new bill as "a farce." The response of the authorities was that they were free to enlist as volunteers in the army. A year after the new bill for military service was drafted, the Chamber of Deputies, i.e., the Lower House of Parliament, had passed only six clauses (April 1910) as further discussions were repeatedly adjourned. For all practical purposes, however, the conscription procedures were eventually put in place as if the whole of the bill had already become law. Most importantly, the new system of recruitment, relinquishing as it did the fiscal benefits issuing from the magnitude of receipts of military exemption tax money, was estimated to cost the Ottoman Treasury about one million British pounds sterling,[37] a huge sum at the time for the poverty-stricken Ottoman state.

Despite all these initiatives, however, the fundamental obstacles of the problem could not be overcome. Not all Armenians were eager to serve in the Turkish army and the overwhelming majority of the Muslims were vehemently opposed to that idea. The reasons were complex but basically they involved disdain, bordering on contempt, of the *raia* subjects, who were regarded as objects fit only for subservience to the Muslim overlords. Moreover, there were two ancillary problems besetting the Turks. Military service for non-Muslims was bound to usher in an era of tangible equality for non-Muslims, thus curbing, if not helping to abolish, the dominant status of the Muslims. In addition, all Muslims, e.g., Turks, Kurds, and Circassians, could not see themselves ever being commanded by Armenians, or for that matter, by any non-

Muslim officers. The idea was anathema to them. Yet, for the Armenians at least, accessibility to the rank of officer was a pre-condition for acceptance of the principle of military service. As French historian Le Viscomte de la Jonquière observed, however, this was an impossible demand, as far as attaining the higher ranks was concerned; in his book he described the structural difficulties in this regard.[38] The British author, A. Gallenga, anticipated that "Christian youths in barracks would be exposed to nameless outrages, and that, on the other hand, if attempts were made to enlist Mussulmans and Christians in separate battalions or squadrons, collision between the different corps, whenever they might be brought together, would be inevitable." He further referred to "the prejudice strongly rooted in the Mussulman mind, that the Christian is too ignoble a being to be honoured with the use of the soldier's weapons, and by the, perhaps, more reasonable apprehension that he is too dangerous to be trusted with them."[39]

The persistence of these obstacles, endemic in the theocratic Ottoman state, is reflected in the more or less uniform treatment of Armenians in the 1877–78 war Turkey fought against Russia; in that war the Armenians were relegated to the status of beasts of burden or "pack animals." In this Russo-Turkish War, 20,000 to 30,000 Armenians had to carry on their backs heavy weapons and ammunition for long stretches of territory which were devoid of other means of transport.[40] This treatment was inflicted upon the Armenians in spite of their displays of loyalty and cooperation, as exemplified by the following boastful remark Erzurum's Armenian deputy, Daniel Kharadjian, made in the Ottoman Parliament on 22 December 1877: "Ignoring the Russian pretense of wanting to protect us, we young and old Armenians formed home guard milice units. Despite my status, and abandoning my sense of pride (*bil-iftihar*), I joined these units. The companies we formed grew steadily to become battalions. We shall respond to the Russian offer to protect us with our bayonets. (massive applause)."[41]

When assessing the abortiveness of the efforts to include the non-Muslim subjects of the Ottoman Empire in the plan of universal military conscription, Gallenga prognosticated the catastrophe that befell the Armenian population of the Ottoman Empire during World War I. In discussing "the enrollment of the Christians in the ranks of the army," he "regretted" that the plan was jettisoned and offered this observation.

> The great point at issue in everything connected with the existence of the Ottoman empire is the religious question. You must either make one people out of Mussulmans and Christians, or one of the two races will eventually destroy the other.[42]

Notes

1. *Massis* (Constantinople Armenian newspaper) 28 April 1877, no. 1964.
2. Khoren Kapigian, *Haigagan Hartzu Arevelyan Hartzee Metch 1860–1880* (The Armenian Question within the Eastern Question 1860–1880), (Beirut: n.p., 1962), p. 148.
3. *British Foreign Office Archives* (Kew, London) FO 424/63, Doc. no. 162, 162/1, enclosure pp. 100–1.
4. *British Blue Books.* Turkey no. 1 (1878), Doc. no. 598. 13 December 1877 communication of Turkish Foreign Minister Server Paşa to Musurus Paşa, Turkish ambassador to Great Britain, pp. 543–4.
5. Ibid., Doc. no. 612, 612/1, pp. 561-2. 8 December 1877 report.
6. Ibid., Doc. no. 633, p. 579. 18 December 1877 report.
7. FO 424/67, Doc. no. 502, Registry no. 21, p. 216. Trabzon's British Vice-Consul Alfred Biliotti's 27 January 1878 report to Foreign Secretary Earl of Derby confirming the intent of the sultan that enrollment in the Civic Guard on the part of the Armenians was to be voluntary, not compulsory.
8. Kapigian, *Haigagan* [n. 2], p. 162.
9. E. Engelhardt, *La Turquie et le Tanzimat, histoire des réformes dans l'Empire Ottoman depuis 1826 jusqu'à nos jours* (Turkey and the Tanzimat, history of reforms from 1826 up to our time), vol. 1 (Paris: Cotillon and Co., 1882), pp. 145–6.
10. *The Life of Midhat Pasha: A Record of His Services, Political Reforms, Banishment, and Judicial Murder, Derived from Private Documents and Reminiscences by His Son Ali Haydar Bey*, (London: John Murray, 1903), pp. 111, 127, 129, 137, 141–2. See also Stanford J. Shaw and Ezel Kural Shaw, *History of the Ottoman Empire and Modern Turkey*, vol. 2, *Reform, Revolution and Republic* (Cambridge: Cambridge University Press, 1977), p. 180.
11. Father Minas V. Nourikhan, *Zhamanagagitz Badmoutiun 1868–1878* (Contemporary history), vol. 3 (Venice: St. Lazare Printing House, 1907), p. 363. The date of the publication is indicated to be 28 January 1878, which, in Ottoman practice, is often a routine case of delayed publication.
12. *The Life of Midhat* [n. 10], pp. 142–3.
13. Ibid., pp. 143–4.
14. Nourikhan, *Zhamanagagitz* [n. 11], pp. 362, 363, 365; *The Life of Midhat* [n. 10], pp. 131, 136.
15. Here is a list of them for the first session (7 March–16 June 1877): Roupen (Edirne), Manouk Kharadjian or Karaca (Aleppo), Hovsep Kazazian (Diyarbekir), Daniel Kharadjian and Hamazasb Ballarian (Erzurum), Hagop Shirinian (Sivas), Sahag Yavruian (Hüdavendigâr or Bursa), Krikor Buzdikian (Adana), Sebuh Maksudian, Hovannes Allahverdian or Hüdaverdian (Istanbul); Serviçen became Senator shortly after his election as deputy from Istanbul. For the second session of the Chamber of Deputies (13 December 1877–14 February 1878), the eleven Armenian deputies were more or less the same people except for Melkon Doniloğlu (Ankara), Ispartalian or Ispartalıoğlu Agop (Aydın), Sakayian Aleksan and Hagop Kazezian (Istanbul), Ohannes Güreghian (Trabzon), and Hagop Kazancian (Tuna, i.e., Danube). In both sessions Hovannes Allahverdian, deputy from Istanbul, served as second deputy president of the Chamber without being duly elected by the deputies but only thanks to the intervention of Sultan Abdul Hamit, against which intervention several deputies, including Armenian ones, protested as an unlawful act. Mihran Düzian, together with Serviçen, became

the only Armenian senator in that Upper House comprising thirty members, of whom seven were non-Muslims. Cemal Kutay, *Türkiye Istiklâl ve Hürriyet Mücadeleleri Tarihi* (The history of Turkey's struggles for independence and freedom), vol. 13 (Istanbul: Tarih, 1960), pp. 7531–9; Nourikhan, *Zhamanagagitz* [n. 11], pp. 367, 544. Hamparzoum Yeranian, *Houshartzan Van-Vasbouraganee* (Memorial for Van-Vasbouragan) vol. 1 (Alexandria, Egypt: n.p. 1929), pp. 108–9.

16. Nourikhan, *Zhamanagagitz* [n. 11], p. 545.
17. *Midhat* [n. 10], p. 136.
18. Nourikhan, *Zhamanagagitz* [n. 11], p. 373.
19. Ibid., p. 507, n. 1.
20. Ibid., p. 547.
21. Kapigian, *Haigagan* [n. 2], p. 140.
22. Quoted in ibid., p. 157; Mikayel Varantian, *Haigagan Sharzhman Nakhabadmoutiunu* (The history of the origins of the Armenian revolutionary movement), vol. 2 (Geneva: Armenian Revolutionary Federation publication, 1914), p. 132.
23. *Russes et Turcs: La guerre d'Orient* (Russians and Turks: The war in the east), vol. 1 (Paris: Librairie de la Société Anonyme, 1878), p. 318, right hand column. No author is indicated.
24. Ibid.
25. Ibid., pp. 322, right hand column, 324, left hand column.
26. Varantian, *Haigagan* [n. 22], p. 132.
27. Kutay, *Türkiye* [n. 15], vol. 10, pp. 6502–3.
28. Nourikhan, *Zhamanagagitz* [n. 11], pp. 372–3.
29. Kutay, *Türkiye* [n. 15], vol. 10, pp. 6512, 6524–5; Varantian, *Haigagan* [n. 22], p. 134–6.
30. Nourikhan, *Zhamanagagitz* [n. 11], pp. 374; Kutay, *Türkiye* [n. 15], vol. 10, pp. 6513–4, 6524, 6525–6.
31 *Massis,* 9(21)June 1877.
32. A. O. Sarkissian, *History of the Armenian Question to 1885*, reprint, (Urbana, IL, 1938), (*University of Illinois Bulletin,* vol. 35, no. 80 (3 June 1938), pp. 58–60.
33. These details were culled from the main Armenian newspaper, *Massis*, no. 1985, 7(19) June 1877. In a prefatory statement the editors of the newspaper expressed their appreciation for the display of "lofty humanitarian sentiments" of the two Greek deputies and conveyed "the sentiments of gratitude of the entire Armenian nation, upon which they can lay their indisputable claim by virtue of the sublime patriotic statements they made."
34. Quoted in A. Gallenga, *Two Years of the Eastern Question*, vol. 1 (London: Samuel Tinsely, 1877), p. 186.
35. F. G. Aflalo, *Regilding the Crescent* (Philadelphia: Lippincott, 1911), p. 233.
36. Reproduced in ibid., pp. 235, 236.
37. Ibid., p. 236.
38. Le Viscomte de la Jonquière, *Histoire de l'Empire Ottoman*. New and revised edition, vol. 2, (Paris: Hachette, 1914), pp. 594–6.
39. Gallenga, *Two Years* [n. 34], pp. 183, 197.
40. *The Eastern Question and the Armenians* (pamphlet) (London, 1878), quoted in Varantian, *Haigagan* [n. 22], pp. 143–4.
41. Kutay, *Türkiye* [n. 15], vol. 10, p. 6524.
42. Gallenga, *Two Years* [n. 34], pp. 186–7.

6

The Advent of Armenian Revolutionaries and the Ottoman Turkish Backlash

Victim Responses and Notions of Provocation

In international conflicts, all other things being equal, the decision to escalate and the initiative to direct the course of the conflict belongs to the more powerful nation. Yet, one cannot entirely dismiss the dynamics of mutual relations and the attendant interactive mechanisms as factors affecting the processes and outcomes of such conflicts. Victim responses to actual or anticipated acts of victimization are part of these mechanisms and are subject to constraints which are more or less imposed by the victimizers; these constraints are such as to provoke the victim to be "provocative." In this sense victim "provocations" are a dependent rather than an independent variable in more than one respect. The main thrust of such victim roles is by necessity the goal of obviating or reducing the level of victimization. As such, "provocations" can, therefore, essentially be diverse forms of responses to acts of victimization involving at their point of origin grievance manifestations. Their transformation into violent confrontations are functions devolving upon the more powerful dominant group reacting to the grievance and/or to the devices used in the expression of the grievance. The voluminous reports of consular correspondence published by the British Foreign Office (in 1860, 1867, and in the Blue Books of 1890, 1890–91, and 1892, nos. 1 and 2) support the plausibility of this interpretation of the Turko-Armenian conflict. One also finds in these reports clues to Ottoman-Turkish devices of deliberate conflict-generation and conflict-escalation that had the effect of "goading the Armenians into rebellion," which then would be defined as "provocation" calling for severe repressive measures. The well-informed French diplomat Paul Cambon quoted a high ranking Turkish official telling him early in 1894: *"La question d'Arménie n'éxiste pas, mais nous la créerons,"* that is, "the Armenian Question does not exist, but we shall create it." In his lengthy report, as mentioned above, Cambon also diagnosed the problem as having originated in "the exasperation...of the inoffensive population...which simply was aiming at reforms, and dreaming of an orderly Ottoman administration."[1]

The intrusion into this conflict of immigrant publicists and intellectuals of the Armenian diaspora in Europe despairing of Turkish inertia and of indifference in the face of Armenian pleas and petitions, helped, however, Ottoman authorities to redefine the conflict as Armenian provocation. The outlines of a reactive Armenian movement began to emerge, with spillovers in Russian Armenia in the Caucasus, that led to the onset of Armenian revolutionary activities. These activities gave rise to the theory of provocation, advanced by a group of students of Ottoman history, but which has been recently questioned and criticized by Robert Melson's. As Melson concluded, "...the provocation thesis rests on a simple action-reaction model of human events without making either action or reaction credible."[2]

The Armenian Revolutionaries

The Armenian Revolutionary Movement which certainly helped precipitate but not cause the cycle of Turkish massacres, though provocative from an Ottoman perspective, had its own intrinsic justifications, as far as its small retaliatory raids through its roving squads and small flying columns in the provinces were concerned. These were local punitive forays undertaken against enormous odds, with inordinate stamina and valor, and under the restraints of a Spartan discipline prescribing unlimited self-sacrifice and proscribing violence against the innocent, particularly women and children. Directed mostly against Kurdish brigands and regular Turkish army units and the gendarmerie defending them, these forays by the *fedayee* squads, and the legends surrounding them served to refurbish the psyche of multitudes of cowed Armenians.

The merits of these revolutionaries were succinctly acknowledged by no less a man than Cemal Paşa, the third ranking member of the Ittihad oligarchy. The last chapter of his memoirs deals with "The Armenian Question" and starts with the declaration: "We like the Armenians, especially their revolutionaries, more than the Greeks and the Bulgarians, for they are more gallant and heroic (*mert ve kahraman*) than these two elements. They do not practice two-facedness...."[3] A

German author, who spent more than a decade in Turkey and closely observed these "freedom fighters," could not resist admiring "that something inordinately attractive about them...their willingness to endure boundless sacrifices that included their lives...their passion for freedom blended with a daredevil's intrepidity...."[4] From a different perspective, however, these *fedayees* were risky provocations. The following two observations are germane to a more judicious review of theories of the provocation-repression cycle. First, the revolutionaries were not a solid bloc with a uniform program of emancipation from Ottoman rule. In fact, the two major revolutionary groups in many respects were counterposed to each other as rivals, and more importantly, disagreed on the immediate and distant goals attached to the reforms. The Huntchaks essentially aspired for total emancipation and separation from Ottoman dominion, while the Dashnaks advocated more or less a system of administrative autonomy under Ottoman suzerainty. Apart from other considerations involving demography, ideology, and presumed advantages to accrue to Russia as a result of the actions of Armenian revolutionaries, Turkish leaders rightly projected into the future and viewed such limited autonomy as nothing but a stepping-stone toward eventual independence. This projective and anticipatory bent of the Ottoman response to demands for reforms and local autonomy merits particular attention. Secondly, there is general agreement that the revolutionaries were not only opposed by the bulk of the Armenian population and of its ecclesiastical leadership, but in fact comprised a very small segment of that population. The opposition to the revolutionaries was not only due to an aversion against violence but reflected the fact that "the mass of Ottoman Armenians remained loyal subjects" with most of the Armenian leaders supporting the concept of Ottoman sovereignty.[5]

When James G. Bennett, American newspaper man and publisher of the *New York Herald*, became skeptical of the veracity of reports on the 1894–96 massacres, generally described as examples of unparalleled savagery, he prevailed upon Sultan Abdul Hamit to obtain permission to have the story of the massacres impartially investigated by a team. A member of this team was American author and Civil War observer George Hepworth, who also described himself as having a "rather keen appetite for facts." With a retinue of Turkish military officials, including a colonel, a lieutenant colonel, a secretary, and a bodyguard, the team proceeded to the sites of atrocities and conducted a two-month investigation. In 1898 Hepworth summed up his findings and in doing so he prognosticated nearly two full decades before its actual incidence—the Armenian genocide:

> Now to summarize. When I say that the Armenian massacres were caused by Armenian revolutionists, I tell a truth, and a very important truth, but it is not the whole truth. It would be more correct to say that the presence of the revolutionists gave occasion and excuse for the massacres. That the Turks were looking for an occasion and an excuse, no one can doubt who has traversed that country. Way down in the bottom of his heart, the Turk hates the Armenian. He will swear to the contrary, but I am convinced that the statement is true nevertheless. The reasons for this are abundant, as I have tried to show in other chapters of this book. The Turk is extremely jealous of the Armenian, jealous of his mental superiority, of his thrift, and business enterprise. He has, therefore, resorted to oppression, and his steady purpose has been and is now, to keep his victims poor. Equal opportunities for all are a delusion and a snare. They do not exist.[6]

> During my travels in Armenia I have been more and more deeply convinced that the future of the Armenians is extremely clouded. It may be that the hand of the Turk will be held back through fear of Europe but I am sure that the object of the Turk is extermination, and that he will pursue that end if the opportunity offers. He has already come very near to its accomplishment for the Armenians of today are an impoverished people, hopeless and in despair.[7]

For a variety of reasons the authorities rarely concerned themselves with the principles of fairness and judiciousness that required, among other things, the observance of the standard norm of separating the revolutionaries and other assorted activists from the rest of the people. Entire communities were punished for individual acts, and the Armenian nation was repeatedly decimated for the acts of dissident or militant groups, which the authorities purposively identified with the entire nation. Through their own rather frivolous definitions these authorities persisted in labeling certain kinds of discontent and grievances as "treason," and in a sweeping compass of attribution of guilt collectivities were targeted for retribution. The case of Boghos Noubar, an Armenian notable, selected by the Supreme Patriarch of the Armenians to press the Armenian quest for reforms in the capitals of pre-World War I Europe—in light of the failure of the Young Turks to carry out their repeated promises of reform—is a case in point. He was labeled by the authorities and the Turkish press as "a traitor." Yet, he was not only opposed to "revolution" in principle, but disapproved of the revolutionaries and their tactics, while consistently supporting the concept of Ottoman sovereignty and rejecting the idea of Tsarist dominion in eastern Turkey; to him the reforms were as vital for the Turks as for the Armenians. Commenting on Noubar's stance regarding the Ottoman regime, Russia's Ambassador at Paris, Iswolsky, reported to his Foreign Minister Sazonof on 28 February(13 March) 1913: "Nubar repeatedly assured me that Turkish Armenians want neither autonomy nor change of rule [to Russia] but just the implementation of reforms stipulated in the Berlin Treaty and elaborated in 1895 by Russia, France, and England but which still remained dead letters."[8] While still in Europe, B. Noubar was condemned to death in absentia on 18 August 1915. This, in spite of the fact that a pro-Ittihad Turkish daily had published a press release by B. Noubar containing excerpts from the memorandum he had prepared for the Ambassadors' Conference that was convened at that time to elaborate a new Armenian Reform Act. In the press release it is stated that "the Armenians are loyal subjects of the Turkish Empire who neither desire autonomy nor the protection of another power."[9] The protracted controversies surrounding these reforms served to imperil the overall safety of the Armenians. On the eve of World War I, their condition was "as bad as ever."[10]

Apprehensive Reactions by the Authorities

In the final analysis the Ottoman failure to implement reforms in the "Armenian provinces" was not due to administrative incompetence or weakness but rather to an inveterate political urge to deny the Armenians the attainment of conditions implicit in such reforms. It was feared that through such reforms the Armenians might not only upset the superordination-subordination relationship obtaining between Turks and Armenians, but might even reverse it in the eastern regions billed as "historical Armenia." Equal opportunity and equality (*müsavat*) were considered stepping stones in that direction. In a memorandum to the recently appointed Inspector of Eastern Provinces, Raif Paşa, Abdul Hamit aired his anxiety in this regard when exhorting him to resist European pressures for reforms in the six provinces which may result in the establishment of "an Armenian principality, and the domination (*hakim*) of a minority over Muslims."[11] In his extensive report analyzing "The Causes of the Massacre" of Adana in April 1909, England's Adana Vice-Consul Major Doughty Wylie alludes to Turkish charges of seditiousness by Armenians wanting to establish a principality in and around Adana. But when diagnosing the more substantial grounds of the Turkish enmity resulting in the 1909 twin Adana massacres Wylie offered the following observation: "The Turks, masters for centuries, found their great stumbling block in equality with the Christians. [In the 1908 Ittihad revolution]...The Turks hated the idea that they were no longer masters. The Armenian wanted to rush into Home Rule... Among the fiercer professors of Islam resentment grew. Were God's adversaries to be the equals of Islam? In every café the heathen were speaking great mouthing words of some godless and detested change...." After the atrocities, "Cheers were given for Sultan Abdul Hamit. He had set the fashion of massacres."[12]

Notwithstanding the plight of rampant poverty among the masses of Armenians in the provinces, in the capital, in coastal and in large cities many Armenians were thriving as bankers, merchants, tradesmen, and artisans; their access to military and governmental careers were pre-empted by religious dogmas and tradition as they were subjected to the discriminatory practices of debarment and exclusion. The scattered office-holders in the Sultan's Treasury, Foreign Office, the Mint [Dadians] and a few other ministries, such as Post and Telegraph, constituted exceptions. Similar exceptions comprised the dynastic favorites of the sultans, e.g., the Balians, renowned for their contributions to the religious architecture of the Empire, and their dubious role as creators of palatial splendor. On the other hand, however, Muslim monopoly of government employment was 95.4 percent.[13] Where oppression was minimal or bearable, the Armenians tended to surge forth in every sphere in which they applied themselves. Their levels of success and ascendancy, however, were always handicapped, if not fragile or tenuous, as they remained hostages of their own successes. Irrespective of the type of success, they essentially remained "inferior infidels" and were nearly always at the mercy of their Ottoman-Turkish overlords for their ultimate safety and security. When highly exercised, the overlord could afford to dare to dispatch "the infidel" with minimum fear of retribution of one kind or another. In this sense Ambassador Morgenthau's following allegory is illustrative: "The Turk had the right to test the sharpness of his sword upon the neck of any Christian." Morgenthau's memoirs, from which excerpts are adduced below, further illuminate this problem. Some regions, with demographically more solid Armenian identity, for example, were immune from this lethal vulnerability. Moreover, when favored by suitable circumstances, the Armenians could pose a danger to the Turks. The realization of this point and its projection into the future weighed considerably in the World War I genocide scheme, as attested to by two of its authors trying to justify it. Talat: "they [the Armenians] are determined to domineer over us," and are responsible "for our failure" in the battlefields of the Caucasus where they militarily "assisted the Russians...Our Armenian policy is absolutely fixed and that nothing can change it." Enver: "I have the greatest admiration for their [the Armenians'] intelligence and industry...they have helped them [the Russians] in this war...It is our own experience with revolutions which makes us fear the Armenians. If two hundred Turks could overturn the Government, then a few hundred bright, educated Armenians could do the same thing."[14] The relative validity of these projective concerns was in a sense certified through the legacy of a few bastions of Armenian military valor. The exploits of the Armenians of Zeitoun, about whom very little is written and known, can be considered as an integral part of this legacy. A short review may therefore be in order.

Notes

1. *Documents Diplomatiques Français (1871–1900)*, vol. XI (Paris: Impremerie Nationale, 1947), pp. 71, 72, 73 (20 February 1894), no. 50 report to French Premier Casimir-Périer.
2. Robert Melson, "A Theoretical Inquiry into the Armenian Massacres of 1894–1896," *Comparative Studies in History and Society* 24, no. 3 (July 1982), pp. 493–5; *idem, Revolution and Genocide: On the Origins of the Armenian Genocide and the Holocaust* (Chicago: University of Chicago Press, 1993), pp. 43, 49–53. The quotation is from the latter work, p. 51.
3. Cemal Paşa, *Hatıralar* (Memoirs), completed and edited by Behçet Cemal, his son, (Istanbul: Çağdaş, 1977), p. 404.
4. Ernst Christoffel, *Zwischen Saat und Ernte* (Between sowing and harvest), (Berlin-Friedenau: Verlag der Christlichen Blindemission im Orient, 1933), p. 76.
5. S. J. Shaw and E. K. Shaw, *History of the Ottoman Empire and Modern Turkey*, vol. 2 (Cambridge: Cambridge University Press, 1977), pp. 201-2.
6. George H. Hepworth, *Through Armenia on Horseback* (New York: Dutton, 1898), pp. 339–40.
7. *Ibid*, pp. 146–7. When extrapolating the portents of the 1894–97 massacres, i.e., the magnitude of the victims, whose number he placed at "about 200,000," the renowned British ethnographer W. M. Ramsay made a similar forecast. He declared in 1897: "The Armenians will in all probability be exterminated except the remnant that escapes to other lands." From *Impressions of Turkey* (New York: Putnam's; London: Hodder and Stoughton, 1897), pp. 156–7.
8. André Mandelstam, *Le Sort de l'Empire Ottoman* (The fate of the Ottoman Empire), (Paris: Payot, 1917), p. 211.
9. *Tercümanı Hakikat* (Turkish newspaper) 7 July 1913; *see* also FO 195/2450/45/5.
10. Roderic Davison, "The Armenian Crisis: 1912-1914," *American Historical Review* 53, no. 3 (April 1948), pp. 491, 500–1.
11. Sultan II Abdülhamid Han, *Devlet ve Memleket Görüşlerim* (My views on state and country), A. Alaeddin Çetin and Ramazan Yıldız, eds, (Istanbul: Çiğir, 1976), p. 199. The memorandum has no date.
12. FO 424/220, enclosure to 48 Report, p. 70.
13. Shaw and Shaw, *History* [n. 5], p. 242.
14. Henry Morgenthau, *Ambassador Morgenthau's Story*, (Garden City, NY: Doubleday, Page, 1918), pp. 280, 337, 338, 345, 347.

7

Zeitoun (Süleymaniye): An Aberrant Episode in the Evolution of the Turko-Armenian Conflict

Introductory Note

In the analysis of the Armenian genocide as the ultimate means of resolving the protracted Turko-Armenian conflict, the institutionalized, pervasive vulnerability of the Armenians as the victim group remains a key factor. To recognize this means to recognize the pivotal role of critically disparate power relations in the enactment of that genocide, and for that matter of any genocide. In the Zeitoun episode the validity of this postulate is confirmed negatively, i.e., the decrease of Armenian vulnerability has served to increase the chances of averting the ultimate disaster of genocide. The 1895–96 Zeitoun uprising constitutes a special phase in the evolution of the Turko-Armenian conflict in terms of its outcome: the Ottoman Turks failed to prevail and the Armenians of the area escaped wholesale massacre which evidently was imminent.

As usual, the sources of the conflict involved a regime of oppression that exacerbated the conditions of chronic misgovernment. Even though he in part blames the Zeitounlis for their "wrong-headedness, obstinacy, ignorance, conceitedness..." Lieutenant Ferdinand Bennet, British Consul at nearby Maraş, summarized the problems of oppression in the summer of 1881 with these words:

> Hatred of the Moslem yoke...a history of grievances and of an age of barbarity... willful misgovernment...the lawlessness of the Kurds, the over-taxation, insecurity, injustice on all sides....[1]

Zeitoun reflected the same picture of governmental ineptness and abuse that existed in all other provinces containing large Armenian populations. But there were some significant elements in the situation of the Zeitounlis that favored them and afforded resistance through rebellion. Foremost among these elements were the twin conditions of topography and demography. The physical configuration and the geography of Zeitoun were such as to render a defensive uprising relatively easy. As to the demographic advantage, Zeitoun was one of those rare towns in the Ottoman Empire which was utterly homogenous in terms of a nearly 100 percent Armenian population. The combined impact of these twin advantages upon the mind-set of the Zeitounlis was powerful enough to help produce a culture of defiant self-confidence bordering on defiant belligerence. Consul Bennet in his above-mentioned report berates the Zeitounlis for they are "strongly convinced that they are a Power of themselves, and that the Turkish government is afraid of them...."

In brief, the Armenians were capable of generating power and overcoming their statutory vulnerabilities when favored by a set of circumstances. Subordination does not need to automatically lead to a degree of submissiveness. Even though the Armenian success in Zeitoun was conditional, episodic, and, therefore, relative, it demonstrated the critical importance of demography in the consummation of a conflict; here, demography proved as a determinant in the shaping of power relations that usually animate such a conflict.

During the last five centuries of Armenian history, marked by foreign conquest and subjugation, four regions managed to maintain a status of semiautonomy and relative freedom. In Transcaucasia, that region was Siunig or mountainous Karabagh. Within the borders of the nineteenth-century Ottoman Empire, the other regions involved were (1) Sassoun, in the mountains south of Muş in historic Daron-Douruperan; (2) Van-Shatakh, in historic Vasbouragan, both in eastern Turkey; and (3) the enclave of Zeitoun, situated forty miles northwest of Maraş in historic Cilicia. Zeitoun was surrounded by the chain of the Taurus mountains, a perfect example of mountain-fastness, and a veritable eagle's nest (*Ardzwepouyn*, in Armenian). Its relative inaccessibility, the parochialism and fetish for endogamy of the mountaineers, and their inveterate aversion to the idea of attracting national attention for any reason contributed to their relative isolation and obscurity. Yet, they have been compared to the mountaineers of Montenegro and of Karabagh as "a sample of a vigorous race," and were characterized as "rude and stern people...a thoroughly militant type of manhood."[2] Within the limited scope of their operations, they practiced the eye-for-an-eye maxim, responding to massacre with massacre, and thereby drastically reduced during the successive episodes of Abdul Hamit era massacres the scale of civilian casualties throughout the region. In this respect alone, they stand out as the only Armenian group which, by resort to effective limited retaliations, vindicated the principle of forceful deterrence, and averted disaster for the inhabitants of a large cluster of Armenian villages in the area. Enrico Vitto, the Italian consul of Aleppo, who, along with the other representatives of the European Powers, took a leading part in the negotiations to end the hostilities and to have the Turks come to terms with the Armenians, could not resist the urge to pay homage to these combatants as "guardians of honor and pillars of freedom." He admiringly wrote: *"Ti saluto, eroica citta di Zeitoun"* (I salute thee, heroic city of Zeitoun).[3]

By a succession of skirmishes and wars, small and large, the mountaineers forged a martial spirit and an ethos of defiance directed against the Turks and the assorted Muslim tribes of the area, and especially against the Ottoman authorities. This overall conflict was sharpened in the 1860s when Zeitoun for the first time was incorporated into the province of Aleppo by becoming one of the four counties (*kaza*) of Maraş, one of that province's three districts (*sancak*). Of the thirty villages of the Zeitoun district, including *yaylas* (summer camping grounds) and *çiftliks* (farms), ten were Armenian, the rest, mostly Turkmen, had mixed populations. The town of Zeitoun was divided into four wards (*tagh*), ruled and administered by four princes (*işkhan*), identified with four different Armenian dynasties, which in turn comprised a mixture of kinship groups with appellations ending with "enk," as distinct from the typically Armenian "ian," which described the dynasties, such as "Kalousdenk." The economy of the area, including outlying villages, was controlled by the four princes, and an assortment of nobles functioning as landed aristocrats. With its considerable land properties, the church was also part of the economic arrangement. In maximum control of the domains through feudal and semi-feudal practices that extended to settling all kinds of internal disputes, the four princes would periodically convene to discuss and administer city-wide affairs. The local Turkish officials primarily served as fiscal agents of the empire, concentrating on the task of tax collection. They were reinforced by the presence of a few law enforcement officials and officers, and of a large garrison outside the town. According to the statistics of the Armenian patriarchate, in the 1870s there were 28,000 Armenians out of a total population of 36,000 in the area, with Langlois in 1862 estimating them at 20,000. Langlois also notes that murder was rare in Zeitoun, murder for theft unheard of, that the mountaineers' "probity is proverbial," and that there is no prison for Armenians in Zeitoun.[4]

Their system of stratification and authority carried over into military organization and operations. It was incumbent upon the four reigning princes to maintain unremitting vigilance, to marshal resources, mobilize warrior detachments, map strategy and tactics, and personally lead in combat. In this capacity many of them proved pioneers of local warfare, innovating and perfecting techniques of combat, setting standards of bravery, examples of self-sacrifice, and altogether creating legends with which Zeitoun history is suffused. One of these princes, Nazaret Yenidünyayan, the younger brother of Babig Paşa, another legendary hero of Zeitoun, was wounded in his leg during the first days of the 1895 insurrection. Medical help not being available, it is said that in the presence of the other chiefs he drew his dagger, slit his wound, cut through his bone, pulled out the bullet, wiped away the fragments of the shattered bone, washed the wound, and after tightly binding it up nonchalantly declared: "Now it is healed." Author Aghassee states that during the entire insurrection this warrior-prince read the Bible every night for half an hour, "before my eyes."[5]

Religion was an integral part of life in this bastion of citizen-warriors as evidenced by a string of churches, chapels, and monasteries dotting the Zeitoun landscape, and by the ubiquitous presence of clergymen who held a powerful sway upon generations of Zeintounlis; in fact, the four princes were ultimately subject to the moral authority of the primate of Zeitoun. These clerics cherished a militancy which gave a distinct flavor to Christianity as believed and practiced in Zeitoun, and distinguished Zeitoun from most other Armenian communities in Turkey. Adeptly blending in the traditions of the area, they molded and were molded by an ethos in which belligerence and humility, secularism and esteem of sacredness became intertwined and through the practice of which, by all accounts, they became intrepid warriors excelling in heroism when engaging in combat.

Some sixteen major, and twenty-five minor, wars were waged against governmental forces,[6] and against the marauding irregulars who were allied with the latter and were identified with such ethnic groups as Turkmens, (especially the Kozanoğlu), the Kurdish Afshan tribe, Circassians, Lazes, Alevis, and Zeibeks. Despite the geography and the topography of the area favoring the Zeitounli warriors, the danger of being overrun by determined government forces was ever present; by the same token, these natives made the most out of their defensive advantages, in the process fostering an ideal for defiant heroism. When discussing Zeitoun with the French Vice-Consul of Maraş, a European author called Zeitoun "the most distinguished city in Armenian history, a militant and heroic city whose history is but a long series of struggles." He quoted an Armenian mother deploring the fact that instead of falling on the battlefield, her son had died in bed during the 1895 Zeitoun insurrection: "My son died a shameful death."[7]

Unlike most other Armenians in the Ottoman system, who were forbidden to bear arms, Zeitoun Armenians had an ongoing love affair with their weapons. The first act of the rites of passage for boys was the obtaining of a gun, of having it blessed by a priest, and performing target practice. It was a common occurrence to go to Church with one's weapon, and to remove it only during the service. Describing the rifles, knives, and swords decorating the walls of every home, a chronicler in 1887 portrayed these abodes as little "garrisons rather than homes," with people running around in the city always armed, and every male and female over ten being capable of using an assortment of firearms.[8] Langlois records the manifestation of this martial spirit during a festive reception the Zeitounlis gave the French visitor.

> They would improvise contests for marksmanship displaying extraordinary skills, would thrust, with their rifles on their shoulders and with complete abandon, in the torrents of an onrushing river and blend with nature in an improvised race to cross a river while armed. They can climb a tree like cats, hide behind leaves, and shoot with deadly accuracy.[9]

The familiarity with and attachment to one's weapon were also the result of widespread hunting, with the partridge being the chief game. Many of the skills acquired in hunting that bird were easily transferred to the type of warfare in which Zeitoun Armenians distinguished themselves. Because the partridge is a highly suspicious and alert bird, the hunter must exercise the utmost care and practice the art of hiding; he must remain motionless and maintain absolute stillness. Unless the bird is allowed to come close by, the shot may miss and the hunt may be eluded with no other opportunity presenting itself that day. In meeting these conditions of successful hunting, they perfected the tactics of defensive and "economical warfare," taking full advantage of the rock infested habitat of the eagle's nest that was Zeitoun. They lurked and lured, and when they struck, they rarely missed.

The 1895–96 Insurrection

Barthélemy, the Gérant of the French Consulate at nearby Maraş, attributed the 1895–1896 uprising to "a circular Grand Vizier Kâmil Paşa had sent to the Kaymakams repudiating the Reform concessions that were granted by Abdul Hamit in October 1895.[10] A British captain attributed the dispatch of that circular to an Ottoman design to "reduce" Zeitoun.[11] In the course of the combat thousands of unsuspecting Turkish soldiers and irregulars from among the invading troops instantly fell victim to the deadly shots of the Zeytounlis. Commenting on this, Ali Paşa, the commander of the Western Forces attacking Zeitoun in 1895, acknowledged to the Armenian chief of operations during armistice negotiations: "Your soldiers were choice marksmen."[12] These combatants functioned like lethal ghosts. Their limited numbers and resources required the utmost budgeting of effort. Highly aware of these limitations, they cherished themselves and each other as members of a precious and rare species that should not be wasted recklessly. In this sense, they called themselves "scarce walnuts" (*hamruadz unguyzner*), the loss of anyone of which would be noticed and painfully felt. This is the main reason why in all the battles they fought against the Turks during November and December 1895, they sustained relatively few casualties, while exacting heavy tolls from the latter. Relying on old flint-locks and muzzle loaders, the insurgents organized and executed a kind of defense through which the ranks of the Turkish Fifth Army Corps, consisting largely of Circassians, officered by Turks, were decimated. In the words of the British consul at Aleppo, Henry Barnham, the Corps "suffered a heavy defeat, with at least five thousand killed."[13] During that defense the Commander Remzi Paşa himself was wounded. When their ammunition was nearly spent, the Zeytounlis were getting ready for a surprise night attack to be launched simultaneously at the different sectors of the western front defended by Commander Ali's 10,000 troops. Commenting on this plan, which was preempted by armistice initiatives, French Lieutenant-Colonel de Vialar praised their skill in that kind of war, declaring: "they handle the dagger with an unbelievable dexterity" (*ils manient le poignard avec une dexterité incroyable*); de Vialar was struck by the crusading spirit with which "the Zeitounlis wage all their wars."[14] Finally, in his summary comment another French author exalted: "This improbably heroic victory of 6,000 Armenians against 50,000 Turks" (*cette victoire invraisemblablement héroique de 6,000 Arméniens sur 50,000 Turcs*).[15] A Turkish author indicates that of these 6,000 Armenians, 2,000 were unarmed.[16]

Having replaced the humbled commander Remzi Paşa with Edhem Paşa, the hero of the ensuing 1897 Turko-Greek war, the sultan approached the Powers with a view to ending the fight. This unprecedented concession to the military feat of the Armenians calls for an explanation. Abdul Hamit was gravely concerned with the repercussions of the Zeitoun resistance, as French Ambassador Cambon and Russian Ambassador Nelidof confirmed. In his 26 December 1895 report to his foreign minister, Cambon wrote: "The Sultan requested our intervention." On 3 January 1896 Cambon confirmed this time the Porte's, i.e., the Ottoman government's identical request, adding that these requests were due to the military failure of the Ottoman troops. On 10 January 1896 Cambon again reported to his foreign minister to the effect that the sultan was virtually begging for cessation of hostilities so as to spare the terrible losses and suffering of his troops not used to the rigors of the Zeitoun winter. The pages of the official French Yellow Book dealing with this episode are illuminating regarding the seriousness of the crisis in which Sultan Abdul Hamit found himself. Here is what on 5 March 1896 the French chargé d'affaires, de la Boulinière, said about this crisis: "Since the occurrence of the troubles, this is the second time that the Powers rendered a great service to the sultan by presently extricating him from a difficult and disturbing situation in Zeitoun (*le grand service de le tirer d'une situation difficile et inquiétante*)...he was only too happy to see the Powers intervene" (*Il a été trop heureux de l'intervention des Puissances*).[17] Finally, reference may be made to the attendant anxieties expressed by Abdul Hamit himself. Conceding that up until then the Imperial Army had been unable to cope with the Armenians, in a memorandum to his Cabinet ministers he opted for the advisability (*münasib*) of having one of the consuls of the six European Powers propose (*teklif*) to "the rebels" that they lay down their arms without fear of reprisals. He wanted to end at once (*bir an evvel*) the combats which were exacting a great deal (*haylice*) of casualties, dead, and wounded among Ottoman military, including "quite high ranking officers" (*oldukca büyük rütbeli zabıtlardan*). He authorized the government to inform the field commander to "at once cease hostilities" one way or another (*işe bir an evvel netice verilmek*).[18]

In commenting on the significance of the intrepidity of the Zeitounlis, British ethnographer Ramsay contrasted them with "the timid and submissive type" of the average Armenian, explaining the difference as a reflection of the difference between free people and oppressed people.[19] Another British author, an ex-naval intelligence officer, who had traveled 1,300 miles across Turkey during a five-month trip, had visited Zeitoun, and who was accompanied only by a Turk, described Zeitoun's "struggle against the Ottoman State" as "a wonderful performance...for there is nothing to equal it in Asia Minor...had the Armenian race at large been of the same nature as these highlanders...there would never have been an Armenian Question...."[20] Another British author, Talbot Mundy, who narrated the 1895–96 uprising, expressed a similar view.[21]

The Zeitoun episode, as described in this chapter, is significant not only as an aberration in the overall picture of the Turko-Armenian conflict, but beyond that it may help explain, to some extent, why the rest of the Armenian population became easy prey for empire-wide massacres at the very time the Zeytounlis were in a state of uprising in the winter of 1895–96. The conditions of these massacres and their outcome will be examined in the next chapter with a view to illuminating the escalating phases and tempo of the Turko-Armenian conflict.

Notes

1. *British Foreign Office.* FO 424/123. Reg. no. 14, pp. 4, 6, 7. Consul Bennet's 7 June 1881 report to the British ambassador to Turkey, Sir William Edward Goschen.
2. The reference to "vigorous race" is in Victor Langlois, *Les Arméniens de la Turquie et les Massacres du Taurus* (The Armenians of Turkey and the Taurus massacres), (Paris: Claye, 1863), pp. 17, 19, and that of "rude and stern people" is in James Bryce, *Transcaucasia and Ararat,* (London: Macmillan, 1896), p. 501.
3. Anatolio Latino (pseudonyme of Enrico Vitto), *Gli Armeni e Zeitoun,* vol. 2, 2d ed. (Firenze: Bernardo, 1899), p. 135.
4. Langlois, *Les Arméniens* [n. 2], pp. 18, 22.
5. Aghassee (Garabed Tour-Sarkissian), *Zeitoun yev eer Shurtchanagneru* (Zeitoun and its environs), (Beirut: Sheerag, 1968), pp. 145, 187. (Revised version of the 1897 original, published in Paris.)
6. Turkish authors insist that the number of these clashes which they describe as "rebellion" (*isyan*) is exactly fifty-seven. Abdullah Yaman, *Ermeni Meselesi ve Türkiye* (The Armenian question and Turkey), (Istanbul: Otag, 1973), p. 80; Inayetullah Cemal Özkaya, *Le Peuple Arménien et les Tentatives de rendre en servitude le peuple Turk* (The Armenian people and the attempts to reduce the Turkish people to servitude), (Istanbul, Ankara: Institut pour l'étude de la Turquie, 1971), p. 121.
7. Ludovic de Contenson, *Chrétiens et Musulmans: Voyages et Études* (Christians and Muslims: Travels and studies), (Paris: Plon-Nourrit, 1901), p. 107.
8. Vaspour Meliksetian, *Zeitounee Herosamarderu* (The heroic battles of Zeitoun), (Yerevan: State Publishing, 1960); Anoushavan, "Zeitounee Antzialeetz yev Nergayeetz," (On the past and present of Zeitoun), in *Araks* (S. Petersburg, Russia) I (November 1887), pp. 105–29.
9. Victor Langlois, *Voyage de la Cilicie et dans les montagnes du Taurus éxecuté pendant les années 1852–53* (Travel in Cilicia and the Taurus Mountains undertaken in the years 1852–53), (Paris: Duprat, 1861), p. 73.
10. *Livre Jaune. Affaires Arméniennes. Supplément, 1895–96,* (Paris, 1897) no. 65, 25 October 1895 report to Ambassador Cambon, p. 52.

11. A. E. Townsend, *A Military Consul in Turkey* (Philadelphia, London: Lippincott, Seeley, 1910), p. 86. See also the 5 January 1896 issue of *La Liberté*.

12. Aghassee, *Zeitoun* [n. 5], p. 301.

13. FO 195/1932, Aleppo, January to 6, 1896 cipher.

14. *Livre Jaune. Supplément*, [n. 10], no. 117, April 1896, p. 85.

15. Contenson, *Chrétiens* [n. 7], p. 32.

16. A. Alper Gazigiray, *Osmanlılardan Günümüze Kadar Vesikalarla Ermeni Terrörürün Kaynakları* (Documentary sources of Armenian terror from Ottoman times to the present), (Istanbul: Gözen, 1982), pp. 148–9.

17. *Livre Jaune. Supplément*, [n. 10], pp. 55, 58, 60, 63, 65, 84.

18. Sultan II Abdülhamid Han, *Devlet ve Memleket Görüşlerim* (My views on state and country), A. Alaeddin Çetin ve Ramazan Yıldız, eds. (Istanbul: Çığır, 1976), pp. 82, 83, 86, 87, the 13(25)December 1895 memorandum.

19. W. H. Ramsay, *Impressions of Turkey* (New York: Putnam, 1897), pp. 214–5.

20. W. J. Childs, *Across Asia Minor on Foot*, 3d ed. (Edinburgh and London: W. Blackwood, 1918), pp. 401–3.

21. Talbot Mundy, *The Eye of Zeitoun*, (New York: McKinlay, Stone, and Mackenzie, 1920), pp. 57–8, 244–5.

8

The Eruption of Empire-wide Massacres:
The Rudiments of Genocide as a Method of
Resolving the Turko-Armenian Conflict

The 1894–96 Massacres

Most of the other areas of the Ottoman Empire containing large concentrations of Armenians were visited upon with a sweep of destruction which not only decimated the Armenian people but crippled them for decades to come, at the same time triggering a series of wide-ranging emigrations. Certainly decimation is not coterminous with genocide. The Abdul Hamit era massacres were limited in several respects. The victims involved were: (a) mostly menfolk, to the exclusion, as a rule, of women and children of both sexes, with the 1894 Sassoun massacre, the 1895 and 1896 massacres of Istanbul, and the December 1895 Urfa cathedral burning of 3,000 women and children being the major exceptions; (b) mostly from urban centers; (c) those who were massacred lost their lives in periods of relatively short duration, ranging from two to four days, (d) killed or burned outright in or around their places of residence or business. In other words, there were no wholesale deportations and massacres, as the main purpose of these massacres involved large-scale economic, cultural, and psychological destruction through selective massacres. Nevertheless, it appears that the massacres were not without a subsidiary purpose, namely, as a probative effort which retrospectively may be characterized as a rehearsal for the subsequent 1915–18 cataclysm. The period of Hamidian massacres was initiated with the August 1894 Sassoun massacre.

The hue and cry in Europe, especially in England, the official remonstrances by the European Powers, and the official report of the Sassoun Inquiry Commission, with which the representatives of England, France, and Russia were associated, proved to be nothing but a mixture of expressions of heroics, impotent indignation, and bluff. The pervasive fears of punitive measures that had gripped the Sultan and his perpetrators prior to the massacres not only evaporated quickly but gave way to a new level of Turkish perception in which the Armenians were defined as an utterly vulnerable nationality. In the subsequent 1895–96 massacres, which engulfed all the eastern provinces, this perception was tested, confirmed, and strengthened. The overall reaction to the 1895–96 massacres was more or less a repeat performance of that engendered in the wake of the 1894 Sassoun massacre. On the level of the scale of casualties, however, the Armenian losses grew exponentially in the ensuing 1895–96 massacres. What follows is a very sketchy documentation of these massacres, distilled from the secret reports of the consular and diplomatic representatives of the European Powers in Turkey. The purpose of adducing these excerpts is to merely highlight the sources of authorization and direction of the pogroms, the techniques of camouflage, the instruments of the massacre, and the various methods of inculpating the victims as part of the plan to deny the crimes. The evolving and continuous massacres[1] and their documentation in German and Austrian sources,[2] and more particularly in Ottoman-Turkish sources,[3] are discussed elsewhere.

On the Sassoun Massacre

The British, French, and Russian Consular delegates of the Sassoun Inquiry Commission submitted a sixty-page joint report. In it, they asserted that "the refusal of seven or eight wards" of a village to pay taxes, or "some isolated acts of brigandage" by an Armenian band, or some Armenian "resistance to the troops" did not constitute "an open revolt" as claimed by the Ottoman authorities. The delegates further maintained that these deeds did not warrant the disproportionately severe measures of repression that included burning victims alive, wounding and killing "without distinction of age or sex," and especially "old people, the sick, and children," who were unable to flee.[4] In a separate memorandum, attached to the Joint Report, the British delegate Shipley dismissed Turkish charges as "the pseudo revolt, or the pretended outrages" of the Armenians, concluding: "…it is not too much to say that the Armenians were absolutely hunted like wild beasts, being killed wherever they were met."[5]

French Documents on the 1895–96 Massacres

Ambassador Cambon, in a report of 22 November 1895 described these massacres as having been "organized."[6] Commenting on the source and origin of the orders for massacre, he wrote: "It is impossible not to recognize more clearly the direction given to the authorities by the Palace." The Turkish foreign minister, Tevfik Paşa, conceded to Cambon that "the authorities allowed all these atrocities," and promised to request the execution "by fire squads of the principal guilty." Cambon added: "I believe in his sincerity, but can anticipate the fate of his proposals. The sultan will never issue orders against guilty Moslems even less so against guilty authorities." His "long audience" with Abdul Hamit, whom he urged "to punish the [Armenian] revolutionaries but to not repress the population, to separate the masses" from the former, led to the fact that "the Sultan thanked me and made the most satisfactory promises." But, "*il n'en tiendra aucune*" (he will not keep any of them).[7] In fact, four months before the start of the massacres, the French consul at Diyarbekir informed his superiors (20 May 1895) that "the Kurds had received permission to exterminate the Armenians."[8] Cambon also mentioned the employment of "emissaries" who carried the verbal orders to the provinces alerting "the Moslem masses to defend Islam" as soon as Hamit was pressured again by the Powers to make concessions on reforms. "Hamit will refrain only if he is convinced that he will be held personally accountable for the blood spilled."[9]

British Documentation

Muş Vice Consul Hampton reported that all Muslims were implicated in the massacres, which were carried out on order from "central authorities," and "of the existence of which [order] I have no doubt." Prisoners were released from prison for this task.[10] Sivas Vice Consul Bulman reported on 4 February 1896 of having "definite proof that the massacres were prearranged."[11]

Harput Vice Consul Fontana provided a clue as to how massacres could be ordered from the Palace without any explicit use of the word itself, or anything similar to it. The Agn [Egin] massacre in the summer of 1896 was the latest in the 1894–96 cycle. It was unleashed after establishing the fact that the leader of the raid of the Bank Ottoman by Armenian revolutionaries was a native of that city. Fontana was able to reconstruct the sequence of events through the disclosures of a Turk who was connected to the state Telegraph Office. That office received a telegram from the Palace ordering Harput province authorities "to take the necessary action" against the Armenians at Agn, who "intended to create a disturbance." The machinery for massacres was immediately set in motion by the Military Commandant issuing the appropriate telegraphic orders to Agn officials. The massacres that began "at the firing of a gun, lasted forty-eight hours," claiming "upwards of two thousand Armenian victims; 980 houses out of 1,150 were put to the torch," and "all were pillaged." Even though the Armenians had "assembled in their church and offered up special prayer owing to the great fear prevalent in their town," their religious plenipotentiary (*murahhas*) "was compelled by the authorities, under pain of death, to telegraph to the patriarch that the Armenians were responsible for the outbreak there." After "discrediting" official versions and accounts, the vice consul concluded by saying, "...many Turkish notables here are deploring the massacres...and declaring that the Armenians gave no excuse for the crime."[12] On the post massacre climate, Fontana commented: "It is difficult to believe that any real reform can be introduced in this atmosphere of anarchy and bankruptcy. The foulest criminals and murderers are at large throughout the *vilayet* (province) and respected for their wealth, the spoil of their victims."[13]

Ambassador Mallet reported to Foreign Minister Grey that during the 1895 massacres Grand Vizier Said Paşa came into possession of "certain incriminating documents which he refused to surrender" to Abdul Hamit and, therefore had to take refuge.[14] Chargé Herbert wrote to Salisbury that "the recent massacres in the Turkish Provinces were the result of secret orders sent by the Palace officials if not by the sultan himself," as evidenced by "a copy of such an order obtained." Citing several consular reports to support this contention, Herbert significantly injected the remark, "it must be borne in mind [that these] consular agents are generally Turkophil and dislike the Armenians."[15] In a 2 September 1895 cipher it is reported that Herbert was "certain that the government organized and armed, for the purpose of killing the Armenians, the mob which committed all the massacres..."[16]

Upon returning to his post in November 1896, Ambassador Currie sent to Salisbury a lengthy report which identified the principal actors involved in the policy of massacres, singling out the following: the minister of interior (Memduh) was an "unscrupulous man," and "the obedient instrument of the sultan's ill-will against his Armenian subjects;" Izzet, the sultan's "principal, if not only advisor, displacing the four most trusted counsellors of the sultan," and given to spying, thievery, and bribery. With reference to Foreign Minister Tevfik Paşa, Currie stated that he "admits with pleasing frankness that he is entirely without influence over the Imperial Master and that his advice is never taken."[17]

An Austrian Report

Aleppo Consul Bertrand described the role of the president of the Criminal Court trying to condemn some Armenians on trumped up charges in order to blame them for the massacres, and to absolve the Turks. In a further report, the Consul focused on the town of Kilis, maintaining that the massacres there were premeditated and prearranged with the complicity of local authorities (*organisés de connivence avec le gouvernement local*), whose casualty figure of Armenian victims is three to four times lower than that of the Consulate.[18]

German Documentation

Even though the Germans studiously avoided pressuring the sultan, or remonstrating against him, Kaiser Wilhelm II's Ambassador Saurma reported on a widely held view that the atrocities were the result of the Muslims having been spurred on by low level local authorities. At the end of his report, one reads Kaiser Wilhelm's following remark suggesting that the German emperor was contemplating opposition to the Turks: "Hence, we surely ought to speak to the Turks with a different tone."[19] In another report, the ambassador alluded to "the ongoing mass murder of the Armenians."[20] But, in a further report he told his Foreign Office in Berlin that "the most diverse sources assure us that the Armenian massacres were enacted mostly as a result of secret orders (*geheime Befehle*)" emanating from the Palace.[21] In still another report, the Kaiser is quoted as saying "...as the Berlin Congress of 1878 in no way protects the Christians, the Turks are free to cut their throats."[22]

Regarding the number of casualties, Saurma, relying on a non-German source, cites British Ambassador Philip Currie's estimate of "about a hundred thousand" Armenians as having been slaughtered."[23] German data, on the other hand are compiled to present a figure of 80,000 killed out of hand (*umgebract*); this is the figure conveyed this time by a German source, Kaiser Wilhelm, to a British authority, i.e., the British military attaché in Berlin, Colonel Swaine.[24] The figure covers, however, only the period reaching up to December 31, 1895. All these figures are, therefore, incomplete, since the series of massacres of the next year, 1896, are not included. Quoting sources close to the Kaiser, and close to General von Goltz, (stationed in Turkey 1883–1895 for the purpose of instituting military reforms), and describing the situation as "frightful" (*épouvantable*), Loze, the French ambassador at Vienna, cites the combined figure of 200,000 as the probable total loss of the Armenians; the actual dead, and those expected to perish from "hunger and cold during the current winter."[25]

The preponderance of British sources that have been used in this study to support certain arguments and to document the massacres of the Abdul Hamit era is cast into special relief by the remark the British chargé at Istanbul appended to the Consular reports on the 1895–96 massacres as he transmitted them to London. It bears repeating here: "It must be borne in mind [that] Consular agents are generally Turkophil and dislike the Armenians" (see note 15). A similar point may be made relative to the preponderance of German and Austrian documentation on the massacres of World War I, during which a host of German ambassadors, including Turkophiles Wangenheim and Kühlmann and provincial consuls inundated their Foreign Ministry with all sorts of accounts on the extermination of the Armenians. All these incriminating statements were made despite their political and military alliance with Turkey and the implicit commitment to guard and protect the interests of their Turkish ally.

In response to the reports on the ongoing massacres in the 1894–96 period, the U.S. Senate unanimously passed a resolution on 22 January 22, 1896 condemning them. When pleading for the unanimous adoption of the resolution, Senator Cullom declared: "…I was appalled by the carnival of blood prevailing…The evidence of the bloody enormities was given by all classes and nationalities until it was beyond the slightest doubt. A Turkish Army had bayoneted, robbed, murdered, and flayed alive the people of Armenia…No event of the centuries called so loudly to the civilized world as the slaughter in Turkey, the greatest in the history of the world.[26]

Notes

1. Vahakn N. Dadrian, *The History of the Armenian Genocide. Ethnic Conflict from the Balkans to Anatolia to the Caucasus* (Oxford and Providence: Berghahn Books, 1997), 4th ed., part 4, "The Inauguration of a Proto-Genocidal Policy," ch. 8, "The Era of Abdul Hamit Massacres, pp. 113–71; ch. 9, "The Portentousness of the Abdul Hamit Era Massacres," pp. 172–6; part 5, "The Wars and Massacres of the New Young Turk Regime," ch. 10, "The 1909 Twin Adana Massacres," pp. 179–84; part 6, "The Initiation and Consummation of the Genocide," ch. 14, "The Implementation of the Genocide," pp. 219–34; ch. 15, "The Disguises of the Law of Deportation and Ancillary Acts," pp. 235–47.

2. Vahakn N. Dadrian, "Documentation of the Armenian Genocide in German and Austrian Sources," in *The Widening Circle of Genocide*, vol. 3. Charny, ed. (New Brunswick, NJ: Transaction, 1994), expanded and published as a separate unit, 125 pp.

3. Vahakn N. Dadrian, "Documentation of the Armenian Genocide in Turkish Sources," in Charny, Israel W., ed., *Genocide: A Critical Bibliographic Review*, vol. 2, (London: Mansell; New York: Facts on File, 1991), pp. 86–138; "The Armenian Genocide in Official Turkish Records: Collected Essays," special issue of *Journal of Political and Military Sociology*, vol. 22, no. 1 (Summer 1994), 208 pp.; "The Naim-Andonian Documents on the World War I Destruction of the Ottoman Armenians: The Anatomy of a Genocide," *International Journal for Middle East Studies* 18 (1986), pp. 311–60; "The Documentation of the World War I Armenian Massacres in the Proceedings of the Turkish Military Tribunal," *International Journal for Middle East Studies* 23 (1991), pp. 549–76; "The Turkish Military Tribunal's Prosecution of the Authors of the Armenian Genocide: Four Major Court-Martial Series" *Holocaust and Genocide Studies* 11, 1 (Spring 1997), pp. 28–59.

4. *Blue Book*, Turkey, no. 1, (1895) part 1, pp. 133–93. Report no. 252, written on 20 July and submitted on 15 August 1895. The quotations are from pp. 170, 171, 173.

5. Ibid., 16 October 1895. Inclosure no. 267, pp. 203–8. The quotations are from pp. 206, 207. The Shipley memo was written on 20 July 1895. For a fuller account of the Sassoun massacre as well as the other massacres perpetrated in 1895 and 1896, see Dadrian, *History of the Armenian Genocide* [n. 1], pp. 113–71.

6. *Livre Jaune. Affaires Arméniennes. Supplément, 1895–96* (Paris, 1897), no. 150, p. 104.

7. *Documents Diplomatiques*, vol. 12 (Paris, 1897), no. 265, 8 January 1896, pp. 394–5; 26 September 1896, no. 459, p. 756.

8. Victor Bérard, *La Politique du Sultan*, 3d ed. (Paris: Michel Lévy Frères, 1897), p. 306.

9. *Archives du Ministère des Affaires Étrangères: N.S. 1, Turquie*, Politique Intérieure. Jeuns Turcs. (Paris, 1897), 11 February 1897.

10. FO (British Foreign Office Archives at Kew, London), 195/1944, 3 January 1896 report.

11. FO 195/1930.

12. FO 195/1944, reports of September 25, 29, 30, and November 8, 1896, folio nos. 224, 228, 253–8, 303. The printed version, bearing the same call numbers has also a six-page long 18 November, no. 58 report, which is described as "Inclosures" no. 1 and 2; in no. 1 is enclosed Ambassador Currie's 2 December 1896 report to Salisbury, pp. 339–41.

13. FO 195/1944, 7 September 1896 report.

14. FO 424/251/9273, no. 241, 10 March 1914.

15. In FO 195/1870 confidential report no. 79, there is a long draft, bearing the date of 13 November 1895.

16. FO 424/188, no. 164, p. 138.

17. 27 November 1895, report no. 868? (last digit not legible as the report was hand-written), FO 195/1870.

18. Austrian Foreign Ministry Archives (Vienna), *Politisches Archiv (PA)*, Abteilung 37: Konsulate: 1896, Karton 303, reports no. 74 (5 March); no. 77 (12 March); and no. 90 (26 March 1896).

19. German Foreign Ministry Archives, 1871–1914. *Akten des Auswärtigen Amtes, 1871–1914, vol. 10. Das türkische Problem 1895*, (Berlin: Deutsche

Verlagsgesellschaft für Politik und Geschichte, 1923), report no. 162/2444, October 26, 1895, pp. 84–5.

20. Ibid., report no. 165/2448 (1 November 1895), p. 95.
21. Ibid., report no. 165/2456, p. 101.
22. Ibid., report no. 165/2463 (21 November 1895), p. 109.
23. Ibid., report no. 233/2479 (16 December 1895), p. 127.
24. Ibid., report no. 2572 (transcript of a letter by the Kaiser on 20 December 1895), p. 251.
25. *Documents Diplomatiques*, [n. 7], no. 256 (2 January 1896), pp. 384.
26. *Congressional Record*, 54th Cong., 1st Sess., vol. 28, part 1.

9

The Outlines of a Genocidal Scheme:
The Saloniki Decision and Its Disclosure
by Dissident Ittihadists

This Hamidian episode of large-scale massacres in the evolution of the Turko-Armenian conflict was not only significant for the scale of its casualties but also for its aftermath, marked as it was by a total absence of legal or political retribution against the perpetrators, from within or without. As the prior lack of effective deterrence had enabled the Ottoman-Turkish authorities to plan and enact the massacres, the subsequent failure of the Powers to mobilize and apply retributive justice, and, concomitantly, exact indemnification for the victims, emboldened the same authorities enough to assume a post-massacre posture of defiance and denial. In effect, as mentioned earlier, the 1894–96 Abdul Hamit era massacres developed as a form of limited ethnocide, paving the ground for the World War I genocide; the former involved mainly an assault on the economic, cultural, and religious infrastructure of the nation, the latter an attempt at the destruction of the nation itself, along with all the artifacts of its ancient culture and civilization. This emerging nexus between ethnocide and genocide is the salient feature of the Turko-Armenian conflict, affording a degree of continuity of destructive methods of conflict resolution. Indeed, the dynamics of victimization in intergroup conflicts are such as to produce a transition from limited to maximum victimization, should the conflict be sustained one way or another and at the same time should the absence of external deterrence persist, or be perceived by the perpetrator group to persist. This is the context in which Ittihad, otherwise called the Committee of Union and Progress Party, eventually charted its course against the Armenians and brought genocide to fruition during the ample opportunities provided by the Great War.

One noteworthy point during that process of charting a course towards genocide were the resolutions and decisions of the 1910 Saloniki Congress of Ittihad, briefly mentioned in the introduction of this work. Even though it was primarily the ongoing tensions in Macedonia and Albania that had triggered these decisions in 1910, one of the main targets covered by the broad sweep of these decisions were the Armenians. Internal secret communications, relayed through letters in 1906 and 1907(nearly four years earlier) disclose the fact that the Armenians were labeled as the arch enemies of the Muslims of Turkey and the Caucasus, "to be dealt with accordingly." The letters were signed by two medical doctors, Drs. Nazım and Şakir,[1] the prime architects of the World War I Armenian genocide, both of whom were condemned to death by the 1919 Turkish Court Martial as arch perpetrators. In his 8 December 1907 letter, Şakir openly conceded, for example, that Ittihad's previous agreements with the Armenians, and the promises made to them, had no value whatsoever. He described these promises as baits to exploit the latter's resources for the benefit of the struggling Young Turks, and for the end of gaining sufficient strength to settle scores with them in due course of time. After reproducing this letter Turkish historian Bayur noted the relative carelessness with which these ominous declarations of future intent were made in writing.[2]

In subsequent exchanges with the Huntchaks, dissident Young Turks in overt as well as covert terms sensitized their Armenian counterparts to these ominous secret designs. The Armenian author of these revelations, a Huntchak party leader, who was in league with dissident Ittihadists, (and who later formed the opposition Turkish Itilâf Party), was personally involved, in the summer of 1906, in five series of negotiations with physicians Şakir and Nazım and their initial mentor, Ahmed Riza. During the late summer of 1908 he was consulting with Prince Sabaheddin, and conducted negotiations again with Şakir and Talât in August 1908, the latter of these negotiations lasting "3–4 hours." The same Armenian author notes how Şakir in particular was incensed upon learning of the Huntchak Party's designs for a future Armenia. The negotiations not only collapsed, but Ittihad ended up coopting the rival Dashnak party, whose program was deemed to be less radical and less threatening to Turkey.

The disclosures of the Ittihad secret decisions were made through:

1. Kurd dissident Bedir Bedirhan;
2. Damad Salih Paşa, who through marital bonds was connected to the

Sultan's family and who was hanged by Cemal Paşa in 1913. He "swore on his word of honor that the Ittihadists had decided to exterminate the Armenians come what may";

3. Colonel Fuad, a Circassian officer, whose wife was Armenian, and who, like the above-mentioned Salih Paşa, was executed on the gallows by Cemal Paşa on charges of complicity in the political assassination of Grand Vizier Mahmud Şevket Paşa. He transmitted Ittihadist plans concerning the Armenians in Van province;

4. Niksar's prefect Ihsan;

5. Military Governor Sabih, who "in 1912 handed over to us a batch of very valuable documents containing sealed instructions" as to how to "liquidate, in due course of time," the Huntchaks in particular, and "the Armenian people in general";

6. The Deputy Governor of Kayseri, "an educated Albanian," who likewise delivered some documents swearing on their "authenticity," and warning the Armenians of the impending danger of massacres;

7. Engineer Sami, who in 1912 supplied "minute details" on the Ittihad conspiracy against the Armenians;[3]

8. Galib Bey, Director of Post and Telegraph in Erzurum, who relayed to his friend, the Armenian dragoman at Erzurum's French Consulate, that Ittihad's plans against the Armenians, as framed in the Saloniki Congress, are such as to "make one's hair stand on end." Unable to endure the ensuing atrocities during the war, he committed suicide.[4]

Some of these revelations were published in *Huntchak*, the monthly organ of the party of the same name, in such a covert way as not to compromise the sources and to protect the informers. This effort of concealment seems to have weakened the value of the information and reduced its potential impact.[5] The alleged documents, as far as it is known, did not find their way into print. However, the revelations were in line with and reflected the root causes of the ongoing tensions and internal feuds within Ittihad. These dissensions resulted in an internal purge, in many resignations in protest by the dissidents, a purge, and in the formation, in November 1911, of the above-mentioned opposition *Hürriyet ve Itilâf* party.

The dissidents decried as "sinister" the secret schemes of the Ittihadist leadership who were seen gravitating toward such goals as agitation against the non-Muslim nationalities and toward designs of ethnically homogenizing Turkey, by force and violence if necessary. This critical development in the career of Ittihad was conceded and confirmed by Turkish historian Bayur, who spoke of the exasperation of the Ittihadists in dealing with the nationalities, especially the Armenians, and revealed their final decision to take care of the problem with the Armenians "through the Army" (*işi ordu ile görmek*).[6]

The Pre-Congress Speech of Talât

Notwithstanding his purported allegiance to Islam, as well as the purported similar allegiance of most of his cohorts, Talât is credited with a speech he delivered on 6 August 1910, some ten weeks before the opening of the annual and Third Ittihad Convention in Saloniki. In this speech he is reported to have declared the fundamental principle of equality before the law of all non-Muslims as being anathema to Islam. When reporting this speech, the British vice consul in Monastir, Arthur B. Geary, assured the Foreign Office that the details of the speech, delivered to a secret enclave of Ittihad leaders, were obtained from "an unimpeachable source."[7] The same speech was also reported in a French diplomatic cipher,[8] and by Monastir Austrian Vice Consul Zitkovsky.[9]

As reported by Vice Consul Geary, cited above, the relevant portion of the speech reads:

> You are aware that by the terms of the Constitution equality of Mussulman and Ghiaur [infidel, a derogatory label applied to non-Muslims] was affirmed by you and all know and feel that this is an unrealizable ideal. The Sheriat [the religious laws of Islam], our whole past history and the sentiment of hundreds of thousands of Mussulmans and even the sentiments of the Ghiaurs themselves...present an impenetrable barrier to the establishment of real equality.... There can therefore be no question of equality until we have succeeded in our task of Ottomanizing the Empire.

Even more significant, he declared in the same meeting that Ittihad needed the army to carry out this plan of homogenizing. He said: "The army is solidly ranged in our support...[hence] we remain all powerful." Equally important, Talât alluded to secret Ittihadist party schemes which, he averred, could not be divulged to the civil servants in the provinces, who, therefore, "ought to remain in ignorance." He then advocated the creation of a network of party branches in these provinces in order to "control" provincial administration, emphasizing the importance of keeping "the reins of power entirely in our hands."

The 1910 Saloniki Congress (1–12 November 1910) and the Fatal Decision

This proved to be a landmark decision, setting the stage for the evolution of what proved to be Ittihad's disastrous career, insofar as it related to the treatment of the empire's nationalities. In less than a decade, that evolution culminated in the dissolution of the Ottoman Empire, the practical elimination of the nationalities, and the demise of Ittihad itself. The central objective crystallizing in the secret deliberations of that Congress was the forcible homogenizing of Turkey, which was seen to be afflicted with centrifugal forms of nationalism, especially animating the non-Muslim but indigenous populations of the Empire. It was proposed at the Congress that measures be taken for their elimination in order to "level" these troublesome nationality differences. This fact alone suggests that the projected extermination of the Armenians was but one phase of a comprehensive plan in which other nationalities, considered to be alien, discordant, and unsettling, were to be targeted.

Recognizing the seriousness of the situation, a host of European governments had mobilized their agents to penetrate the inner councils of the Congress leadership to learn what they could about the direction and secret designs of that party. Involved were particularly the Saloniki consuls of Britain, Bulgaria, France, Serbia, Romania, and Austria-Hungary, of whom the latter two were described as long-time Saloniki intelligence agents themselves. In making this disclosure, the French consul also revealed that a Turkish male secretary of the Congress was a paid agent who took down his notes and supplied them to him; the consul "guaranteed the reliability of the source," and "the authenticity of the document."[10] Britain's Monastir vice consul Arthur Geary characterized his "confidential source [as one] on which perfect reliance can be placed."[11]

According to the same French consul, the secret decision revolved around the use of military force to end the nationalities' dreams for independence. "*Seule la force militaire pourra enlever aux nationalités...l'illusion de leur indépendence.*" A new 11 million Turkish pound budget had been decided to bolster the Turkish army's strength. This new objective of achieving the unison of Turkey "*par la force des armes*" included a penchant for joining Kaiser Wilhelm's Triple Alliance, in preference to the Entente created by England, France and Russia. Quoting from the speech of the secretary general of the Ittihadist Congress, the French Consul referred to a demand by the Edirne branch of Ittihad party pressing, if need be, for a resort to the massacre of Edirne Bulgarians, and of all other Christian nationalities labeled as hostile.[12] The German Consul at Saloniki also reported that "according to a seemingly reliable source," the Turks have decided to resolve their conflict with the Christian populations by "the use of force" (*die Anwendung von Gewalt*).[13] Even the French chargé at distant Hejaz, Saudi Arabia, was able to tell his foreign minister, Pichon, that he had secured a document containing "The Secret Resolutions of the 1910 Saloniki Congress," adding: "I think I can vouch for its authenticity." His disclosures more or less tally with the rest, emphasizing Ittihad's resolve to blend Islam with Turkish nationalism, "to uproot (*déraciner*) the nationalist tendencies" of the non-Turks, and to "deform" them.[14]

According to Harry Lamb, British consul general at Saloniki, most secret decisions were deliberated on and reached "after the end of the plenary sessions…by five or six leading members [including] Nazım."[15] Nazım figures prominently as a most influential extremist within Ittihad. He is described as one of the chief partisans of "severe repression" by one source,[16] as the most powerful member of the local Committee (*einflussreichste*) by another;[17] a third source described him "as the most marked personality…and the moving spirit" of Ittihad's Central Committee, the extreme arm of which is prepared "to order the massacre of the Christians as a last resort."[18] At the Congress under review, Nazım served as vice president, was elected a member of the Central Committee of the party, and secretary general of the Saloniki branch of Ittihad; the incidence of this latter election was kept secret. It should be noted that the Saloniki branch dominated for a long time the overall party organization and its programs. Nazım successfully pushed through the acceptance of budgetary allocations to enable him to undertake large-scale resettlements of Muslims from Russian and Persian border areas in the Balkans, as well as in the "six Armenian provinces," especially the Erzurum area. As a French historian has stated, Nazım was the chief advocate of the goal of completely "Turkifying" the country through massive Muslim resettlements, through coercion, and massacres.[19] In fact, during World War I, he organized and supervised the killer detachments of the Special Organization, and was a member of the secret Supreme Directorate of Ittihad. As mentioned earlier, he was indicted, tried, convicted, and sentenced to death in absentia by the Turkish Military Tribunal on 5 July 1919.[20]

Finally, a comment on the techniques of secrecy and deflection may be in order. As the Turkish Court Martial Indictment pointed out in its introductory part, Ittihad had two faces: one, "the external public" (*zahiri ve aleni*), the other "covert and secret" (*mestur ve hafi*).[21] The British reports on the 1910 Congress underscore this stratagem, with the British ambassador at Istanbul offering the following comment on the Congress decisions: "…it must be confessed that there is a considerable contradiction between their professions and their acts. Besides their published decisions, they are credited with secret ones which inspire their inner workings."[22] The same ambassador, borrowing from the text of his Saloniki Consul's report, some two weeks later characterized "the official version of the decisions" as being intended "to throw dust in the eyes of the world."[23] Consul General Lamb, in his report cited above, dismissed the "official manifesto which purports to be at once a résumé of its decisions and a declaration of its policy…[as] merely a repetition of familiar verbiage bearing no real relation to existing facts and designed merely to throw dust in the eyes of the outside world."[24]

A Note on the 1911 Congress

It is worth noting that at the fourth Annual Congress (30 September–10 October 1911), the idea of maintaining "the prerogatives," and the "diverse religions" of the nationalities was once more reasserted in item Number 11 of the official Text of Resolutions.[25] This reassertion was in part due to the alarm, which dissident Ittihadists during most of 1911 had caused among the subject nationalities by venting their scorn against the party's "fraud, lies, and violation of all the principles of the Constitution" (to quote dissident Riza Tevfik).[26] It was also due to the rise of anti-Semitism among Muslim spiritual leaders and conservative Young Turks denouncing the alleged growth of freemason influence in the ranks of the Ittihadist leadership, and the perceived influence of the Saloniki Jews, believed to be the element exerting that influence. In the words of Austrian Saloniki Vice Consul Gregovich, the Congress ostensibly yielded on the point in order to mollify all these nationalities by assuaging their anxieties. However, the French Saloniki Consulate's chargé, S. Zarzecki, had reported anti-Semitic outbursts in connection with a club gathering, which involved such Ittihadist leaders as Ömer Naci, Yunus Nadi, and Muhiddin agitating against the Jews in this connection.[27] As to pan-Islamism, Nazım is quoted as saying that though "reactionary," Ittihad managed to harness that religious movement to its purpose.[28] Equally noteworthy is the revelation by Austrian Saloniki Consul General Kral that in a pre-Congress memo to the Ittihadists, ex-Grand Vizier Kâmil Paşa advised them not to be "blatant" in their pan-Islamic drives.[29] In a ten-page report Austria's Saloniki Consul General Kral provides additional details on the deliberations of the Congress.[30] The discussion on pan-Islamism is contained in another report by the same Consul.[31] Saloniki's Acting British Consul General, James Morgan, for his part sent two reports, while the actual Consul Harry Lamb sent one report.[32] The two German accounts are part of the correspondence sent from the German Saloniki Consulate.[33]

According to British sources, the 1911 Ittihadist Annual Congress was supposed to last a month.[34] However, Italy on 23 September 1911, sent to Turkey an ultimatum that was to expire in twenty-four hours. Moreover, the Ottoman Parliament was due to reconvene imminently, and most Congress delegates were members of the Ottoman Parliament's Chamber of Deputies. This fact, and Italy's subsequent invasion of Libya, regarding which Italy's ultimatum had been issued, prompted the Ittihadists to cut short their congress. Notwithstanding, the Ittihadist leaders had more or less managed to assuage the anxieties of the nationalities who had been alarmed by the charges and disclosures of the party's dissidents.

The Intricate Relationship between Acts of Conspiracy and Genocidal Designs

The picture that emerges from these party congresses is the dual-track role performance of Ittihad. On the one hand there is the formulation of a platform outlining a party program that is intended strictly for public consumption. On the other hand, there is the clandestine mapping of a sketchy plan that is ominous and undoubtedly sinister in nature, and is, therefore, kept secret from the public, even from the regular organs of the government, and from the lower echelons of the party leadership and naturally from rank and file. The former act is belied by the latter as the main purpose of the duality of such role performance is to conceal and/or deflect from the essential and high-priority objectives of the top leadership of the party. The principal aim is to confound the outsiders by surreptitiously combining overt and covert methods of operations.

Several Turkish authors, historians, political scientists, and biographers, did recognize this secretive modus operandi of Ittihad as its trademark, as far as the attainment of questionable goals and its reliance on lethal violence were concerned. Tevfik Çavdar, the biographer of Ittihad party boss Talât, explicitly admitted to "the dual character of the organization" of Ittihad party whose "secret nature was nurtured and explored through a separate organizational component. The entire body exactly resembled an iceberg comprising visible and invisible parts."

Speaking of Talât as the party boss, Çavdar declared that he knew how to exploit the potential of that secret component of the party by way of "readily sliding in the position of man launching illegal undertakings."[35] Sina Akşin, a historian and an expert on Ittihad, pointed out that the party's "secrecy was meant to cover the discrepancy between its program of Ottomanism and its application of a program of Turkism. Moreover, the resort to secrecy was probably due to the mentality of an organization which did not recoil from murdering people in pursuit of its political goals (*Siyasal amaçlarına ulaşmak için adam öldürmekten kaçınmıyan*)."[36] For his part Tarık Z. Tunaya, the late dean of Turkish political scientists, declared: "Ittihad was a power-wielding monopolistic clique which issued orders from behind the curtains (*her şeyi perde arkasından hükmeden*)...the great Empire was in the hands of these eight individuals...operating secretly and in an organized way behind a mysterious curtain...a secret oligarchy which resorted to weapons whenever it could not silence ideas."[37]

The most salient feature of this almost pervasive secretiveness of Ittihad was the extension of that secretiveness to the regular organs of the Ottoman state organization, organs which were not directly identified with the party apparatus and as such were treated as alien elements. This is exactly the modus operandi Talât had projected in the above mentioned pre-Congress conclave of top Ittihadist leaders in Saloniki in August 1910. He stated that the goals of the party, especially with respect to the provinces, could not be attained unless the provincial officials of the government were kept "in ignorance."[38] This is an attitude in which lethal schemes of conspiracy can readily germinate, including the scheme of organizing of the mass murder of a targeted population group; the actualization of such a scheme all but may become contingent upon the onset of propitious opportunities.

Notes

1. Y. H. Bayur, *Türk Inkilâbı Tarihi*, vol. 2, part 4, (Ankara: Turkish Historical Society, 1952), pp. 85–7, involving two letters dated 23 November 1906, and 22 September 1906; for the 3 January 1908 letter see pp. 125–6; for the same letters see also Ahmed Bedevi Kuran, *Inkilâp Tarihimiz ve Ittihad ve Terakki* (The history of our revolution and Union and Progress), (Istanbul: Tan, 1948), pp. 214, 215.
2. Bayur, *Türk Inkilâbı Tarihi*, [n. 1], p. 130.
3. Sabah-Kulian, *Badaskhanadouneru* (The responsible ones), (Beirut: Donikian, [1916]1974), pp. 239–40, 329–30, 198–213, 244, 250–5, 329–31.
4. For a review of these disclosures see Vahakn N. Dadrian, "The Secret Young-Turk Ittihadist Conference and the Decision for the World War I Genocide of

the Armenians," *Holocaust and Genocide Studies* 7, no. 2 (Fall 1993), pp. 179–80.

5. *Huntchak.* 26, no. 2 (February 1913), pp. 9ff; Ibid., no. 3 (March 1913), pp. 6ff.
6. Bayur, *Türk Inkilâbı Tarihi*, [n. 1], p. 13.
7. *British Documents on the Origin of the War 1898–1914*, 9, part 1, (eds. G. P. Gooch and Harold Temperley), (London, 1926), p. 208.
8. *French Foreign Ministry Archives* (Paris), N. S. Turquie: Jeuns Turcs, vol. 7, pp. 92–7.
9. *German Foreign Ministry Archives*, Türkei 159, no. 2, band 12, A18643, no. 69 secret, 14 October 1910 report.
10. The Consul was Max Choublier, 17 November 1910 report in *N. S. Turquie* [n. 8]; his description of the respective discoveries of the Romanian and Austrian Consuls as intelligence agents are in ibid., 22 November 1910 report.
11. FO 195/2359, folio 273, 13 December 1910 report.
12. *Consul Choublier* [n. 8], 15 and 17 November 1910 reports.
13. The Consul was Mutius, *Türkei* 198/6, A18779, 8 November 1910 report.
14. *N. S. Turquie*, [n. 8], vol. 8, 26 January 1911 report.
15. FO 420/250, p. 4; FO 195/2359, folio 338, 16 December 1910 report.
16. *Max Choublier*, [n. 8], 22 November 1910 report.
17. Germany's Saloniki consul *Mutius*, [n. 13], A20309, 5 December 1910 report.
18. FO 195/2359, No. 149, Britain's Saloniki Consul Lamb's 19 November 1910 report.
19. René Pinon, "La Liquidation de L'Empire Ottoman," *Revue des Deux Mondes.* 53 (September 1919), pp. 131, 139–40.
20. *Takvimi Vekâyi*, (The judicial journal of the Ottoman government, whose "supplements" (*ilâve*) covered many portions of the proceedings of the Turkish Military Tribunal trying the authors of the Armenian genocide), no. 3604, 22 July 1919, p. 219; On 26 August 1926 Nazım was executed in Ankara on conviction of charges of complicity in the plot to assassinate Mustafa Kemal.
21. *Takvimi Vekâyi*, no. 3540, 5 May 1919, p. 8.
22. Ambassador Sir Charles Marling's 22 November 1910 report to the foreign secretary, Sir Edward Grey is in FO 371/1017, section 2, p. 1.
23. Ibid., 7 December 1910 report section 5, p. 1.
24. Ibid., 19 November 1910, section 2, p. 2, and FO 195/2359.
25. *N. S. Jeuns Turcs*, [n. 8], vol. 8, French Saloniki Consul Jousselz's 10 October 1911 report.
26. Ibid., Saloniki French Consul S. Zarzecki's 28 January 1911 report.
27. Ibid., 3 April 1911 report.
28. Ibid., 7 April 1911 report.
29. *P.A.* XXXIII/414, no. 145, p. 3 of 31 October 1911 report.
30. Ibid., no. 141, 23 October 1911 report.
31. Ibid., no. 155, 13 November 1911.
32. Morgan's reports are dated 28 September and 11 October 1911 and that of Lamb 10 December 1911. All three are to be found in FO 195/2382, folios 262–4, 323–4, and 503–5 respectively.
33. *Türkei* 198. Die Jungtürken, vol. 7, A14462, Mutius's 8 September 1911, and Schwörbel's A182, 26 January 1912 reports.
34. FO 195/2382, folio 323.
35. Tevfik Çavdar, *Talât Paşa* (Ankara: Dost, 1984), pp. 190, 210.
36. Sina Akşin, *100 Soruda Jön Türkler ve Ittihad ve Terakki* (The Young Turks and Ittihad in the context of 100 questions) (Istanbul: Gerçek, 1980), p. 156.

37. Tarık Zafer Tunaya, *Türkiyede Siyasi Partiler 1859–1952* (Political parties in Turkey 1859–1952), (Istanbul: Doğan Brothers, 1952), p. 182.

38. See note 7 above.

10

The Twisted Interconnections between Armenian Military Roles and the World War I Armenian Genocide

The Dilemmas of Military Service as Citizens

The doubts of Turkish authorities about the benefits for the Ottoman state of introducing a system of universal military conscription without regard to race, creed or nationality were real; they were predicated upon the recognition of the fact that the introduction of such a system was intrinsically risky for the internal security of the empire. The predominant view was that universal military conscription was at best a double-edged sword: on the one hand it could facilitate the process of integration of the string of non-Muslim nationalities of the multiethnic Ottoman Empire in the sociopolitical fabric of the Ottoman system; on the other hand, however, it could also foster a martial spirit and correlative martial aptitudes among these groupings whose loyalties to the empire were tenuous, if not questionable, and could, therefore, not be taken for granted. In other words, when trained and equipped, these Ottoman subjects could acquire a negative potential, thereby becoming a liability rather than an asset, especially in times of war. The long history of inequities, persecution, and episodic massacres punctuating the dominant role of the Turks in the fractious social universe of Muslim–non-Muslim relations was such as to make possible, if not to warrant, the emergence of such a potential.

Wartime conditions posed a particularly troubling problem. Like some other minorities, the Armenians were connected in many ways with substantial masses of a diaspora which had established themselves in territories adjacent to the territories of the Ottoman Empire, especially in the Caucasus and the Balkan peninsula. Even more significant, these Armenians in overwhelming numbers were either refugees from Ottoman Turkey, or were the progeny of these refugees. The regional anti-Armenian massacres attending the three waves of Russo-Turkish wars of 1828–29, 1853–56, and 1877–78 had unleashed a series of mass migrations, a large-scale exodus from Ottoman Turkey. These populations were identified in the host countries as direct and indirect casualties of Turkish persecution; their immigrant life was a constant reminder of the source of their problems of suffering and hardship associated with forced dislocation. But the bulk of these diaspora Armenians were the survivors and the progeny of these survivors of the cycle of the 1894–96 empire-wide massacres that decimated and seriously crippled the Armenian community of the empire; they are examined in some detail in chapter 8. With but few exceptions these survivors, many of them the orphans of the Abdul Hamit era massacres, were still under the spell of the horrors of these massacres. Their animosity against Turkey and the Turks was almost inveterate and apparently constituted the very core of their sense of ethnic-national identity. Similar sentiments prevailed among Armenian immigrants in the rest of Europe, North and South Americas, and the Near and Middle East. As a rule immigrants of this type are too absorbed in the struggle to survive in a strange land and to cope with the elements of culture shock. But when opportunities suddenly spring up to inflict upon those who may be broadly identified as the source of their past or current misery, the struggle for acculturation is often overwhelmed by an impulse for retaliatory reckoning. Wars do offer such opportunities in the sense that the young and the able-bodied among the dislocated immigrants are afforded a chance to join the ranks of the enemies of what they consider to be their sworn enemy.

This fact compounded the plight of the Armenian population of Ottoman Turkey during the two wars the Ottoman regime fought prior to its ultimate demise in 1918. In the 1912–13 Balkan war but especially in World War I that population to a large extent became hostage to Armenian initiatives in the diaspora; these initiatives involved plans to provide contingents of volunteers to those armies which were arrayed against Turkey in those wars. Under such conditions, all other things being equal, there is always the acute danger of scapegoating that can assume lethal proportions; military setbacks are attributed to, or mainly explained in terms of such interventions from the outside. Worse yet, the external initiatives on the part of ethnic-national groups, identified with corresponding kinship groups within the targeted country aiming at marshalling volunteer corps, may serve as a pretext to activate deadly schemes of "ethnic cleansing" internally, i.e., against these kinship groups.

In the present case the issue was further complicated by the fact that the quasi introduction of universal military conscription in the 1909–10 period, noted above, had led to the rudimentary preparation of Armenian cadres which were militarily trained by Turkish officers and drill sergeants. As a result the Armenians, while trying to aid and abet their patron-states, ended up fighting for opposite ends, and ultimately against each other. Far more critical was, however, the disaster that engulfed the Armenian nation in connection with this development of military involvement in Turkish wars. This is the more significant when one considers the fact that in both wars Armenians, whether individually or in groups, fought with valor in the ranks of the Turkish army—despite the incidence of occasional desertions which, however, at times assumed epidemic proportions, as far as the Turkish deserters were concerned. In order to fully understand the web of interconnections between these military involvements of the Armenians and the World War I Armenian genocide, a brief account may be in order.

The Balkan War as a Test Case for Harnessing the Martial Aptitudes of the Armenians

When the first Balkan war erupted in October 1912 the conditions producing that result were not much different from those prevailing in the Asiatic provinces of Turkey. There was the contagious animus of nationalism among the Ottoman Empire's subject nationalities as well as among the emancipated ones in the Balkan peninsula. The latter's feuds and mutual rivalries were overshadowed, however, by their common antagonism against Ottoman authorities. The legacy of sustained oppression contributed to aggregate anti-Turkish hostility that culminated in the formation of the Balkan League. It involved an expressly anti-Turkish military alliance that was forged among the Serbs, Bulgarians, Greeks, and Montenegrins with the tacit support of the Russians. But cumulative developments and their expression in an alliance need not necessarily yield a bloody war. What, as a rule, is needed is the onset of a precipitating factor, and the Turks were not long in producing that factor by resorting to their standard device of repression through ghastly massacres. In the summer of 1912 large numbers of Macedonian Bulgars in Berana, but especially in Kotchana, southeast of Üsküp or Skolpje, were cold-bloodedly slaughtered. On 14 August

1912, these atrocities provoked massive demonstrations in Sofia, the capital of Bulgaria. Some two weeks later the decision was made to declare war against Turkey in October of that year.

The prospect of fighting against the Turks in a war of what they regarded "liberation" drew thousands of Macedonians, mostly Bulgars, to the Macedonian Corps of Volunteers that comprised nearly 15,000 men. Despite their relatively small size, the Armenians of Bulgaria, especially of the city of Varna, enthusiastically joined this volunteer movement. In no time there materialized the Armenian Company which, exceeding the standard size of 150–160 men, contained 230 volunteers; by the end of the war it had grown in size, counting 270 men, including officers and staff. Some of the volunteers were from other parts of the world including a large number of artisans from Romania. The unit was integrated into the overall Corps of Volunteers, becoming the Second Company of the Twelfth Battalion of the Third Brigade. It underwent intensive training under the leadership of Karekin Njteh, an Armenian captain in the Bulgarian army. Eventually the overall command was given to Antranik (Ozanian) whose exploits in his fight against Turkish and Kurdish "despots" in the interior of Turkey in the preceding two decades had elevated him to the status of a legendary folk hero. He assumed his command with the rank of captain that the Bulgarian High Command granted him. According to Armen Suni, MD, who was in charge of the Sanitation and Health Section of the Company, the Armenian volunteers were driven by a passion to break the centuries-old yoke of the Ottoman Turks. The volunteers' firm resolve was emblematic of the Armenian people's craving for a "revenge which had permeated every fibre of their heart and for five centuries had been tearing asunder the inner recesses of their souls."[1] Kuneyef, the Bulgarian commander of the Twelfth Battalion, witnessing the military feats resulting from this vengefulness of the volunteers, is reported to have exclaimed after a certain victory, "Oh, they are lions, veritable lions these volunteers."[2]

Within two weeks after their entering into combat at the Kırcaali sector of the front, the company helped score a spectacular victory against General Ali Yaver (Paşa); he was the commander of the First Turkish Army Corps.[3] After having been pushed back to the area of south of Mestanlı on 19 and 20 October 1912, the general some three weeks later was forced to surrender.[4] The circumstances of his capture are of sufficient significance to merit a brief description here; that significance is accented by the fact that whereas Turkish sources provide hardly any detail about it, Armenian sources are quite specific. After capturing Dedeağac and entering the village Osmancık, the command of Macedonian Corps of Volunteers allowed the Armenian Company to take up positions in the vicinity of Merhamlu village, at the banks of Maritza (Meriç) river, where the main body of the First Army Corps was entrenched. Instead of a frontal attack against well-fortified positions, Commander Antranik, using all the skills he had acquired as a guerrilla fighter in Turkey some decades earlier, decided to circumvent these positions. In a swiftly executed swinging movement his forces swooped down an adjoining valley and from there climbed up the slopes facing general Yaver's positions from a new angle. Realizing the near hopelessness of his trapped condition, Yaver Paşa decided to surrender with his staff and army corps units. The spectacular success of this bold movement had a chance element; because of a mechanical defect in it, Antranik could not hear the trumpet, through which his superior, commander Alexander Protokerof, had signaled an order to stop his risky undertaking.

The aftermath of the surrender appears to be no less significant. Captured along with General Yaver were 10,000 soldiers, three colonels and 242 officers of the First Army Corps.[5] When surrendering his sword as part of the military protocol, General Yaver was both surprised and dismayed to see Antranik, the Armenian folk hero, in the position of the victor receiving that sword. He is reported to have retorted bitterly, "Had I known that you were my opponent, I would have fought to the bitter end and never would have surrendered." Upon hearing these words, Antranik gallantly returns the sword.[6] Apprehensive that as irregular forces the Armenian volunteers could ignore the standard rule of respecting the inviolability of military prisoners and act mercilessly against them, Yaver Paşa requested that their transportation to Berecik as a way-station to captivity in Bulgaria proper be handled by the regular forces of the Bulgarian army.[7] When asked as to why he surrendered with so many forces and canons at his disposal, General Yaver is reported to have exclaimed: "The see in the rear, the swines [the volunteers] in front; what can I do?" *"Dalda deniz, kapakda domuz. Ne yapayım?*).[8] After kissing his cheeks three times, Colonel Protokerof in a ceremony in Rodosto (Tekirdağ) decorated Antranik with the Golden Cross for Military Heroism, declaring: "You Armenians, you all are heroes and are fighting like lions. But the Cross for Heroism can only be awarded to the hero of heroes." Captain Karekin Njteh received the Officer's Cross. Subsequently Antranik was honored with the additional decorations of fourth- and third-degree silver crosses and second-degree golden cross as King Ferdinand of Bulgaria bestowed upon him the honor of Bulgarian citizenship and made him a regular officer of the Bulgarian army. Moreover an additional thirty-five Armenian volunteers received various decorations for valor, of whom sixteen were promoted to the rank of sergeant and eight to that of second lieutenant.[9]

Unlike many of the volunteers under his command Antranik throughout the Balkan war maintained a strict military code of confining hostile operations to military personnel and targets; this posture was consistently maintained by him in nearly all of his encounters in the past, whether as a guerrilla fighter or a regular army officer confronting the Turks and the Kurds. During an interview with Leon Trotsky in Sofia this is how he summed up his rationale in this respect. "I never engaged in hostile acts against the peaceful Turkish population; I only fought against the Beys and against the government. I am not a nationalist. I recognize only one nation: the nation of the oppressed."[10] As one Armenian volunteer admitted, however, "it was difficult to subdue our inveterate urge for revenge as our memories of the Armenian massacres were still vivid." Nevertheless Antranik, who otherwise was an unrestrained warrior, in every way endeavored to contain this urge for revenge in combat operations, especially "when the enemy did surrender, when one was face to face with an unarmed man."[11]

Counterposed to this Armenian contribution to the military initiative of the Balkan League was the larger contribution of Armenian fighters conscripted in the Ottoman-Turkish army under the new system of universal military service. The noted British scholar George Young estimates their number at 8,000, adding that, of all the other non-Muslim subjects of the Ottoman Empire these Armenians "alone fought well."[12] A similar view is expressed by noted Ottomanist Roderick Davison who speaks of the Ottoman Armenian soldiers' "valiant service in the Balkans,"[13] despite the fact that the Young Turk Ittihadists had "stifled Armenian hopes" for reform, and "the constitutional regime had done little for the Armenians."[14] These frustrations stood, however, in sharp contrast with the willingness of thousands of young Armenians many of whom rushed to the draft boards with a zeal to serve Turkey. The following eyewitness account of such a scene illustrates the point: "A contingent of soldiers of the new mixed Turkish army proceeded from Topkapı, one of the centers of recruitment, to the War Ministry, where the barracks of the recruits were situated. The crowds everywhere applauded, chanting the war song *Ey gaziler*, and the military band provided the accompanying music. Many of the recruits in the procession were Armenians who were rejoicing in this unprecedented event: the advent of the system of nondiscriminatory military service for the defense of the sacred fatherland... An old Turk, standing next to me, said, 'Nobody can overpower Turkey any more:"[15] The testimony of prominent Turks is corroborative in this regard. War Minister Nazım Paşa, for example, was quoted by the *Times* of London stating at the end of the first Balkan war that "the Armenian soldiers had done their duty as well as the Turks, and that there were practically no cases of panic among them."[16] About the same time an influential Young Turk publicist and educator published under the title, "The Armenians and Us" an article in the Turkish newspaper *Ikdam* in which he wrote:

> Presently when the other people murdered before our very eyes our fleeing wives and children, the Armenian soldiers who had enrolled in our army fought with a heroism that knows no higher degree. The officials whom the Armenians had put at the disposal of our government were the last ones leaving their posts when the cities that were threatened by the enemy were being evacuated. Their families were the ones which opened their doors to the fleeing citizens with the plea, "Don't go away. Don't destroy your hearth. Let us live together until such time when the unhappy days are over."[17]

Nevertheless, for the Armenians of Turkey the pendulum began to swing decidedly in the opposite direction. In the overall picture of gloom and doom in late 1912 and early 1913, the Turks, especially the members of the radical wing of Young Turk Ittihadist leadership, were in no mood to appreciate to any significant degree the Armenian acts of heroism in the war Turkey disastrously had just lost. The enormous scale of Turkish losses and the attendant state of Turkish despair have been described elsewhere.[18] Two allied factors served to accentuate the dilemmas of the Armenians rendering them highly vulnerable for destructive targeting. Both factors would subsequently prove as major contributing factors for both the scheming and the organization of the World War I Armenian genocide. One was the joint decision of Armenian clerical and political leaders to reactivate the dormant Armenian reforms issue by the formation of a special delegation that would seek the intervention of European Powers for the final realization of these reforms. This decision was in part prompted by the steady deterioration of the plight of the provincial Armenian population; but, more importantly, it was prompted by an eagerness to take advantage of the weaknesses of a militarily defeated and generally dispirited Turkey.

This Armenian initiative would provide an opportunity to the minority radical wing of Ittihad party, led by physician-politicians Nazım and Şakir, to do some more persuading and eventually prevail upon the rest of the members of the Central Committee of the party to seriously consider the adoption of radical anti-Armenian measures.[19]

The other factor was that of migration involving the influx into Turkey of tens of thousands of Muslims fleeing from the inferno of death and destruction that the military victories of the Greeks, Serbs, and Bulgarians had wrecked in the Balkans. Their condition of destitution and misery was matched and even exceeded by their intense animosity to the sources of their suffering which they conveniently subsumed under a single category, namely, the Christians. This depiction of and focusing on the religious factor would later prove devastating for the Armenian population of Turkey. As the Turkish editor, cited above, observed, "Each episode of violently executed exile brings with it much misery and suffering but, even more, hatred and animosity in the areas in which the refugees are settled. As was the case in 1877, this time around too the refugees from Rumeli will bring in the villages and towns of Anatolia an awful urge for revenge on account of the misfortunes and afflictions and the hardships to which they were subjected. Given the kind of despondency and bitterness animating this urge for revenge, one cannot determine as to against whom it should be directed." But Suphi had no doubt as to whom eventually the target would be. He continues, "What a shameful error we would be committing, however, should we proceed to discharge against the Armenians the hostility that grew in our hearts." As if wanting to forestall such a development and fight against the specter of his own ominous premonition, Suphi issues the following admonition to his fellow Turks and Muslims: "We Muslims and Turks a long time ago should have been cognizant of the importance of the Armenians for the welfare and salvation of the Ottoman fatherland and of the fact that how much this welfare and salvation is dependent upon them."[20]

But, to no avail; it was not to be. As Fridjof Nansen observed, "The Turkish defeat in the Balkan war made things still worse for the Armenian Christians...thousands of Turkish emigrants from Macedonia and Thrace arrived in Anatolia full of hatred for all Christians, in which they were encouraged by the Government."[21] That encouragement confirmed the ominousness of the premonition of Suphi cited above; the Armenians would become the target of a massive discharge of aggression at the opportune moment. Sensing this grave danger, the Armenian Patriarch in vain tried to seek, through his 12 May 1913 petition, the intervention of the grand vizier. In that petition the patriarch bitterly complained about the violent abuses of the new settlers in the Armenian communities and that "the Armenians were continuously being killed, wounded, forcibly converted to Islam while the perpetrators are being left untouched. The weapons of the Armenians are being taken away (under the terms of the 1908 Constitution, the Ittihadists allowed the Armeniasns to bear arms) while the Muslims are being allowed to keep theirs."[22] A German specialist of Ottoman-Turkish affairs and a confidant of many Ittihadist leaders disclosed that the Turkish authorities in 1913 were in the process of resettling in Asiatic Turkey half a million Muslim refugees from the Balkans.[23] The specific and studied utilization by the Ittihadist decision makers of the multitudes of these refugees as primary tools in the organization and implementation of the wartime genocide will be the subject of a separate discussion in chapter 11, "Demography."

The World War I Crucible

If one could consider the first Balkan war and its devastating outcome for Turkey an event foreshadowing the Armenian genocide by way of intensifying the simmering Turko-Armenian conflict, by all apparent evidence, World War I, on the other hand, functioned as a catalyst for the precipitation of that genocide; the dynamics of that war were such as to provide opportunities for the violent explosion of that conflict. As in the case of the Balkan war, so in World War I, Armenian loyalties and contributions to the war effort were not only dual in character but were patently antithetical as well. Whereas the Armenians residing in Turkey were conscripted to assist in the war effort of Turkey, and indirectly of the Central Powers, Germany and Austria, in particular, the rest of the Armenians throughout the Armenian diaspora without hesitation gravitated to the camps of the opposing Entente Powers, mainly Russia, France, and England, the enemies of their envisaged common enemy, Turkey. As in the case of the 1912 Balkan war, in this case too, the phenomenon of military prowess and feats of bravery displayed by the Armenians in the operations launched by mutually hostile armies, locked in a deadly fight against each other, once more came into the limelight of public attention. Already at the start of the war, 1,500 Armenians had enrolled in the Reserve Officers Training School that was set up in Istanbul in the summer of 1914. Even more significant, according to a German account, this number exceeded that of the Turkish enrollees.[24]

Within weeks after the start of military operations against Russia, Armenian soldiers of the Third Turkish Army, which was conducting these operations, had distinguished themselves in combat. This fact was broadcast by no less an authority than the de facto Commander-in-Chief of Ottoman Armed Forces and Minister of War Enver. In fact Enver had temporarily assumed the command of that army during that army's gigantic offensive against the Russians in the 1914–15 winter. On two occasions he went out of his way to express his appreciation for the quality of the Armenian soldiers' performance in the battlefield. On his way back from the front to his General Headquarters in Istanbul in January 1915, he had stopped by in Erzincan and Konya where he made references to what he described as the praiseworthy exploits of the Armenian soldiers. Upon his return to the Ottoman capital, he put this praise in writing and sent it to the primate of Konya, Karekin Khatchadourian, emphasizing that he "personally had observed" these acts of bravery.[25] The second time Enver expressed himself on this topic was on the occasion of the Armenian patriarch visiting with him in February 1915. Enver not only repeated to the patriarch his respective words of praise but injected a highly revealing personal note in his utterances. It developed that Enver and his staff were virtually saved from certain capture by the Russians through the adroit and swift tactical move of Armenian lieutenant Hovannes Aginian, a veteran of the Balkan war. Without any authorization Aginian and the men under his command had acted in such a way as to prevent the surprise Russian assault on the temporary field headquarters from which Enver and his coterie were directing the movements of the Third Army. The Patriarch sought and obtained Enver's permission to publicize these details personally supplied to him by the war minister himself.[26] An Armenian chronicler states in his description of the family background of Aginian that Enver not only on the spot promoted Aginian to the rank of captain but sent from Istanbul a certificate of congratulations and thanks. The document was emblazoned in gold inlaid letters, and bore the Imperial monogram (*Tuğra*). These acts proved, however, nothing but gestures of tragic irony. Shortly after the episode described above, Aginian was killed in battle, and the government reported that his father was also killed, but not in battle. He was part of a convoy being deported from Sivas to Surudj. The killer bands had set upon and massacred the entire convoy. Therefore, Aginian's family could not receive Enver's certificate.[27]

The other side of the picture was such, however, that whatever significance one might want to attach to such happenings, and to everything else they denote and connote, that significance was overshadowed and overwhelmed by the specter of a peril looming large in the horizon. There were not only large numbers of Armenians fighting as volunteers in the armies arrayed against the Turks and Turkey, but even more critical, they were recognized by the Turks as ancillary forces contributing in good measure to the latter's military setbacks. The Armenian volunteer movement that sprang up in the Caucasus comprised multitudes of young Armenians from Russia, Persia, Europe, and the United States who, like the volunteers in the Balkan war, were animated with intense feelings of hostility and revenge against the Turks. Among them were many who were natives of Turkey; others were veterans of anti-Hamidian guerrilla warfare, or of the 1912–13 Balkan war. What was perhaps the most signal aspect of this movement was the involvement in it of Antranik, the folk hero, and more specifically, the hero of the 1912 Balkan war. In fact Antranik played a major role in upsetting the Ittihadist pan-Turanian plan by defeating General Halil Kut's First Expeditionary Force at Dilman in Iran (south of Khoi and northwest of the Urmia salt lake) on 18 April (1 May) 1915. Halil's mission was to swing around the positions of the Russian Caucasus Army through a gigantic encircling movement, trap and destroy that army in order to clear the way for a direct march all the way to the dream-land of Turan in Turkistan. But once more, Antranik, in full command of his detachment of some 1,300 Armenian volunteers, and assisted by 300 Cossacks, repulsed Halil's repeated attacks, forcing the latter's expeditionary unit of 13,000 men (augmented by some 4000 irregulars) to embark upon a humiliating and torturous retreat, all the way to Bitlis—after sustaining heavy casualties. Once more Antranik seemingly proved to be the nemesis of the Turks, and once more he was embraced, honored, and decorated by the high command of the host country involving Tsarist Russian officers.[28] The Turkish reaction was summed up by Halil's cohort, Turkish general Ali Ihsan Sabis who declared that the Dilman defeat was a "major defeat" (*büyük mağlubiyet*), it was "a tragedy" (*felâket*) entailing "heavy losses" (*ağır kayıplar*) and causing retreat that took place under "miserable" (*perişan*) conditions. "With that defeat the plan to conquer Azerbaijan, Dagistan, and to push behind the Russian lines and to instigate rebellions in the hinterland of Russia was completely foiled. This was a heavy blow to people who are in pursuit of daydreams" (*hulya peşinde*). The Dilman blow was necessary to learn to refrain from indulging in daydreams and to act heedlessly."[29]

The Dilman defeat was but one link in a chain of other catastrophic Turkish military defeats involving hostile Armenian participation in the production of these defeats, in particular at Van and at Sarıkamış. Whether true or false, or whether exaggerated, Ittihadist leaders in part blamed the Armenian volunteers for the colossal defeat in the Sarıkamış battle. Talât is reported to have told American Ambassador Morgenthau that the Armenians "assisted the Russians in the Caucasus and our failure there is largely explained by their actions." Enver is reported to have said almost the same thing to the same ambassador.[30] Beyond these major military debacles, the defeat at Van was perhaps the most devastating, not only strategically, but in terms of lacerating the Turkish psyche. Fighting behind make-shift barricades, 500–600 Van Armenians, assisted by some 1,000 support personnel, rose up to prevent the Turks from deporting and destroying the Armenian population of the city and its environs. Despite repeated attempts to encircle and reduce that population, the regular and irregular Turkish forces, mainly consisting of twelve veteran battalions that comprised the Van Gendarmes Division, not only failed to overwhelm the defenders but after suffering heavy losses were forced to discontinue their operations and flee from Van. The rapid advances of Russian troops from the east, spearheaded by Armenian volunteers, had posed a serious threat to the attacking Turkish forces. Thus, in the end, the Armenians of Van, after successfully repulsing the enemy during their 20 April–17 May 1915 uprising, prevailed, and in the process inflicted a severe blow to Turkish military self-confidence and pride.

Contrary to persistent Turkish claims that the Van uprising was part of a wide Armenian conspiracy, intended to cripple the Turkish war effort, Vice Marshal Pomiankowski of Austria, who throughout the war was attached to the Ottoman General Headquarters, asserted that the uprising was an act of "desperation" (*Verzweiflung*) to avert "a general slaughter."[31] The accounts of a Turkish-speaking Venezuelan officer, in charge of the Turkish artillery that was used against the Armenian defenders, are more trenchant. He revealed, for example, the fact that Turkish authorities had initiated the attack against the Armenians by launching massacres against the civilian population. "The *Belediye Reisi* (mayor) who was directing the orgy...astounded me by replying that he was doing nothing more than carrying out an unequivocal order emanating from the governor of the province...to exterminate all Armenian males of twelve years of age and over." According to his own admission, this Venezuelan officer had blasted the Armenian positions with "16,000 bombshells" and the Armenians still held. Continuing his rare first-hand account from the Turkish side of the confrontation Commander de Nogales praised "the heroic city of Van...the intrepidity of its [Armenian] defenders...their invention of a sort of auger," and conceded that "I have rarely seen such furious fighting as took place at Van, it was an uninterrupted combat, sometimes hand to hand or with only a wall between. Nobody gave quarter or asked it... The Armenians fought with a courage undreamt of by our Circassians.... The resistance of the Armenians was terrific, and their valor worthy of all praise." Yet he berated the Armenians for their strictly defensive posture. "If 30,000 or 40,000 Armenians shut up in Van...had undertaken the offensive, and arming themselves with cudgels if nothing better were available, and axes, and knives, had attempted a sally en masse, who knows if they might not have crushed us at length and perhaps even have obliged us to retire to the province of Bitlis. This would have cut off the retreat of our expeditionary army in Persia and have saved the lives of thousands of their own brethren who were perishing daily in neighboring towns and throughout the vilayet of Van..." Speaking of a similar mistake at Muş, he again criticized the Armenians as mere defenders: "There the Armenians committed their usual strategic error, entrenching themselves in the principal buildings and in the churches, which naturally the Ottoman artillery speedily reduced to ruins."[32] Confirming the purely defensive and almost hopeless condition of Van Armenians, Ambassador Morgenthau observed:

> The whole Armenian fighting force consisted of only 1,500 men; they had only 300 rifles and a most inadequate supply of ammunition...the Armenians fought with the utmost heroism and skill; they had little chance of holding off their enemies indefinitely, but they knew that a Russian army was fighting its way to Van and their utmost hope was that they would be able to defy the besiegers until these Russians arrive.[33]

The Dysfunctional Dynamics of Armenian Military Successes and their Lethal Consequences for Ottoman Armenians

The hardships and the attendant humiliations suffered by the Turks as a result of these calamitous setbacks were such as to inject a new dimension in the Ittihadist scheme of liquidating the Armenians. Inordinate anger, bordering on fury, galvanized the perpetrators to invest their exterminatory undertaking with a zest for boundless fiendishness, examples of which are provided and graphically described by the only Christian who personally had witnessed them as a member of the Turkish command structure namely, the above-mentioned Venezuelan officer, de Nogales.[34] The combined Armenian populations of Van and Bitlis provinces, the heartland of historical Armenia with the highest degree of density of Armenian population, were not even subjected to the pretense of "deportation" and were mercilessly slaughtered *in loco*. Of the 80,000–90,000 Armenians residing in the 100 or so villages of Muş plain, the large majority were burned to death in haylofts and large stables. Even Third Army Commander General Vehip was aghast at personally observing a year later the charred remains of multitudes of women and children in the village of Tchreeg, five kilometers northeast of Muş city.[35] These bloodbaths took place under the authority of General Halil Kut, the vanquished army commander of the battle of Dilman. Shortly after his retreat to Bitlis, on June 7, 1915, he was appointed to the post of general commander of the combined forces of the First Expeditionary Force and the Van Gendarmes Division or, what was left of them. In 1919 Halil himself admitted to have killed approximately 300,000 Armenians.[36] He was assisted in this genocidal task by the governors-general of the two provinces involved, i.e., Van and Bitlis. What is even more striking, all three men had family and kinship ties to the two principal authors of the Armenian genocide, namely, Talât and Enver. Van governor Cevdet was Enver's brother-in-law; he had married Enver's sister. Bitlis governor Mustafa Abdulhalik (Renda) was Talât's brother-in-law; his wife was Talât's sister. General Halil (Kut) was Enver's uncle; Enver's father was his brother.

The ultimate catastrophe befalling the Armenians in connection with World War I was thus conditioned by their involvement in military affairs affecting Turkish national interests; specifically, it concerned the wartime application of the 1909–10 Turkish universal military service law. Subject to the related provisions of conscription, the bulk of the able-bodied Armenian population was inducted into the Turkish army following the proclamation of General Mobilization on 2 August 1914, immediately after the signing of the secret Turko-German military and political alliance pact. Within weeks after this act of conscription that eventually encompassed all Armenian males, ages 15–60, on 11(24) September 1915, to be precise, an order was issued by the Third Army commander to disarm the recruited Armenian soldiers and to begin forming Turkish "milis"[37] units that later became the Special Organization killer bands. Three weeks later, i.e., several weeks before even Turkey entered the war, Hans Humann, the German Marine attaché at the Ottoman capital, disclosed that the Armenians, along with the Greeks, were being segregated in labor battalion formations.[38] This process would last several months and was nearly completed in March 1915. These dates are most important since they refer to time frames when there was neither an Armenian uprising, nor any Turkish charge of Armenian rebellion in any part of Turkey. The disarming of the Armenian soldiers, followed by their isolation as "labor battalions" paved the way for the implementation of what appears to be a preplanned exterminatory scheme. As Pomiankowski, Austrian vice marshal and military plenipotentiary to Turkey, wrote, "the massacre of the able-bodied Armenians served the purpose to render the rest of the people defenseless (*wehrlos zu machen*).[39] German state archives are replete with accounts documenting this mass murder of the conscripted Armenians.[40]

It is fair to conclude, therefore, that contrary to all Armenian hopes and expectations, the new Ottoman system of universal military conscription not only failed to help the Armenians improve their lot in Turkey but, in the vortex of swiftly unfolding wartime developments, it helped dispatch them en masse into the inferno of genocidal annihilation. Ambassador Morgenthau's narration, adduced below, provides an apt portrayal of that inferno.

Let me relate a single episode which is contained in one of the reports of our consuls and which now forms part of the records of the American State Department. Early in July, 2,000 Armenian "amélés"—such is the Turkish word for soldier's who have been reduced to workmen—were sent from Harpoot to build roads...practically every man of these 2,000 was massacred, and his body thrown into a cave. A few escaped, and it was from these that news of the massacre reached the world. A few days afterward another 2,000 soldiers were sent to Diarbekir. The only purpose of sending these men out in the open country was that they might be massacred. In order that they might have no strength to resist or to escape by flight, these poor creatures were systematically starved. Government agents went ahead on the road, notifying the Kurds that the caravan was approaching and ordering them to do their congenial duty. Not only did the Kurdish tribesmen pour down from the mountains upon this starved and weakened regiment, but the Kurdish women came with butcher's knives in order that they might gain that merit in Allah's eyes that comes from killing a Christian. These massacres were not isolated happenings; I could detail many more episodes just as horrible as the one related above; throughout the Turkish Empire a systematic attempt was made to kill all able-bodied men, not only for the purpose of removing all males who might propagate a new generation of Armenians, but for the purpose of rendering the weaker part of the population an easy prey.[41]

The mass execution of tens of thousands of Armenian soldiers by fellow soldiers and officers within a single army organization is an act of perpetration rarely encountered in modern history. The victims were all citizens of the same state of which the army was an integral part, with a presumed mission to protect and to defend it and its subjects. It becomes evident, however, that the perversion of that mission was part and parcel of a comprehensive and gigantic plan to eradicate an entire minority group to which the victim soldiers belonged, and whose destruction in good measure rendered the execution of that plan, as anticipated by the planners, affordable.

Notes

1. Armen Suni, *Haigagan Vashdu Antranigee Aratchnortutiamp 1912–1913 Tuaganneroun Balkanian Baderazmoum* (The Armenian Company in the 1912–1913 Balkan war under the leadership of Antranik) (Baku, 1914), p. 38.
2. Ibid., p. 77.
3. Mahmud Mukhtar Pascha, *Meine Führung im Balkankriege 1912* (My leadership in the 1912 Balkan war) 5th ed. Imhoff Pascha, trans. (Berlin, Mittler und Sohn), p. 6.
4. Yusuf Hikmet Bayur, *Türk Inkilâbı Tarihi* (History of the Turkish Revolution) vol. 2, part 2 (Ankara, Turkish Historical Society, 1983), pp. 20, 22.
5. Suni, *Haigagan Vashdu,* [n.1], pp. 145–7; Arsen Marmarian (pen-name of Vahan Totoventz) *Zoravar Antranig yev eer Baderazmneru* (General Antranik and his wars) (Istanbul, 1920), p. 226.
6. *Panper Hayasdanee Archivneree* (Bulletin of Armenia's Archives, Yerevan) vol. 1, no. 10 (1965), p. 9.
7. Antranik Tchelebian, *Zoravar Antranik* (General Antranik) (Yerevan, Arevig, 1990), p. 267.
8. Ibid.
9. Ibid., p. 268; Dzadour Aghayan, *Antranik. Tarashrtchan. Tebker. Temker* (Antranik. An epoch. Events. Figures) (Yerevan, IHFA Publication, 1994), pp. 344, 348; Colonel A.H. Haroutunian, "Antraniku Vorbes Mardig yev Zoravar" (Antranik as a fighter and as a general) *Badmapanasiragan Hantes* vol. 28, no. 1 (1965), p. 118; A.N. Munatzaganian and H.G. Hagopian, *Zoravar Antranik* (General Antranik) vol. 1 (Moscow, Vernadoun, 1991), pp. 166–7.
10. The interview appeared under the name of Andit Odon, Trotsky's journalistic pen-name, in *Kievskaya Misl,* a political-literary daily newspaper in Kiev. 19 July 1913.
11. Aghayan, *Antranik* [n.9], p. 349.
12. George Young, *Constantinople* (New York, Barnes and Noble, 1992; reissue of 1926 London edition), pp. 268–9.
13. Roderic Davison, "The Armenian Crisis, 1912–1914" *American Historical Review* vol. 53, no. 3 (1948), p. 491.
14. Ibid., p. 483.
15. *Püzantion* (Istanbul Armenian newspaper), no. 6620, 12 June 1918.
16. *Times,* London, 20 December 1912.
17. Hamdullah Suphi, "The Armenians and Us" *Ikdam,* 17 December 1912. Suphi came from a distinguished Turkish family whose members for generations oc-

cupied the highest ranks in the Ottoman state system and whose parental home was a gathering place for the contemporary literati.

18. Vahakn N. Dadrian, *History of the Armenian Genocide: Ethnic Conflict from the Balkans to the Caucasus to Anatolia.* 4th ed. (Providence/Oxford, Berghahn, 1997) pp. 192–99.

19. Ibid., see especially pp. 195–8.

20. Suphi, "The Armenians and Us" [n.17].

21. Fridjof Nansen, *Armenia and the Near East* (London: George Allen and Unwin, 1928), pp. 296–7.

22. Doğan Avcıoğlu, *Milli Kurtuluş Tarihi 1838 den 1955e* (History of the National Liberation from 1838 to 1995) vol. 3 (Istanbul: Istanbul Publishers, 1974), p. 1128.

23. Ernst Jäckh, "Vorderasien nach dem Balkankrieg" *Asiatisches Jahrbuch* (1913), p. 14.

24. Johannes Lepsius, *Der Todesgang des armenischen Volkes* (Berlin-Potsdam: Missions Verlag, 1930), p. 161.

25. Ibid., p. 162; this matter was publicized in the 26 February 1915 issue of the *Osmanischer Lloyd*, a German language newspaper in Istanbul, the mouthpiece of the German Embassy.

26. Zaven Arkyebiskobos, *Badriarkagan Housherus. Vaverakirner yev Vugayoutiunner* (My Patriarchal memoirs: Documents and testimonies) (Cairo: Nor Asdgh, 1947), pp. 96–7.

27. Garabed Kapigian, *Yegernabadoum Sepasdio* (The Holocaust of Sıvas) (Boston, Hairenik, 1924), pp. 187–8.

28. Tchelebian, *Zoravar Antranik* [n.7], pp. 304–5, 309–15; *Zoravar Antranigee Govgasian Djagadee Badmagan Orakroutiunu, 1914–1917.* (General Antranik's historical diary about the Caucasian front, 1914–1917) (recorded by his adjutant) (Boston, Baikar, 1924), pp. 18–21; Aghayan *Antranik* [n. 9], pp. 429–35; Munatzaganian and Hagopian, *Zoravar Antranik* [n. 9], pp. 121–7; Kevork Gharibdjanian, *Zhovourtagan Heros Antranik* (Popular Hero Antranik) (Yerevan, Haiasdan, 1990), pp. 73–80.

29. Ali Ihsan Sabis, *Harp Hatıralarım* (My war memoirs), vol. 2 (Ankara, Güneş, 1951), pp. 129, 157, 205, 217, 221.

30. Henry Morgenthau, *Ambassador Morgenthau's Story* (Garden City, NY, Doubleday, Page, 1918), pp. 337, 347.

31. Joseph Pomiankowski, *Der Zusammenbruch des Ottomanishen Reiches* (Vienna, Amalthea, [1928]1969), p. 160.

32. Rafael de Nogales, *Four Years Beneath the Crescent*, Muna Lee, trans. (New York, Scribner's, 1926), pp. 60, 68, 70, 76, 80, 89, 95, 135.

33. Morgenthau, *Ambassador Morgenthau's Story* [n.30], p. 299.

34. de Nogales, *Four Years* [n.32], pp. 85, 123–4, 133–5, 219–20.

35. Vehip's Affidavit, prepared upon the request of the Inquiry Commission that was attached to the Turkish Special Court Martial prosecuting in 1918–20 the authors of "the Armenian deportations and massacres," is deposited at the Jerusalem Armenian Patriarchal Archive. Series H. 17. File Nos. 171 and 182.

36. Halil Paşa, *Bitmeyen Savaş* (A fight without end) M.T. Sorgun, ed. (Istanbul, Yedigün, 1972), p. 274.

37. The order was issued by General Hasan Izzet. *Askeri Tarih Belgeleri Dergisi*, vol. 32, no. 83 (March 1983) Armenian Documents Series, Special Issue no. 2, Doc. no. 1894, p. 7.

38. A.A. Türkei, 142/41. A27535. Report no. 241. 16 October 1914.

39. Pomiankowski, *Der Zusammenbruch* [n.31], p. 160.

40. A.A. Türkei, 183/44, A24663, enclosure no. 3; 183/38, A28019; Botschaft Konstantinopel no. 90/B, 1950, enclosure 1.
41. Morgenthau, *Ambassador Morgenthau's Story* [n.33], pp. 303–304.

11

The World War I Law on Deportation and the Final Solution Formula

In the key indictment of the Turkish Court Martial containing the testimony of a Turkish Governor-General, Nazım is quoted as declaring that the extermination of the Armenians was meant to "solve the Eastern Question" (*hall edecek*).[1] This declaration of intent finds corroboration in a document purporting to be a translation of the secret memorandum (*tezkere*) which Interior Minister and Ittihad party boss Talât is said to have attached to his proposal to Grand Vizier Said Halim; the latter's Cabinet in May 1915 approved the proposed draft of the Temporary Deportation Law. That proposal was sent on 13(26) May 1915 to the Grand Vizier, who formally approved it only on 16(29) May, one full day before the Cabinet formally sanctioned that law, as it was legally empowered to do through a wartime Enabling Act. Talât, however, did not wait for any of these legal formalities. Irrespective of these gaps in dates involving official state acts, on 14(27) May 1915 the promulgation of the law was proclaimed through the press even though it was not formally sanctioned either by the grand vizier or the Cabinet he headed, and even though deportation procedures had been set in motion weeks before. Referring to Talât's unusual hastiness and his maneuvers to railroad the law, historian Bayur described it as a compulsion to create "an accomplished fact."[2]

The hint of "a final solution" is contained in the memorandum alluded to above but apparently is excised from the one produced by Turkish historian Bayur and practically all other historians. So far as it is known, Muammer Demirel is the only Turkish author to discuss that memo in connection with the Temporary Deportation Law without, however, reproducing it in full, or commenting on those components of the memo that reveal a prewar decision on genocide. Addressing Said Halim as "princely Grand Vizier, felicitous and eminent" (*devletlu ve fehametlu*), Talât right away launches an attack against "separatist tendencies" being fostered in "the Armenian community" (*Ermeni cemaat*) by certain "elements." He then inveighs against the efforts to involve foreign powers in the matter of reforms in the provinces that would have meant "local privileges, foreign supervision, and control." In the past, he goes on to say, such reforms imposed by foreigners led to the "partition" (*inkisam*) and "the dismemberment" (*tecezzi*) of the fatherland. The need to preserve and sustain the territorial integrity of the Ottoman Empire on the one hand, and to prevent foreign involvements on the other, have preoccupied the organs of the State. "The removal of this anxiety is one of the vital tasks of the government"; therefore, he goes on to say, "*a radical solution is needed to end and to completely wipe out the problem (külliyen izalesi).*" He then proceeds to outline his program of deportation, which is reproduced in Bayur's work. The memorandum bears the number 280 and is dated old style, 13 May 1331 (or according to the Gregorian calendar, 26 May 1915); it also bears Grand Vizier Said Halim's initials appended to his word of authorization, namely, "to be implemented as proposed" (*mucibince amel*).[3]

Even though Talât makes allusions in that secret memorandum to certain wartime acts of sabotage and atrocities "by a group of Armenian inhabitants," the above-cited expressions, revolving around the thorny issues of reforms, which antedate the war and represent the kernel of the Turko-Armenian conflict, are the central themes. They betray the existence of elements of a prewar posture focusing on larger, strategic considerations affecting the fate of the entire Armenian people in Turkey, independent of the wartime conduct of certain "elements of the Armenian community."

As far as it is known, this is the first time that one encounters the expression "radical solution"—in an avowedly official but highly secret Turkish document—serving as a euphemism for genocide, and emanating from no less a figure than the supreme chief of Ittihad, and the government identified with it.

The Turkish Perspective on Functionality

Throughout this work attention has been focused on the Turko-Armenian conflict as a problem intrinsic to the structure of the Ottoman state system and its destructive by-products. But from a Turkish perspective there is a functional dimension to the problem, which renders the principle of destruction a sufficient means to a necessary end, hence functional. Referring to the practical results of the World War I deportations, the Turkish author of a massive volume on this subject confirmed the eliminational intent of these deportations by declaring: "The Armenian deportations radically solved (*kökünden çözümledi*) the Reform problem, which for centuries had become a headache for the state."[4] In other words, these "deportations" served a purpose, as they were intended to do; they were, therefore, useful, or functional. A German scholar goes so far as to suggest that the desire to extricate themselves from the grip of the Armenian Reform shackle had influenced the Turks' decision and their timing to intervene in World War I on the side of Germany. These Turks were "animated with a drive to solve the Armenian Question in such a radical way that would preclude any future projects for reforms. The 8 February 1914 [Reform] Agreement signed by Russia and Turkey on behalf of the Powers ushered in the first chapter of the great tragedy of the Armenian people...[that included] undeniable (*nicht ableugnbare*) massacres. The Turkish measures served their purpose...one million Armenians died."[5] At the fifteenth sitting of the Yozgad trial series, 27 March 1919, held by the postwar Turkish Military Tribunal, the Presiding Judge read out a cipher by Gendarmerie Commander Tevfik, one of the three defendants, in which the latter is depicted exhorting his subaltern who was assisting him in the operations of the ongoing mass murder that "the Armenians are to be eradicated" (*köklerini kazmak*).[6] Hoca Ilyas Sami, the Kurdish-Turkish Deputy for Muş, where massacres took the form of mass immolations in a string of haylofts throughout the Muş Plain, and were most dramatic in terms of casualties, is reported to have boasted that : "I have eradicated the Armenians thoroughly" (*kökünden kazdım*).[7]

Thus, the issue of Armenian Reforms emerges here as the central and abiding issue around which the Turko-Armenian conflict crystallized throughout the eras of Abdul Hamit and the Young Turk Ittihadists. In his memoirs, drafted in Berlin before his assassination in March 1921, Talât openly declares that 1912–13 was the high point of the Turko-Armenian conflict, when he finally concluded that the Armenian clamors for reform actually aimed at autonomy and eventual independence through Russian intervention. When he and his Ittihad cohorts tried to dissuade the Armenians through private conferences, and to persuade them to rely on projected new Turkish initiatives for reform, it became clear that "the Armenians were bent on exploiting Turkey's weakness" resulting from the latter's defeats in the 1912 Balkan War.[8]

In his memoirs, Archbishop Zaven, the Armenian patriarch, states that when he pleaded with Talât to stop the severe anti-Armenian measures, Talât retorted that during 1912–13, "you ran from capital to capital in Europe seeking intervention in our governmental affairs." This exchange took place on 19 September 1915, in Talât's office.[9]

As a matter of fact, several Ittihadist leaders went out of their way to warn the Dashnak leaders of dire consequences for the Armenian people in Turkey should these leaders continue to espouse the newly resuscitated Armenian reform movement. At the time, Boghos Noubar, representing the supreme patriarch of the Armenians, the Catholicos, was pleading for European intervention in several European capitals. In a historic meeting in the home of Bedros Haladjian, a loyal Armenian Ittihadist, a deputy in the Ottoman Parliament, and a former minister of public works with close personal ties to Talât, the Turkish representative threatened large-scale massacres against the Armenians unless these leaders and their party publicly opposed the new reform initiative. The latter balked at the Turkish demand.[10] In another setting, Cemal Paşa, a member of the Ittihad triumvirate, personally issued a threat to the Dashnak Party through the intermediary Vartkes, another Armenian Parliamentary deputy. In the same September-December 1913 period, Cemal repeated that threat to several Armenian students. The gist of these threats was that exterminatory massacres against the Armenians would be inevitable, should the Powers once more proceed to impose reforms upon Turkey.[11] When the new Reform Act finally materialized on 8 February 1914, despite all Turkish efforts to avert it,[12] this is how Behaeddin Şakir, one of the chief architects of the Armenian genocide, expressed his ire: "The Turks are upset that the Armenians raised the issue of reforms involving the Powers. We had expected that they would proclaim their satisfaction with the Turkish regime which was willing to accommodate them...The Patriarchate and the parties should have reached an agreement and terminated the services of Boghos Noubar Paşa...."[13]

Nor is the assessment of the advent of the Kemalist republican regime free from the burden of identifying that regime with similar notions of functionality. The prevalent view is that the Kemalist regime would have encountered serious obstacles at its very inception had the Armenians not been eliminated during the previous Great War. In interpreting the Kemalist War of Independence, and the ensuing formation of the modern Turkish Republic, a prominent ex-Ittihadist, privy to the secrets of the inner councils of that party, also noted the functional feature of the destruction of the Armenians. In so doing, for the first time such a prominent public figure used the term "genocide" when describing and characterizing that act of organized mass murder. He was first engaged in the Special Secretariat of the Interior Ministry of Talât, with whom he travelled to Bucharest prior to World War I. During that war, as a reserve lieutenant, he became the private secretary of Cemal Paşa, and the chief of Department II of the General Staff of his, Cemal's, Fourth Army. He rose to prominence in the Turkish Republic as a Kemalist stalwart, parliamentary deputy, and editor-in-chief of the influential Ankara daily, *Ulus*. As he condemned the "genocide," describing it "as one of the gravest crimes against humanity involving the extermination of a race, a religious community, or a nationality," and as he blamed the Ittihadist mentality of Şakir, who had exterminated the Armenians in a drive "to wipe out Armenianism" (*Ermeniliği yokederek*), he proceeded to agree with the rationale of it, which was to avert "the danger of the formation [in Turkey] of an Armenia." He declared: "Had the Armenians by 1918 still remained concentrated in the East [of Turkey], there is no doubt that there would have been formed an Armenia during the Armistice."[14] In a later, autobiographical book he further commented: "What a pity that without the Armenian tragedy Atatürk's National Pact movement wouldn't have been able to gain a foothold."[15]

Another prominent editor and postwar Kemalist, who had obtained an American Ph.D. in Sociology, served as a correspondent during the war for *Tanin*, the mouthpiece of Ittihad, and visited Germany several times as a war correspondent, was interned as a dangerous nationalist in Malta by the British; interned along with him were also those top Ittihadists who were slated for trial before an International Tribunal for high crimes committed against the Armenians during the war. His exchanges with these party leaders led him to conclude that: "The deportations...for certain influential Turkish politicians meant the extermination of the Armenian minority in Turkey with the idea of bringing about racial homogeneity in Asia Minor. [They argued that] 'A dense Armenian population in the Eastern provinces has proved to be a danger to the very existence of Turkey. We are acting as instruments to remove this danger. We know that, successful or unsuccessful, we shall be universally despised and condemned'"[16]

This rare, candid admission underscores the need to focus on the historical dimensions of a conflict, the final resolution of which proved to be a means to an end, and therefore functional.

In touching on this problem, the Key Indictment of the Turkish Military Tribunal court-martialing the authors of the Armenian genocide in 1919 alluded to the Young Turk Ittihadist attempt at a final solution. It charged that the suspects at the dock "resorted to terror to solve once and for all the lingering troublesome problems and conflicts involved (*mesaili muallâka ve gavaili muaddileyi...ilkai dehşetle hall ve fasl....*)." These problems were identified in the same indictment as those relating to "the Eastern question," namely, the Armenian question which the wartime anti-Armenian measures were meant to "solve" (*Bu teşebbüsün Şark meselesini halledeceğini*).[17] Nor was the resort to terror the only component of functional efficiency in the enactment of the Final Solution. As conceded by a Kemalist Cabinent minister in one of the secret sessions of the Grand National Assembly of the fledgling Kemalist regime, a crucial component in this respect was the element of surprise through which the defenseless population was trapped and destroyed—under the cloak of a wartime plan of deportation and relocation. As this Cabinet Minister put it, "the Armenians instantly submitted (*inkiyad*) because the country was under the control of enormous armies (*muazzam ordular*) and they [the Armenians] had no inkling as to what was in store for them under the scheme of deportation; they had no previous experience with deportation. Thus the plan was implemented swiftly."[18]

Given the dimensions of the conspiracy and the requisite vast network of the conspirators, no genocidal scheme can entirely escape some type or some degree of notice, no matter how secretive the schemers may be. Such notices may come about through espionage, defections, or accidents. In this sense neither the Armenian population, nor the Armenian leadership was completely taken by surprise by the initiation of the Ottoman-Turkish authorities of the deportation procedures. Apart from lingering suspicions abut wartime Turkish intentions vis-à-vis the Armenians and some dark premonitions of an impending calamity threatening to engulf the Armenian population of the Ottoman Empire,[19] there were already some public disclosures about lethal secret Turkish designs in this regard. As early as January 1914, for example (namely, some seven months before the outbreak of the war), the Russian newspaper in Moscow, *Kolos Moskoy*, in its 26 January (8 February) 1914 issue had stated that there existed a secret Turko-German plan for the massive deportation of the Armenians of eastern Turkey. The statement was denounced the next day as totally unfounded and absurd by the Turkish newspaper *Ikdam* which raised the following rhetorical question: "How is it possible to exile hundreds of thousands of Armenians to Mesopotamia?"[20]

Another disclosure was made by British parliamentarian Aneurin Wiiliams who in the aftermath of the 2 August 1914 secret Turko-German alliance pact had learned about Turkish plans of liquidating the Armenians, and about the latter being "in great fear of a massacre." In relaying this informatio to Sir Edward Grey, British Foreign Secretary Williams alluded to the resolve of Turkish Interior Minister Talât's to eradicate the Armenians. He stated that "...it is the settled policy of one, at least, of the highest placed Turkish ministers to rid the contry of the subject Christian races..."[21]

Among those Western historians who do not hesitate to recognize the grim realities of the Armenian genocide, there are some who seem to be placing a higher premium upon the functional utility of that genocide; within this perspective, the tragedy of the demise of the victim nation is virtually dismissed by emphasizing the blessings attributed to the avowed national regeneration of the perpetrator. In other words, even though the Ottoman Armenian population perished, there is to behold the specter of a revitalized, homogenous modern Turkish Republic. The statement below by Lewis Thomas epitomizes this posture.

> By 1918 with the definitive excision of the total Armenian Christian population from Anatolia and the Straits area...the hitherto largely peaceful process of Turkification and Moslemization had been advanced in one great surge by the use of force... Had Turkification and Moslemization not been accelerated by the use of force, there certainly would not today exist a Turkish Republic, a Republic owing its strength and stability in no small measure to the homogeneity of its population, a state which is now a valued associate of the United States."[22]

In a nutshell, *the recreation and forging of a new nation, free from the tribulations and woes of a protracted conflict besetting the old system, for all practical purposes, presently required the wanton destruction of another nation.* In this sense the importance of understanding the relevance of the cumulative aspects of that conflict, antedating by decades the cataclysm of World War I, is once more cast into relief.

Clearly, one is dealing here with the paramount factor of vulnerability and concomitantly with exceedingly disparate power relations. But one has still to explain the conditions of the genesis and persistence, if not incremental growth, of a potential victim's vulnerability. Involved here are such factors as that vulnerability's structural roots, national and international politics, and the onset of a variety of crises creating massive dislocations, and imbalances in the distribution of existing power relations. In other words one has to refocus on the essential conditions through which the Turko-Armenian conflict crystallized itself, intensified, and escalated to the point of a violent explosion, i.e., genocide. As this is precisely the main purpose of this study, these fundamental conditions will be discussed in the following chapter. More particularly, interrelationships among key determinants of the Turko-Armenian conflict will be summarized thereby constructing a framework through which the Armenian genocide may best be understood.

Notes

1. *Takvimi Vekâyi*, no. 3540, p. 8.
2. Y. H. Bayur, *Türk Inkilabı Tarihi*, vol. 3, part 3 (Ankara: Turkish Historical Society, 1957), p. 38.
3. Muammer Demirel, *Birinci Dünya Harbinde Erzurum ve Çevresinde Ermeni Harektleri* (Armenian actions in and around Erzurum in World War I) (Ankara: General Staff, 1996), pp. 52–3. See also the following two works from both of which have been excerpted the same quotation used in the text. H. Khazarian, *Tzeghasban Turku* (The genocidal Turk), (Beirut: Hamazkayeen, 1968), pp. 324–8; *Hairenik* (Boston, ARF Armenian daily) 13 August 1964. The author, a survivor of that genocide, for the study of which he dedicated his life (thereby producing a whole series of works on the various aspects of it), was a reserve officer in the Ottoman Army. During the war he served in the Fifth Division of the Second Army Corps stationed at Adrianople (Edirne).The British Navy, as part of the Allied Occupation Army in Istanbul, had engaged him during the Armistice as an interpreter in the Ottoman Marine Ministry's Records Office (*Evrak Odası*), of which the Inter-Allied Marine Control Commission was in charge. Before that he was engaged as a member of the Intelligence Section of the British Army of the Black Sea. He had located the original of the memorandum while combing and scrutinizing the records there; he surreptitiously copied the entire text in long hand, and after translating it into Armenian, published it. Demirel's text confirms the accuracy of Khazarian's claim that he had indeed managed to secure access to secret Ottoman documents during his Armistice-time employment by the British Navy. Talât's key words *inkisam* and *tecezzi* (partition and dismemberment), reproduced by Kazarian, are translated by Demirel into modern Turkish (*parçalayıp*), and the even more revealing words *külliyen izale* (completely wipe out) are presented by him in a rather diluted way as meaning: the resolution of the trouble is to be achieved in a fundamental way (*bu gailenin esaslı bir şekilde çözümlenmesi*).
4. Mehmed Hocaoğlu, *Tarihte Ermeni Mezâlimi ve Ermeniler* (Armenian atrocities in the course of history and the Armenians), (Istanbul: Anda, 1976), p. 521.
5. Kurt Ziemke, *Die neue Türkei: Politische Entwicklung* (The new Turkey: Political development), (Berlin: Deutsche Verlags-Anstalt, 1930), pp. 271–2.
6. *Jogovourtee Tzain* (Armenian daily) *Renaissance* (French daily) (dailies in Istanbul during the Armistice and covering the courts martial), 28 March 1919.
7. *Jogovourtee Tzain*, 4 April 1919.
8. *Talat Paşanın Hatıraları* (Talat Paşa's memoirs), Enver Bolayir, ed., (Istanbul: Güven, 1946), pp. 51, 55.

9. *Haygashen* (Almanac), vol. (1922), p. 161.
10. "Dzerougeen Hishadagneru: 1915–1918" (The memoirs of an old man: 1915–1918), *Djagadamard* (Armenian daily, Istanbul) no. 95 (1916) 2 March 1919.
11. For more details on these threats by Cemal see Vahakn N. Dadrian, *History of the Armenian Genocide: Ethnic Conflict from the Balkans to Anatolia to the Caucasus,* 4th ed. (Providence, RI: Berghahn Books, 1996), p. 211, n. 23.
12. For details about Turkish efforts of sabotaging the new scheme for Armenian Reforms see ibid., pp. 212–6.
13. *Püzantion* (Istanbul Armenian daily) no. 5276, 15(28) February 1914.
14. Falih Rıfkı Atay, *Milliyet,* 17 and 19 February 1932; *Dünya,* 17 December 1967.
15. *Çankaya* (Istanbul: Sena, 1980), p. 450. See also *Zeytindağı* (Mt. Olive) (Istanbul: Ayyıldız, 1981), pp. 63–4.
16. Ahmed Emin, *Turkey in the First World War* (New Haven, CT: Yale University Press, 1930), p. 220. Before he lapsed into partisan revisionism, a prominent student of the Ottoman Empire cogently summarized the whole picture in describing the ramifications of the Turko-Armenian conflict as "the deadliest of all threats…Now a desperate struggle between them began—a struggle between two nations for the possession of a single homeland, that ended with the terrible holocaust of 1915, when a million and a half Armenians perished." Bernard Lewis, *The Emergence of Modern Turkey,* 2d ed., (New York: Oxford University Press, 1968), p. 356. It should be noted here that the idea of a struggle between two nations for a single homeland was first advanced by the eminent Ottomanist George Young. See his *Constantinople* (New York: Barnes and Noble, [1926] 1992), p. 224.
17. *Takvimi Vekâyi,* no. 3540, pp. 4 and 8.
18. *T.B.M.M. Gizli Celse Zabıtları* (The transcripts of the secret sessions of the Grand National Assembly of Turkey), vol. 3 (Ankara, 1985), p. 394. The minister was Hasan Fehmi (Ataç), minister of finance. The fifty-first sitting took place on 10 June 1922.
19. Dashnak leader Haroutian Shahrigian (Adom) in an editorial in *Azadamard,* the organ of the Dashnak party, sounded such an alarm in the wake of the 2 August 1914 Proclamation of General Mobilization in Turkey. That proclamation coincided with the signing of the secret political and military alliance between Imperial Germany and the Ottoman Empire. In that editorial the Armenian political leader declared that "the Armenian people will be struck with calamities that are unparalleled in history." "The Memoirs of Dzeroug" (The memoirs of an old man) *Djagadamard,* 2 March 1919.
20. Püzant Bozadjian, "Tebee ayash. Heen u Nor Housher" (To Ayash: old and new memories) in *Houshartzan April Dasnumegee* (Memorial for 11(24) April (Istanbul: O. Arzuman, 1919), p. 96. On p. 97 the author, who was one of the 24 April arrestees, declares that one of his Turkish friends, who was of Albanian extraction and who had close ties with Bedri Bey, the omnipotent police chief of Istanbul, alerted him early in April 1915 with the words , "A great catastrophe will befall you Armenians very soon. God have mercy on you. I am fond of the Armenians and it pains me to tell you this." It should be noted that the date in *Houshartzan* about the Turkish daily *Ikdam,* 17 January 1914, is a misprint; it should read 27 January.
21. FO 371/2116/51007. Williams's letter is dated 18 September 1914, quoted in Akaby Nassibian, *Britain and the Armenian Question, 1915–1923* (New York: St. Martin's Press, 1984), p. 31.
22. Lewis Thomas, and Richard Frye, *The United States and Turkey and Iran* (Cambridge, MA: Harvard University Press, 1951), p. 61.

12

The Three Arch-Determinants
of the Turko-Armenian Conflict
and Its Violent Resolution

In this concluding chapter, the fundamental premise of this work bears repetition: a valid study of the Armenian genocide is contingent upon a proper study of the rise and growth of the Turko-Armenian conflict. The root causes, the protracted phases, the escalation, and the violent consummation of that conflict are factors that require the application of a broad and composite perspective of study. Several levels of consideration are involved but they may be subsumed under three major categories: theocracy, demography, and power relations.

Theocracy

Theocracy in any form has two components. One of them is the theological aspect relating to dogmas, doctrines, and an overall belief system. The other refers to the patterns of application of that belief system in the arrangements of the social system and the associated body politic. From its very inception, the Ottoman state system was predicated upon Islam and was thus favored as well as burdened with its mandates and its legacy. Notwithstanding its pervasive spirit of piety, many of its ethical exhortations, and its professed recognition of the merits of the other two variations of monotheism, i.e., Christianity and Judaism, Islam had certain other features which, overshadowing these attributes, proved liabilities for the multiethnic political system that the Ottoman Empire was. Foremost among these features were, on the one hand, its inexorable divisiveness, by which the social universe was split into two irreconcilable, basically hostile camps, namely believers and unbelievers, and on the other, its martial spirit bent upon conquest, subjugation, and expansionist dominion. The plight of the non-Muslim nationalities of the Ottoman Empire was created under these conditions. In their distinct, if not aberrant, interpretation and implementation of Islam, the leaders of successive Ottoman regimes established a social structure that was pregnant with religious and political conflict from its very inception. This social structure primarily consisted of an arrangement involving a more or less fixed distribution of superordinate and subordinate statuses with corresponding roles of domination and submission assigned to the Muslims and non-Muslims, respectively. The Muslims in the Ottoman system persisted in considering themselves as overlords vis-à-vis the non-Muslims, who at best could be tolerated. But toleration is a discretionary exercise not easily amenable to legally secured guarantees; as such it can be withdrawn at will and even transform itself into its opposite, intolerance and persecution.

The Armenian reform movement, as distinct from the subsequent revolutionary movement, which was much less supported by the masses than the former, was geared to forestalling such developments by seeking civil rights, especially equality for all before the law, and their irrevocable institutionalization. Relying on their traditional practices of the Şeriat, i.e., the Islamic Sacred Law, considered to be a banner of fixed infallibility and therefore unchallengeable, the Ottoman authorities in tandem with the various strata of Muslim clerics, as well as the populace, held equality to be not only inimical but essentially anathema to Islam. The decree and the eventual promulgation of laws regarding the principles of equality remained pro-forma and expedient acts, as they were largely sabotaged by a vast array of provincial religious and secular officials as well as the populace. The abortiveness of a strictly reformatory effort on the part of the Armenians, as yet completely removed from any aspirations of emancipation from Turkish rule, had three major consequences that served to derail the prospects of mutual accommodation between Turks and Armenians.

1. Their being permanently relegated to an inferior status was a condition that condemned the Armenians to suffer the consequences of a "structural blockage." It was the kind of status which encumbered the cultivation by Muslims of new channels of social intercourse with non-Muslims, precluding opportunities of inevitable assimilation of the latter, promoting and sustaining segregation, that, perhaps inevitably, ended up fostering centrifugal ethnocentrism. This arrangement served to direct the thusly blocked subjects into paths of trade and commercial activities in which many urban Armenians inevitably perfected their skills and excelled—as military, civil service, and political careers were

generally off-limits for nearly all of them. The resulting relative prosperity for pockets of Armenian urban dwellers led to an economic ascendancy for this segment of the Armenian population, thereby creating problems of "status inconsistency." Given their otherwise inferior position, the relatively superior nature of their prosperity that was visible and even conspicuous, aroused the inveterate cupidity even and the ill-will of many of the less prosperous and the poor among the dominant Muslims.

2. By assigning political meaning to what was distinctly a civil rights movement, the Ottoman authorities injected a new dimension into the conflict. Grievances regarding depredations in the provinces, that included, for example, murder, rape, abduction, robbery, extortion, and the venality of a court system which allowed all this, were misconstrued and defined as political seditiousness. Appeals to Europe in the face of persistent governmental inaction were branded as separatism. In other words, the Armenian quest for mere administrative remedies provoked the resentment of the Turks and after a while became the Turkish excuse for a campaign of persecution through which the existing inequities were compounded. A renewed emphasis on religious differences on the part of the dominant Turks, through which the Armenians were degraded and scorned as infidel (*gâvur*) Christians, and an attendant cooptation of certain Muslim but non-Turkish tribes and ethnic groups in the provinces, particularly Kurds, helped intensify this new campaign.

3. On the one hand, exercised by the futility of the reform movement, and on the other, encouraged by the successes of the Balkan nationalities, notably the Greeks, the Montenegrins, and the Bulgarians, groups of young Armenians banded together to pursue change through a degree of militancy. This transition from a peaceful quest for reform to a penchant for violent revolution coincided with a transition in Turkish response: oppression turned into sanguinary repression, as acts of random depredations were amplified and by administrative fiat were raised to the level of organized massacres. Led mostly by Armenians from the diaspora and the Caucasus, the revolutionary movement on a rather modest scale spread across the Ottoman provinces. Native Armenians were recruited and pressed into militant service. They were to carry out small punitive raids against local oppressors and their cohorts, execute a number of assassinations, and resort to bravado in the hope of intimidating internal and external foes. Perceived by many Armenians as "freedom fighters," but denounced by the Turks as "bandits," these *fedayees* it has to be acknowledged, achieved remarkable

success in developing a sense of combativeness, ideals of heroism, and a proclivity for Spartan discipline: some of their exploits against superior Ottoman army and gendarmerie forces assumed legendary proportions.

The following excerpt from a piece of diplomatic correspondence succinctly portrays these developments. In a 20 February 1894 report to Paris entitled *Exposé historique de la question arménienne,* the veteran French ambassador Paul Cambon traced the genesis of the "Armenian question" to what he considered to be the provocative ill-will of Turkish authorities. He wrote:

A high-ranking Turkish official told me, "the Armenian question does not exist but we shall create it."...Up until 1881 the idea of Armenian independence was nonexistent. The masses simply yearned for reforms, dreaming only of a normal administration under Ottoman rule...The inaction of the Porte served to vitiate the good will of the Armenians. The reforms have not been carried out. The exactions of the officials remained scandalous and justice was not improved...from one end of the Empire to the other, there is rampant corruption of officials, denial of justice and insecurity of life....The Armenian diaspora began denouncing the administrative misdeeds, and in the process managed to cause the transformation of the condition of simple administrative ineptness into one of racial persecution...As if it were not enough to provoke Armenian discontent, the Turks were glad to amplify it by the manner in which they handled it. In maintaining that the Armenians were conspiring, the Armenians ended up engaging in conspiracy; in maintaining that there was no Armenia, the Armenians ended up conjuring the reality of her existence....The harsh punishment of conspirators, the maintenance in Armenia of a veritable regime of terror, arrests, murders, rapes, all this shows that Turkey is taking pleasure in precipitating the events [in relation to] an inoffensive population.[1]

Yet, all these Armenian initiatives invariably tended to produce adverse consequences. They fragmented the Armenian *millet* on many levels, pitting most of the clergymen, for example, against the militants, and the latter against each other, each competing for the loyalties of their co-nationals on preferred divergent beliefs, ideologies, and party programs. Moreover, the Huntchaks were seeking near total emancipation, which they described as "political autonomy," whereas the Dashnaks avowedly were pursuing "administrative-local autonomy" within the sovereign jurisdiction of the Ottoman state. Furthermore, the revolutionaries as a whole were pitted against the masses of Armenian pacifists, reformers, and those with vested interest in the status quo. The resulting dissensions, schisms, factionalism, and attendant mutual enmities seriously impaired an already weak, fractious, and vulnerable community.[2] As far as the Ottoman authorities were concerned, however, it was the Armenian nation that as a whole was guilty of provocations and collective designs that were deemed to be serious transgressions, whether politically and/or from a theocratic standpoint,[3] and in their eyes deserved, therefore, severe repression. That sense of Armenian violative behavior largely derived from the fact that several European statesmen, publicists, and Church leaders set out to champion the cause of the Armenians as a Christian nation, at the same time assailing the Ottoman Turks as sworn enemies of Christianity.[4] This in turn provided ammunition to the Ottoman authorities to inflame the Muslim masses and incite them further against the Armenians. Thus, religion was singled out as a determinant in the Turko-Armenian conflict throughout that conflict's developmental phases while ordinary Armenians continued to be denied, in line with the proscriptions of the Şeriat, the right to bear arms to defend themselves in a perilously hostile environment.

Demography

The Problem of Migrations and New Muslim Settlements

Before the reform-oriented Mahmud II started to restructure Ottoman society following his accession to the throne in 1808, the Armenians in the provinces were the beneficiaries of a system of symbiosis through which they were more or less immune from rampant molestation and depredation. They were protected by a feudal system in which the *derebeyi* lords vouched for their relative safety in return for the rendering of certain tributes and services. Only the frequent upheavals of war threatened to disturb this arrangement. Upon the eradication of the troublesome and dangerous *yeniçeries* and the consequent formal abolition of provincial feudalism, this monarch instituted a centralized regime, without, however, being able to completely abolish feudalism and semi-feudalism in the distant provinces. The result was the onset in the remote parts of the empire of a system of dual and mostly competing authorities, with parallel tax and other obligations, which many Ottoman subjects ended up incurring. In other words, the central authorities in Istanbul proved inefficient and unable to reintroduce law and order in the distant corners of the land, especially in areas to which access was either encumbered by the absence of suitable roads, or was blocked by mountain ranges. Several Armenian enclaves in the east thus became subject not only to Ottoman authorities but also to the exactions of outlaws and self-appointed rulers.

This practice became immensely aggravated by the continuous infusion of Muslim emigrants from the Caucasus and from the Balkan peninsula. Though encouraged by Ottoman governments to emigrate, the majority of them were nevertheless reduced to destitution, due to governmental mismanagement and fiscal weakness. Thus, multitudes of hard-pressed Circassians, Rumeli (Balkan) refugees, Lazes, and Kurds from Persian border areas, injected a new dimension of anomie in areas heavily populated with Armenians, especially the peasant population in rural areas. The northward migration of large numbers of Kurds from the southern regions of the Empire, such as Diyarbekir, and the seasonal movements of nomadic and seminomadic Kurdish tribes, gave a further impetus to social unrest and lawlessness. This Kurdish migratory movement started in the middle of the sixteenth century as "the Kurds expanded from their ancestral seats west and northward into the Taurus and into the Armenian interior...."[5] This movement gained a momentum after the signing in 1878 of the Berlin Treaty the terms of whose Article 61 had special provisions to curb Kurdish depredations against the Armenians. As if to defy these provisions the Kurds, assisted by the Ottoman authorities, accelerated their migration northward and by the outbreak of World War I 100,000 additional Kurds had settled in districts containing large and dense Armenian populations such as Muş, Van, and Erzurum.[6] Nor other Armenian settlements were protected from the assaults the Kurds launched against them from "the south and southeast, so-called Kurdistan; they proceeded to attack everywhere where they found Armenian settlements."[7] Highway robbery, brigandage, confiscation of agricultural lands and products, and theft of cattle, among other forms of depredations, became rampant in certain areas, which at times affected other population groups, including sedentary Muslim Turks and Kurds as well. Unlike the unarmed Armenians, however, being Muslims, these victims were better equipped to defend themselves under certain conditions.

As a result, two major developments set in which proved particularly consequential for the future of Turko-Armenian relations. With the influx of the new Muslim settlers, new sources of interethnic antagonisms emerged as new problems inevitably sprang up and proliferated. These problems remained as irremediable as before, however. More importantly, with their estimated number of two million, (in a period of half a century leading up to World War I), the new settlers drastically altered the existing demographic balance. Lumped together as "Muslims," without regard to their ethnic differences, they were exploited by successive Ottoman regimes as undiversified and uniform statistical material, tipping the delicate demographic balance in "historical Armenia" in favor of the dominant Turks. The Armenians were thus reduced in their own ancestral territories to numerical minorities, as far as the overall population figures were concerned.

The Expedient of Redistricting and
Rearranging the Provincial Boundaries

In order to further promote this objective of securing numerical Muslim preponderance, specific and concrete measures of redistricting were initiated in the last two decades of the nineteenth century. The boundaries of certain provinces with heavy concentrations of Armenians were redrawn by detaching from these provinces chunks of territories that contained dense Armenian populations and attaching them instead to others that had only, or mainly, Muslim inhabitants. The main, if not only, purpose was to effect new formations of clear numerical Muslim majorities. The result was that the Armenians were in fact reduced, province by province, to the position of a minority throughout eastern Turkey. Though in some cases this resort to gerrymandering was governed by practical administrative concerns, a close examination of the overall pattern of redistricting in eastern Turkey points to underlying political designs involving drastic demographic changes at the expense of the Armenians.

Several European authors, treating at various levels the demography of Ottoman provinces with large concentrations of Armenians, clearly recognized this fact. When discussing "the new vilayet Van" in 1877, for example, a German author found it necessary to remark in a footnote that the government was prompted to "detach a large part of southeast Armenia from Erzerum vilayet most probably on the basis of political-ethnographic rather than administrative considerations."[8] Another German student of the Near East some twenty years later, when redistricting in the eastern provinces was nearly complete, and after having traveled through some of them, wrote the following: "The question in Turkey actually revolves around the Armenian population. Soon after the Berlin Congress when Turkey was expected to introduce reforms in her Armenian provinces, she carried out a very transparent manipulation...entailing the rearrangement of the regions inhabited by the Armenians. When this program was completed, strangely no Armenian majority could be found in any of these vilayets. Thereupon the

Turkish statesmen concluded that no reforms could be imposed on non-Armenian majorities for the sake of Armenian minorities at odds with the latter. The matter was thereby settled...."[9] An American author expressed the same view, namely that the redistricting was done in such a way as "to give the Moslems a majority in every district."[10] As late as the summer of 1914, the Ottoman authorities were still determined to treat demography and census, as they related to nationality issues, as the organic components of a political scheme. Indeed, at the session of the Ottoman Parliament (30 June[13 July]1914), Ali Münif, undersecretary in the Interior Ministry, requested one million *kuruş*, instead of the proposed 250,000, to defray the cost of the projected census, arguing that the need for the census was "politically dictated." The issue involved proportional representation for the Armenians in the Parliamentary elections of the provinces of Van and Bitlis.[11] In fact in October 1913 the Armenian Patriarch in a *takrir* (memorandum) to the Justice Ministry proposed that the Armenian share of proportional representation be twenty Armenian deputies based upon a two million Armenian population in the Ottoman Empire at the time.[12]

Given this modern practice of gerrymandering, a brief history of the provincial arrangement of the Ottoman Empire in the period preceding the Abdul Hamit era may be in order. The principal unit in that arrangement was the *eyalet*, instituted for the first time by Sultan Süleyman (Kanuni, 1520–66), and developed by Murad III (1574–95). In 1834, Mahmud II reorganized the system into twenty-eight governmental units, to which were attached thirty-one *sancaks,* or districts. Subsequently there was a reversion to the eyalet system coinciding with the Tanzimat period. In 1853, for example, there were thirty-six eyalets subdivided into *livas* and *kazas* i.e., districts and counties. As far as the geographic entity of Turkish Armenia was concerned, there were three eyalets which were identified with it: Erzurum, Diyarbekir, and Harput. In an effort to centralize authority, Mahmud II (1808–39) began the process of converting *eyalets*, (a term which denoted the geographic concentration in vast regions of indigenous, ethnic populations of the Empire, such as the appellation *Ermenistan Eyaleti*, i.e., the Armenian Province), into smaller administrative units. This resulted in the break-up of this region, comprising the northeastern provinces, into four units: Van, Diyarbekir, Erzurum, and Harput. During the reign of Mahmud II's second son, Abdul Aziz (1861–75), especially in the 1865–75 period, the Erzurum unit, variously called Eyalet and Vilayet, comprised the following *mutesarrıflıks*, i.e., the sub-units (identified as districts), of

Çıldır, Kars, Erzurum, Erzincan, Bayazit, Van, and Muş. After the 1877–78 Russo-Turkish War and the ensuing loss to the Russians of Kars and Çıldır, Erzurum Eyalet was transformed into four separate vilayets: Erzurum, Van, Hakkâri, and Muş. (This redistricting process had begun earlier in the Danube-Tuna province in accord with the 1864 vilayet law, revised in 1871.) With the onset of the Abdul Hamit regime (1876–1908), the process of redistricting for political purposes reached its acme, especially in the decade 1880–90.

In the regions of Van, Muş, Erzurum, and Harput, Armenian population densities were consequently diluted by the standard technique of gerrymandering. Districts were detached, attached, and new ones were created with a view to rearranging provincial boundaries through which Armenians would become distinct minorities. For this very same purpose, the Ottomans even created a totally new province, namely Bitlis, which purposively disrupted and ended the contiguity of territories containing massive clusters of Armenian populations. That area, Daron-Douruperan, which encompassed the expansive historical regions of Van and Muş in particular, was considered the cradle of the Armenian nation and a foremost cultural center, where, for example, that nation's fifth-century Golden Age came to fruition. This new arrangement ideally served the purpose of breaking up and artificially separating from each other blocs of Armenian populations in a large segment of territory inhabited by a cohesive and entrenched native Armenian population. In 1880 Bitlis was initiated as a new and third-class vilayet, for which purpose Muş was severed from contiguous Van. Muş was to be incorporated into this new province, to which was attached the largely Muslim district of Sıırt, a city fourteen hours from Muş, (and which was in turn severed from the province of Diyarbekir). In August 1889, Bitlis was raised to the rank of second class and, in December 1895, in the middle of the empire-wide Hamidian massacres, was again elevated to the rank of a first-class vilayet. In 1884–5, Hakkâri, with a 90 percent Muslim population, mostly Kurdish, was reattached to Van province, thereby critically decreasing the majority proportion of the Armenian population of that province. In July 1880 the vilayet Mamuretülaziz, or Harput, was created by detaching from Diyarbekir the districts (*sancak*) of Harput and Malatya. Its boundaries were further enlarged in May 1888 by dissolving the existing Dersim vilayet, and attaching it as an additional district to that province. In 1893 the county (*kaza*) of Kuzican was detached from Dersim district and attached to that of heavily Armenian populated district of Erzincan in

Erzurum province, and was given the new county name of Pelumer. Moreover, Khnus (Hınıs), which was an integral part of Douruperan in historical Armenia, was detached from Muş and attached to Erzurum province. The territory of the ancient Armenian principality of Sassoun was likewise truncated. Lidje (Lice) was attached to the district Gendje (Genç) in Bitlis province and Farği was attached to Diyarbekir. Sassoun was further amputated by detaching from it Khouyt and Musarzan and attaching them to Bitlis. Chadakh and Purnashen were attached to Muş. Khulp (Kulp), Khiank, and Dalvorig were attached to Gendje (Genç) and Pusank, Aghtzun (Kharzan) and Rundvan were attached to Sıirt. Similar truncations and reconstructions took place later on in Cilicia, certain portions of which were detached and attached to Aleppo, which was part of Syria, which was Arabic in nature and in most any other respect. By the same token, İçili was attached to the western part of Cilicia, i.e., the province of Adana. The artificiality of most of these arrangements is apparent by the fact that most other existing provinces occupied an area of at least 100,000 to 120,000 square kilometers, whereas the newly created Bitlis province, for example, was about three to four times smaller, i.e., about 30,000 square kilometers.

This provincial reorganization was essentially due to the policies of Grand Vizier Said Paşa, who in the initial stages of his career was alarmed by Midhat's liberal reform projects and as the sultan's private secretary was able to prevail upon Hamit to oppose them, in particular the reforms affecting provincial Armenians. Glimpses of the motivations of Said's policy, which was based on his fears that unless the demographic bases of the pressures for these Armenian reforms were eliminated, the Empire would face eventual truncation, are revealed in his memoirs.[13]

It appears that not all efforts to reduce the Armenians to numerical minorities were free from violence and massacre. General Giesl, the Austrian military attaché at Constantinople, who served more than two decades in Turkey, up to the end of the Abdul Hamit era, cites in his memoirs a secret document he personally saw. Conversant in Turkish, he read the following message a provincial governor had sent to Abdul Hamit: "In the period 1894–6 (the period of the massacres), 50,000 Armenians fled across the border, 30,000 are still hiding in the woods, 45,000 have converted to Islam and 10,000 probably died. *Thanks to your Majesty's wise measures the Muslims are now everywhere in the majority*" (italics added).[14] This line of coercive alteration of population ratios based on religion was reportedly espoused even by Midhat

Paşa, the pillar of reform and constitutionality in the Ottoman government. According to a French author, Midhat personally deplored that "Our ancestors are guilty of failure to impose Islam upon our subjects in Europe. Oh! If it were only possible to start again. We should at least try to employ every means for the purpose of modifying to our benefit the numerical ratio of the two religions."[15] An Armenian historian, for his part, confirms this fact by declaring that Midhat Paşa regretted the fact the "the Christians in the past were not forcibly converted to Islam when it was opportune to do so."[16]

As stated above, the almost single purpose of the scheme of redistricting was to rearrange the composition of the Armenian provincial population with a view to reducing the Armenians to absolute minorities in the newly demarcated provinces of eastern Turkey, especially in the six provinces covered by Article 61 of the 1878 Treaty of Berlin. The disputes arising since then about Armenian population figures, in absolute numbers, and in terms of proportions relative to the total number of Muslim Turks on the one hand, and all other Muslims on the other, basically still remain unresolved.[17] But the intimate relationship between Ottoman politics of redrawing provincial boundaries in "Turkish Armenia" to recreate new demographic realities and the subsequent elaboration of tables of Ottoman statistics on Armenian population is a fact that is less subject to dispute. The specifics of this relationship have been recently examined in depth in a monograph written by Levon Marashlian.[18]

The high density of the Armenian population in the Muş-Bitlis-Van triangle is demonstrated in one of the best European analyses of Ottoman population statistics. The Armenian patriarchate tables appear in this German source only in raw form, with no adjustments on the part of the patriarch, containing at the same time European upward corrections of 20–25 percent, uniformly applied to the Ottoman and patriarchate figures. For example, though the Armenian population was spread throughout nine vilayets, (the six provinces, i.e., Sivas, Harput, Diyarbekir, Erzurum, Van, and Bitlis, plus Trabzon, Adana, and Aleppo), two-thirds of that Armenian population, or 913,750 people, were concentrated in the five eastern vilayets representing what historio-geographically was called Greater Armenia (Erzurum, Bitlis, Van, Harput, and Diyarbekir).[19] That figure was obtained by applying to the 1880 official Turkish figure a 30 percent adjustment to account for the fifteen-year (1880–95) growth rate, yielding a 69 percent versus 24 percent, i.e., Muslim versus Armenian, population ratio. However, in five counties (*kazas*) of Van district the proportion of the Armenians ranged from 54 to 67 percent. In seven Van counties (*kaza*), and in two Bitlis counties (Muş and Bulanık), the Armenians comprised 50 to 74 percent of the total population. Thus despite everything else, in an area of 18,190 square kilometers, representing the core of "historic Armenia," the Armenians represented two-thirds (65 percent) of the total population, or double the proportion of the Muslims.[20]

An additional demographic factor further contributed to the vulnerability of the Armenians, namely, the dispersal of rather large segments of the Armenian population in all corners of the Empire, despite the simultaneous maintenance of a major Armenian presence, in terms of a high population density, in certain provinces in the East. The problem was largely created by the unabating depredations and attendant persecutions in the provinces. There developed a continuous exodus through emigration; this movement served to deplete the ranks of the rural Armenian population anxious to relocate in the Caucasus, in Europe, and/or the United States. Other groups of Armenians, in order to secure European protection and escape persecution, chose to convert to Catholicism, Protestantism, or the Russian Orthodox creed by way of seceding from the Mother Church, that represented an autonomous branch of Christianity called Apostolic and Gregorian. The episodic mass conversions to Islam by hundreds of Armenian villages prior to, during, and in the wake of massacres, with more than 500 such villages embracing Islam during the 1895–96 Abdul Hamit massacres alone,[21] caused even greater atrophy in the ranks of the indigenous Armenian population of the Ottoman Empire.

These developments, which led to the overspread, fragmentation, and ultimately to the emasculation of their nation, alarmed the Armenian revolutionaries, who proceeded to force the issue by charting a course of confrontation with the Ottoman authorities. At the same time, however, they were banking on what proved to be an abortive effort of coopting the more or less aloof and manipulative European Powers.

*The Lethal Potential of Forced Migrations—The Pivotal
Role of Balkan Refugees in the Armenian Genocide*

Apart from ethnography and statistics, the new Muslim immigrants were coopted in due course of time by successive Ottoman regimes to serve under the banner of Islam and holy war as instruments of anti-Christian persecution and massacre. The reforms, especially the Armenian reforms, were presented to them as a Christian gimmick to subdue and crush Muslims. The raising of the specter of new Christian overlords in the minds of gullible masses, burdened with memories of persecution inflicted on them by Christians in Tsarist Russia and the Balkans, especially by such *raias* as the Balkan Christians (Greeks, Bulgars, Serbs) who were identified with the *raias* of the Ottoman dominion (Armenians), was alarming enough to unite them against the targeted Armenians. The promise of ample spoils and loot was the additionally needed stimulus to galvanize most of these hard-pressed, deprived, and bitter people.

Following the series of military setbacks in the first Balkan war in the fall and winter of 1912, thousands and thousands of Muslim refugees took refuge in Istanbul in pitiful conditions.[22] Unable to receive effective assistance from the Turkish government, they were perishing day in and day out in large numbers. "...[C]holera broke out among the immigrants and in the army...one saw an entire population dying in the mosque yards under the icy grip of winter, the sight of the misery in Constantinople seemed too grim to be true."[23] In a most graphic description of the details of these hardships another Turkish author wrote that "Neither doctors, nor hospitals were able to cope with the unfolding tragedy gripping these multitudes of refugees thousands of whom were dying and for whom there were neither transport means to remove them nor any space left in the city's cemeteries. The number of cholera victims alone rose to 20,000 in Istanbul."[24]

It is against this backdrop that one has to examine and evaluate the Ittihadist policy of resettling the survivors of these calamitous expulsions and dislocations in various Armenian-inhabited regions and spots in the interior of Turkey in the 1913–14 period. That policy's portentousness is directly connected with Ittihad's emerging new policy towards the Ottoman Armenians, the bare outlines of which were set forth in Saloniki during the Ittihadist annual convention of 1910. As Fridjot Nansen noted in his book, "the settlement of Muslim refugees in the Christian sections of Armenia was carefully prepared and promoted. After the Balkan defeat thousands of Turkish refugees from Thrace and Macedonia arrived in Anatolia full of anti-Christian hatred which was inflamed by the government."[25] The report of a British consul at Erzurum confirms the existence of a deliberate governmental policy to pave the ground for operations to be launched at an opportune moment against the Armenians. In an 28 August 1913 report from Erzurum Consul Moynahan refers to Turkish provocations, stating, "Since the Balkan war a great number of agents have been sent into various regions of Asia Minor, carrying on a violent propaganda against the Christians. Crimes committed against Christians is considered in Turkish Armenia as heroism; if a crime is committed by an Armenian then even the family of the accused are at once arrested." Attached to the same communication is a cable from Van, dated 30 August(12 September)1913 declaring that "the Rumeli (Balkan) gendarmes are continually threatening the Armenian population." Around the same time another report from Karakilise in Bayazid sancak in eastern Turkey states that "the local police chief and his cronies from Rumeli are perpetrating sexual crimes against young girls which they didn't even commit in the ancient regime [of Abdul Hamit]. Under the guise of searching for deserters, pretending to ascertain the sex of children and women every day the honor of Armenian families is violated."[26] As Toynbee summed up the picture, "the arrival of the Rumelian refugees from the end of 1912 onwards produced an unexampled tension of feeling in Anatolia and a desire for revenge."[27]

In the meantime two critical policy developments further revealed the ominous nature of these incremental assaults against provincial Armenian populations. Pursuant to the provisions of a new Provincial Administration Law, an entirely new gendarme organization was established, and what is most significant, its control, then subject to the authority of the War Ministry, reverted to Talât's Interior Ministry.[28] Second, Talât, in an exchange with Russian Ambassador Giers, told him that he intended to use thousands of soldiers from the army in Thrace as gendarmes for the seven provinces in eastern Turkey for which Armenian Reforms were being envisaged. After communicating this news item to his foreign minister, Sazonof, Giers wrote, "In general the Young Turks are seeking to bury the Armenian question."[29]

When these gendarmes finally took up positions in areas heavily populated by Armenians, British Colonel Hawker, Inspector of Gendarmerie in Turkey, in his report of 31 October 1913 wrote: "Lately about 800 gendarmes from Macedonia have been to these vilayets—Sivas, Harput, Mush, Khinis, mostly Van—but many complaints were made...The transferring of the Macedonian gendarmes to these vilayets is almost a negative measure and more likely to do harm than good."[30] In one of his exchanges with American Ambassador Morgenthau, Turkish Foreign Minister Halil during the war, "admitted that...the gendarmes... committed some of the worst crimes against them [the

Armenians].[31] It is thus evident that the scale of that harm materialized during the wartime Armenian deportations and massacres. As if to maximize the instrumental usefulness of these Balkan refugees, Ittihad's Central Committee made sure that the key organizers and supervisors of these anti-Armenian measures were themselves refugees from the Balkans, carrying with them the same baggage of a bitter sense of uprootedness. As one Turkish chronicler of Ittihad's secret operations conceded, "An important portion of the Ittihadists were from Rumeli, from such places as Saloniki, Manastır, Üsküp, Işkodra, Yanya, Kosova. They all were smarting from the sense of despair that often grips a man who lost everything at the gambling table; they were all filled with rage."[32] Turkish as well as official German testimony clearly demonstrate that these gendarmes played a pivotal role in the execution of the majority of massacres committed against the countless Armenian deportee convoys. Cupidity, reinforced by the elemental force of simmering rage, found an ideal target in the multitudes of defenseless and trapped Armenian deportees. As one Turkish author admitted, "Even before the enactment of the Deportation Law, the contingents of the Muslim volunteers from the Balkans (and the Caucasus) launched their operations. The Armenians were subjected to raids, pillage and killings."[33] Taner Akçam likewise asserts that the refugees of the Balkan war were obsessed with "revenge" and in fact became "the willing executioners of the Armenians."[34] Finally reference may be made to the formal proclamation of Berlin's Turkish Patriotic Association in which, in an effort to assign blame, the refugee gendarmes from the Balkans are depicted as the arch villains in the enactment of the Armenian genocide. "They allowed their hatred to gain the upper hand and committed murder and pillage."[35]

The transfer of the mechanisms of control of the new gendarme organization from the Ministry of War back to Talât's Interior Ministry was an adroit act of empowerment and as such underscores the paramount role of the factor of power, in this case the formal power of the Interior Ministry, in the organization and implementation of genocide. Hence, this factor needs to be examined and assessed separately.

Power Relations

Generally speaking, domination is a function of power, whether in its latent form or it actually being exercised; in the latter case it becomes force. In the multiethnic Ottoman system, social and political relationships among many elements of that system were compressed into dominant group versus minority group relationships. Here, the terms dominant and minority do not refer exclusively to numbers. Rather they both have reference to power, and more specifically, to disparity of power relations. Domination presupposes power of one kind or another without necessarily implying numerical superiority on the part of the group exercising domination. As has been pointed out in the preceding section, as well as in the Appendix, throughout most of their history the Turks remained a numerical minority, ruling over a host of quantitatively superior nations and nationalities, which accordingly acquired the status of so-called minorities within the domains of the Ottoman Empire. In the case of non-Muslim minorities, Turkish preponderance of power became Turkish monopoly of power, as the former were structurally denied any significant access to the resources of power, economic power being tenuous and fragile as the wielders of such economic power were always at the mercy of the wielders of political and military power. In the formation and ascendancy of the Ottoman Empire, domination was a by-product of conquest consistent with the Turkish practices of the Islamic creed. The traditional Turkish motto, "by the right of my sword" (*kılıcımın hakkı ile*) epitomized this attitude. Such a monopoly meant, however, an inverse ratio in the distribution of power relations; the more the Turks invested themselves with power as a dominant group, the more their subject nationalities became divested of the same. In this superordination-subordination equation, the potency of one party entailed a commensurate impotency in the other, yielding the structural vulnerabilities of the subject nationalities. In the evolving stages of the Turko-Armenian conflict this structurally built-in impotency seriously handicapped Armenian efforts to reshape the disparate power relations, in the firm grip of which the Armenians were kept hostage to their more or less structurally preordained vulnerabilities.

With the internationalization of that conflict at the 1878 Berlin Congress these vulnerabilities acquired a new dimension, as persistent anti-Turkish pressures and threats from European Powers agitating for Armenian Reforms and insisting on supervision, if not control, signaled the growing weakness of the Ottoman state. Not only was the economy in shambles (the 1874–75 financial collapse of the Empire), but the Empire itself was shrinking steadily through the emancipatory thrusts of a succession of subject nationalities, which, in turn, entailed sizeable territorial amputations. This imperial decline translated into external weakness, if not impotency, in so far as the emancipatory move-

ments in the Balkans, in Lebanon, and Egypt were aided and abetted by
the Powers who additionally wrested from that Empire, with minimal
efforts, colonial territories for themselves. In a sense these losses essentially signaled internal weaknesses, for the spark of nationalism
animating these separatist nationalities was to a large degree ignited by
what has been generally called Ottoman "misrule," a condition which
often is symptomatic of a state of internal weakness.

After reviewing a mass of Consular reports from four eastern provinces, British Ambassador Lord Dufferin decried this misrule as "the
same tale of wrong, misery, corrupt, and incapable administration."[36]
Some two decades earlier E. Joy Morris, minister of the United States
to Turkey, wrote to Secretary of State W. H. Seward: "The Turkish
Tribunal are all stained with the vice of venality and their corruption is
so notorious that recourse to them is avoided as much as possible...[this
corruption] overspread the whole surface of Turkish administration,
corrupting every branch of it to such a degree as to stifle both the sense
of honor and duty..."[37] Instead of taking protests and grievances against
such chronic abuses seriously and treating the problems as being re-
flective of what England's Consul at Van in 1883, i.e., six months earlier than Lord Dufferin, called "utter corruption and incapacity of the
authorities,"[38] these authorities persisted in relying on military response
that was always violent, sanguinary, and repressive. More often than
not, the authorities disdainfully rebuffed the idea of accommodation
through reform by invoking the standard Ottoman maxim of "the
conqueror's inveterate right," and accordingly summoning the martial
spirit of retaliation.

In commenting on the Ottoman state's legacy of lethal violence
against its own subjects, a Turkish military commander and historian
not only deplored the suborning of the Ottoman military to achieve the
ends of such lethal violence but he also prognosticated the grim and
fatal outcome of this legacy. The allusion is to Turkish general (*Birinci
Ferik*) and commander of cavalry (*Süvari Kumandanı*), Izzet Fuad Paşa.
He was the grandson of the famous Ottoman statesman Keçecizade
Fuad Paşa, who, during the years 1863–66, twice served as Grand Vizier, and during 1856–60 likewise twice served as Ottoman foreign
minister. General Izzet Fuad had received his military training in France
and in the Abdul Hamit era he additionally had served as ambassador
to Spain. In 1908 in Paris he published a volume analyzing the 1877–
78 Russo-Turkish war and the errors and missed opportunities associated with that war. This is what he wrote in the preface of that book:

But why these wars against our own subjects or vassals?...The imperial Government employed brutal force against peaceful and weak people, who were ventilating their grievances, by mobilizing against them entire armies in order to prevent them from seeking from God, the protector of the oppressed, deliverance from their miseries. And God heard the non-Muslim populations. What was the end result of the engagement of these combative permanent armies: the loss of the most beautiful provinces of the Empire, the material and moral ruination of the Turks. Fatal mistakes, irreparable mistakes.

Here is the *fuller* and original French text:

Puisqu'il y avait des insurrections, il fallait bien y affecter des troupes; mais pourquoi ces guerres contre nos propres sujets ou vassaux? Pour quel motif notre chère armée perdrait-elle son noble et précieux sang en combattant ses frères?

Pour réparer les torts de notre administration!

Cette armée devenait ainsi une gendarmerie puissante, pour réparer les abus des gendarmes qui étaient bien plus habiles et prompts à les engendrer que capables d'agir pour calmer les crises rationales qu'ils faisaient naître.

Le bien-être national, la fraternité si nécessaire entre les éléments qui composent l'Empire, l'amour du même drapeau, la convergence indispensable des intérêts, au lieu d'être assurés et obtenus par des moyens normaux et paternels, avaient pour ennemis acharnés nos coupables et féodaux administrateurs, nos valys, nos mutessarifs, nos caïmacams, nos alaÿs beys et nos defterdars, qui agissaient de manière à opprimer par la force brutale les paisibles et les faibles et qui obligeaient le gouvernement impérial à faire marcher des armées entières contre des mécontents, pour les empêcher de demander au Dieu protecteur des opprimés la fin de leurs misérers.

Et Dieu écouta les populations non musulmanes!

Et quel fut le résultat de ces armées permanentes qui combattaient les idées des uns et les revendications des autres: la perte des plus belles provinces de l'Empire, et la ruine matérialle et morale des Turcs!

Erreurs fatales, erreurs irréparables![39]

The disparity between the general's diagnosis of a major problem with which the Ottoman Empire was afflicted, and Ittihadist party chief Talât's following statement, made about a decade later in disregard of the root causes of that problem, is most significant; in fact, it goes a long way to explain the ultimate demise of that empire. The statement was made to American ambassador Morgenthau, who recounted it thus in his postwar memoirs: "Talaat explained his national policy: these different *blocs* in the Turkish Empire, he said, had always conspired against Turkey; because of the hostility of these native populations, Turkey had lost province after province—Greece, Serbia, Rumania, Bulgaria, Bosnia, Herzegovina, Egypt, and Tripoli. In this way the Turkish Empire had dwindled almost to the vanishing point. If what was left of Turkey was to survive, added Talaat, he must get rid of these alien peoples. 'Turkey for the Turks' was now Talaat's controlling idea."[40] It should be noted here parenthetically that at this new phase of Turkish nationalism not even Muslim nationalities were spared this treatment, as evidenced in the cases of the Ittihadist oppression of the Albanians and the Arabs.

In his analysis of Ottoman imperialism, C. Max Kortepeter attributed the ultimate dissolution of the Ottoman Empire to the inability of Ottoman authorities "to respond to the grievances of the various [ethnic] units of the Empire…The net result was that the Turks…were forced to divest themselves of Empire and to create a nation-state."[41] The more the Ottoman losses aggregated, the more the urge developed to increase the level of repression against remaining subject nationalities. The realization of a rapid decline in external power, with all the humiliations and frustrations implicit in it, prompted a corresponding drive to consolidate and augment internal power. In the interval between the calamitous Balkan war, 1912, and World War I, 1914, this drive for power was optimized and was primarily targeted against the Armenians, the only remaining non-Muslim nationality in the heartland of the Ottoman Empire, still agitating for reform.

The drive to consolidate internal power as a weapon against the dangers of the dissolution of the Empire was initiated and implacably pursued by Abdul Hamit. In 1876 Hamit had acceded to the throne with a promise to institute constitutional reforms but restored instead a level of absolutism. By virtue of this switch he discarded Midhat Paşa, the pillar of the 1896 Constitutional Act, and the leader of the Constitutional Reform movement. Moreover, Hamit had feigned an accord with Midhat; that accord involved a condition for displacing and replacing his brother Murad V as Sultan, but, as discussed in detail in chapter 5, subsequently Midhat too was discarded; he was eventually banished, and ultimately, in 1883, he was strangled in the distant prison of Taif in Arabia. Consequently Hamit transferred the seat of government from the Sublime Porte to the Palace, thereby concentrating all governmental power in his hands. From a constitutional-legal point of view, this act of monopolizing power was quite legitimate, for Article 5 of the 1876 Constitution invests the monarch with practically unlimited power and authority. ("His Majesty the Sultan is irresponsible [i.e., is responsible to no one]: His person is sacred.") The exercise of this power proved, however, a double-edged sword. As the internal and external pressures for "Armenian reforms" mounted, Hamit resorted to a series

of massacres to coincide with the formal promulgation of these reforms—as if to register his defiance against the Powers and to "teach a
lesson to the Armenians." The tempo of the decline of the Empire in
terms of dominion and shrinkage of territories accelerated, however,
concomitantly.

But even Abdul Hamit's imperial power had its limitations when it
confronted a particular segment of the Ottoman Armenian population
that had distinct attributes, by virtue of which it stymied that power by
successfully resisting it. The reference is to the highlanders of Zeitoun
to whom an additional chapter in this study has been devoted in order
to underscore the critical significance of power relations in the outcome of a conflict. It has been demonstrated in the emergence of this
aberrant case that a small fraction of the Ottoman Armenian population
more or less could prevail, however temporarily, in the outcome of a
special phase of the Turko-Armenian conflict. The four attributes, the
skillful utilization of which afforded the Zeytounlis relative triumph
over vastly superior Ottoman army units (including multitudes of irregulars), involved: (a) a homogenous Armenian population dominat-
ing Zeitoun and its outlying villages; (b) the possession of a modicum
of weapons, however primitive, and the requisite tested skill to use
them with deadly efficiency; (c) the will to fight and to die heroically,
borne out of a cultivated martial spirit and allied martial aptitudes; (d)
the topography of the mountainous habitat of "The Eagle's Nest" Zeitoun
that rendered an assault against it perilous and potentially costly.

The configuration of these four attributes was such that it served as
a matrix of limited Armenian power impelling, if not compelling, the
ruling Ottoman sultan to seek the intervention of the Powers to stop the
fighting "at once" in order to forestall further "considerable" Ottoman
losses, including the loss of "quite high ranking army officers."[42]

One lesson one may draw from this episode is that the vulnerability
of the Armenian population in general was due to a set of constraints in
the clutches of which they remained trapped indefinitely. Absent these
constraints, vulnerability may vanish and one may witness the spec-
tacle of the 1895–96 epic of Zeitoun. It is significant that before the
Ittihadists in 1915 formally embarked upon the destruction of the Ottoman Armenian population at large, they targeted and eliminated first
and foremost the Armenian population of Zeitoun and its environs.

This successor Ittihad regime, identified with the Second Constitutional Era (1908–18), embarked upon a pattern of power accumulation
and power wielding similar to that of its predecessor. Operating through

a tightly organized party apparatus, Ittihad managed to concentrate power in a small oligarchical clique whose designs, modus operandi, and manipulative defiance of the Powers, which were still pressing for Armenian reforms, in many respects proved to be an extension and amplification of Hamidian policies.

In assessing the exercise of power in a setting in which the wielder of power has substantial advantages, international conflicts need to be examined in a context reaching beyond the individual power positions of the antagonistic parties. Alliances, religious and/or kinship ties among the leaders involved, substantial economic stakes, and projective strategies animating external powers to assume certain postures in relation to the antagonists involved cannot be discounted; they often impinge upon the power differential either impairing or enhancing the position of the more powerful party.

The main reason practically all non-Muslim subject nationalities succeeded in extricating themselves from Ottoman domination and eventually attained independence was not so much demography, as claimed by some authors, but the intrusion into this equation of disparate power relations of this external factor. The 1822 Chios massacre of the Greeks by the Turks (followed by the 1866–68 and 1896 anti-Turkish Cretan insurrections); the 1876 "Bulgarian Horrors," the Batak massacre by the Turks (followed by the losses the Turks incurred through the terms of the subsequent Berlin Peace Treaty of 1878); and the 1860 massacre of Christian Maronites in Lebanon (followed by the 1860–61 insurrection in Lebanon), became turning points in the evolution of movements aiming at Greek and Bulgarian independence, and Lebanese autonomy. The reason for these successes scored against the Turks, was obvious. Russia, England, and France, one way or another, actively intervened, and when necessary, militarily prevailed upon the Ottoman rulers, who had to yield. There was absolutely no such intervention at any time from any camp in all the episodes of massacres against the Armenians. Instead, there was a constant barrage of loud protests, diplomatic Notes and Memoranda containing veiled threats, and public agitation belaboring the Muslim versus Christian angle of the conflict. In the course of all this the Powers played out their mutual suspicions, rivalries, and intrigues as their relations to each other and to the successive Ottoman regimes shifted from one pole to another.

The key point common to these international reactions to the series of atrocities against the Armenians is that all the remonstrances and threats of one kind or another were patently belied by a sustained, actual hands-off attitude by all the Powers involved. Fully cognizant of this consequential difference between purport and intent, between public pretense and actual governmental policy, the Ottoman authorities in nearly every instance knew how to call its bluff and proceeded accordingly. Unlike in the case of their Treaty and Accord commitments vis-à-vis the other nationalities, in the case of the Armenians these Ottoman authorities contemptuously ignored and eventually, one by one, discarded as scraps their internationally contracted engagements incorporated in Article 61 of the 1878 Berlin Treaty, in the 1895 Reform Act, and in the 1914 Reform Accord, all of them exclusively dealing with Armenian Reforms in the provinces and variously involving England, Germany, Russia, France, Austria-Hungary, and Italy. Ottoman Armenians had neither a parent-state the Ottomans could or should reckon with, nor were they believed to have overriding strategic or economic significance, as far as the vital national interests of these Powers were concerned.

It may be argued that the incidence of this negative external factor, i.e., the predictable absence of external deterrence, in the overall constellation of effective power relations proved more crucial in the genocide of the Armenians than the latter's impotence in the Ottoman power structure. That impotence may well be characterized as a dependent, and the external factor as the independent variable; the significance and effects of the impotence of Ottoman Armenians in the final analysis depended upon the presence or absence of external deterrence. Given the external weaknesses of the Ottoman state, the impotency of the Armenians in itself didn't need to be disastrous for them, as it was not disastrous in the case of the other nationalities, for the Powers were in a position not only to avert disaster but to treat and help remedy its root causes. In brief, external deterrence was then potentially the most viable antidote for such a disaster, a type of deterrence which, at the very least, could neutralize the Turkish leverage of a power differential threatening to become an instrument of mass murder. In other words, the structural vulnerability of the Armenians, who were embroiled in a conflict with a powerful dominant group, essentially proved to be a potential invitation for their destruction in the absence of credible external deterrence.

Legal enactments involving the promulgation of reforms, more or less imposed from the outside, by definition are hollow when they are devoid of muscular strength, are not intended to be implemented, and are substantially in conflict with the entrenched traditions, interests, and outlooks of uninformed masses liable to agitation and manipulation by leaders opposed to the enactments. But, given the vulnerability of the collectivity expected to benefit from them, these enactments can also become provocative and dangerous. The enactment of successive Armenian Reforms, however vital a necessity for everyone concerned, including the Ottoman regime itself, was not only abortive, but counterproductive as well. It strained the inner recesses of the already taxed and exacerbated Turkish psyche in need of an outlet to ventilate its cumulative frustrations, borne out of manifold difficulties, crises, and humiliating national setbacks. In a society permeated with the vestiges of an exclusionary theocracy and the legacy of martial traditions, more enduring than any combination of alien statutes, codes, and legal provisions, the overriding ethos of superiority and superordination in relation to impotent or weak minorities is capable of apoplectic defiance and rage, as was the case in the genocidal explosion of the Turko-Armenian conflict.

In harnessing that ethos, which was brought to bear on their lethal anti-Armenian measures, Abdul Hamit and Ittihad resorted to parallel methods of power accumulation and power application. Both came into power with commitments to the principles of freedom, equality, and constitutional government, and both reneged after establishing themselves firmly; paradoxically, Ittihad had denounced and deposed Hamit for his reneging, and for his subsequent resort to tyranny. Both persisted in their efforts to purge opponents, dissidents, and potential rivals by a system of internal security that was designed to maintain continuity in the exercise of monolithic and near-absolute power. Both concentrated that power in small cliques, involving, on the one hand, Hamit and his Palace camarilla, and, on the other, Ittihad's Central Committee, billed as the Shadow Cabinet, with the attributes of a Supreme Directorate. Both relied on trusted emissaries, informal orders, and covert instructions to authorize massacres in order to be able to feign ignorance, to conduct farcical investigations in response to outcries against the perpetrators, and ultimately to deny governmental involvement. Both perpetrator camps went so far as to indulge in such acts of perversion as role reversal through which they would try to denounce the victims as a whole as fomenters of disorders and as actual victimizers. Both tested European reaction to massacres by initiating limited, local massacres as trial balloons before embarking upon incremental and more comprehensive ones. The 1895–96 large scale Hamidian massacres, for example, were preceded by the limited 1894

Sassoun massacre; the World War I Ittihad-engineered genocidal massacres were preceded by the 1909 regional Adana massacres. In the aftermaths of all these episodes there was very little accounting and much less retributive justice as the Powers persisted in their choice of inaction as the most desirable option among several other options. In retrospect, the Hamidian massacres as a whole emerge as a prelude to, if not as a rehearsal for, the World War I genocide.

In this connection it is worth noting that the top leaders of Ittihad, especially Talât, on a number of occasions, consulted Abdul Hamit about the ways in which to handle the emerging new phases of the Turko-Armenian conflict. In his memoirs Fethi Okyar (a leading Ittihadist, and after the war, a leading Kemalist serving in several cabinet posts, including that of premier of the Ankara government, in which capacity he served twice), hints at Abdul Hamit's advisory role in connection with the wartime enactment of the Armenian genocide. Talât, in the fall of 1909, had sent two confidential letters to Okyar, in which, through the intermediary of the latter, he was asking the advice of Abdul Hamit regarding, among other things, issues which, "touching as they did on the matter of the very foundations of the country, in those days were life and death issues" (*hayati meseleler*). At that time, Hamit was exiled to Saloniki following the abortive 31 March(13 April)1909 anti-Ittihadist counterrevolution, and Okyar was the military commander of the detachment guarding the monarch in the villa Alatin in Saloniki. When Okyar brought Hamit's answers to Talât's queries, the top leadership of Ittihad was invited to Talât's home to consider Hamit's views and discuss them. Among those present were the principal authors of the Armenian genocide, namely Nazım, B. Şakir, Enver, Yenibahçeli Nail, and Ittihad's secretary general, Midhat Şükrü. From the recorded reaction of Nazım, it may be inferred that Abdul Hamit had proposed a radical solution to the problems Talât had specified and to which Nazım is said to have angrily retorted: "he is proffering us a prescription for our woes and we don't have the guts to ask him why he himself didn't use it for thirty years." According to Talât, the remedy suggested by the ex-monarch was "to pull out by the roots" the problem besetting the Ottoman state (*kök sökeceğiz*). The care with which covert or implicit words are used, either at the meeting of the Ittihadist leaders, or through careful paraphrasing by the intermediary, Okyar himself, is most evident here. In any event, the allusion is, of course, to the idea of eradicating the discordant nationalities, the troublemakers. As if to clarify the matter, Economics Minister Cavid, who was also there, reportedly told his cohorts present at that gathering that Abdul Hamit's advice was meant to be carried out only "when favorable conditions can be created" (*Şartlar temin edilirse*).[43] In their respective memoirs, both Talât and Okyar refer to Abdul Hamit's growing concern that non-Muslims might be able to take over Turkey in the foreseeable future on the strength of their numbers, population growth rate, their vitality, and their enterprising spirit. Hamit reportedly was alarmed in particular about the system of parliament and parliamentary elections, through which he projected the possibility of appointing a non-Muslim to the post of grand vizier (*sadrazam*) and different cabinet ministries. This, he reportedly vowed, "must be prevented by all means."[44]

The revelations of Yakup Kadri Karaosmanoğlu are even more relevant. He too relates an episode of similar exchanges in the party headquarters of Ittihad, i.e., in the office of one of the architects of the genocide, namely, Behaeddin Şakir; the event took place sometime in the summer of 1913 when Ittihad, having purged all the dissidents, was in complete control of both government and people. Yakup Kadri was a legally trained man of letters, a literary authority who in the regime of the Turkish Republic additionally occupied several ambassadorial posts and for some years also served as editor-in-chief of *Ulus*, the principal Kemalist newspaper in Ankara. According to his account, present at the meeting were Talât, Şakir, Cemal Paşa and the ideological guru of the Ittihadists, Ziya Gökalp. Disagreeing with Cemal's espousal of the ideals of Ottomanism, the others endorsed the ideal of a strictly new Turkish nationalism, arguing that it was no longer possible to embrace and unite under the banner of Ottomanism all the diverse and discordant nationalities. Talât emphasized the need to expand and strengthen the party organization in order to successfully carry out "the bloody clash with [discordant] nationalities." *(Kanlı bir anasır kavgası)*, which Şakir insisted was inevitable and imminent. Talât's motto in this connection was: "We must act in unison but the things we do must remain secret."[45]

What is evident in this overall picture is the continuity of the sway of an ethos that overwhelms all legal restraints and other inhibitions when contemplating draconian measures against targeted subject nationalities—in the presumed and anticipated absence of external deterrence. Both regimes co-opted disaffected Muslim tribes, ethnic groups, and refugee settlers who were used and misused as principal instruments of destruction, and were appropriately rewarded.

Notwithstanding, the injection at this juncture of the summary of a caveat may be in order. One may discern the elements of convergence in the massacres committed by seemingly two disparate re-gimes and thereby depict a pattern of logical continuity in extermina-tory behavior. However, one could not possibly theorize that the World War I genocide was, therefore, inevitable. As in all other similar cases, one has to make allowance for the incidence of what might be called the intervening variables. The two episodes of Armenian massacres are linked together in a context highlighting the paramountcy of "the opportunity structure." At the time of the Hamidian massacres there was neither an external nor a global war. The global character of World War I in which the Ittihadists entered without provocation helped cre-ate the array of opportunities afforded by such a world-wide confla-gration. Moreover, the same Ittihadists had the benefits of the experience acquired by Sultan Abdul Hamit, namely, the realization of the utter vulnerability of the Armenians, the predictability of inac-tion of the Powers, and above all the impunity accruing to the perpe-trators. Equally important was the realization that in due time the unpunished crime could be, would be, consigned to oblivion. Abdul Hamit had none of these advantages and, uncertain of the actual re-sponse of the Powers, had to exercise the constraints described in the text dealing with the limitations of the Abdul Hamit era massacres. In the final analysis, however, what emerges here as a single common denominator is the ethos of massacre, prevalent in the regimes of both Sultan Abdul Hamit and Ittihad. That ethos remained inexorably woven with a persistent post-massacre ethos of denial that is orga-nized, provocative, and insidious. Consequently, the elements of the historical Turko-Armenian conflict continue to fester as the Catastro-phe of 1915, and the lingering memory of that Catastrophe, remain, to quote a British author, "unexorcised"[46]—despite the incidence of candor by some prominent Turks who on occasion have shown a will-ingness to admit to the organized mass murder of the Armenians un-der review here. The two epigrams adduced at the very start of this volume illustrate the point. Far more ominous for the future of Turko-Armenian relations, however, is the evident frame of mind of a num-ber of Turks past and present. Reflecting the twin conditions of impunity and denialism associated with the Armenian genocide, the core element of that frame of mind seems to be the truculent readi-ness to again resort to mass murder when threatened by manifestations of Armenian aspirations on what are now Turkish territories, which many, but not all Armenians inveterately consider historic Armenia destined to be reclaimed and recovered at some future time. In the

eighty-fifth sitting of the fledgling Grand National Assembly of Turkey, presided over by Mustafa Kemal (Atatürk), Mazhar Mufit, then
deputy from Hakkâri province, and subsequently and abiding and close
collaborator of Mustafa Kemal, was vehemently denouncing the Armenians for coveting the provinces of Van and Bitlis, calling them
"pigs." He then intoned in the assembly hall: "A repetition of the
mass murder [against the Armenians] cannot be ruled out" (*Tekrar kı-
yam muhal değil efendiler*).[47] Eighteen days later when the Kemalist
armies were poised to march into Yerevan, the capital of the fledgling
Armenian republic—after having invaded Armenia without any declaration of war—that threat of a new massacre proved to be a reflection of Ankara's resolve to extend the wartime Armenian genocide to
Russian Armenia in quest for a really Final Solution. In a top-secret
cipher telegram, dated 8 November 1920, the Kemalist government's
acting foreign minister, Ahmet Muhtar, conveyed to General Kâzım
Karabekir, the commander-in-chief of the invading Turkish army, the
order of Ankara's government to "politically and physically wipe out
Armenia" (*Ermenistanı siyaseten ve maddeten ortadan kaldırmak*)."
Muhtar in the same cipher underscored the fact that this order reflected "the real intent" (*makasidi hakikiyesi*) of the then-functioning
Kemalist government. But in order to deflect and cover-up the projected mass murder, the Turkish general was advised to act with circumspection; he was to "mislead" (*iğfal*) the targeted Armenians, and
to "fool" the Europeans by an appearance of "peace-lovingness." To
further conceal this genocidal intent and trap the targeted victim population, the same foreign minister on the very same day, 8 November
1920, sent another telegram to the despairing Armenian government
in Yerevan. In it, Ankara tried to reassure the Armenians of its "pro-
found and genuine friendship" (*amik ve samimi*) for the Armenian
people, invoking sentiments of "humanity" (*insaniyet*), and making
pledges for economic assistance in order to help Armenia recover and
thereby achieve "complete independence and security" (*temamii istikâl
ve emniyet*).[48]

Even though the prompt Sovietization of Armenia through the intervention of the Eleventh Red Army, which was stationed nearby, averted
the liquidation of the imperiled remnants of the Armenian people, the
six-month long occupation of chunks of Russian Armenia by General
Karabekir's army still produced a small-scale mass murder, a sort of
mini-genocide. According to British historians Grant and Temperley,
"at least a hundred thousand more [from Russian Armenia] were added

to the death roll [of the Armenian genocide]."[49] Armenian and Soviet sources, however, maintain that twice that many Armenians perished as a result of this onslaught.[50]

As Hikmet Bayur, the late dean of Turkish historians, had prognosticated, the resolution of the acrimonious and protracted Turko-Armenian conflict would ultimately be resolved through the engagement of the Turkish army (*işi ordu ile görmek*), (see ch. 9, note 6). An army is the ultimate repository of power that at the end of a victorious war can exercise that power by applying unlimited force. Having been defeated rather swiftly, the Armenians were once more at the mercy of the Turks. Once more the Western powers chose to forsake Armenia, even though they had emerged victorious from the Great War and in the process had resoundingly defeated the Turks who belonged to the Central Powers, the enemy camp. The proverbial Armenian vulnerability in this respect is succinctly described by Paul Helmreich:

> None of the European states had ever intended to become heavily involved in Armenia, despite all their pious pronouncements. Now, finally faced with the necessity of making a decision, they coldly and ruthlessly pushed aside the Armenians and their newborn state.[51]

As explained above, the factor of critical disparity of power relations between a potential perpetrator and a potential victim in itself is not always a decisive factor for the materialization of genocide as a form of radical conflict resolution. In the ever-changing landscape of international relations, where political and military alignments are in a state of constant flux, the presence or absence of effective external deterrence on behalf of a potential victim group is perhaps the most crucial determinant in the calculus of genocide. Were it not for the ideological bent of incipient Soviet Communism that intervened in November-December 1920 and thwarted Turkish genocidal designs, Armenia too, like so many other ancient peoples, might have disappeared in the dustpan of history.

Notes

1. Diplomatic Archives of Foreign Ministry of France (*Documents Diplomatiques Français 1871–1900*), vol. 11, Doc. no. 50, pp. 71–4 (1947). See also *Livre Jaune. Affaires Arméniens. Projets de réformes dans l'Empire Ottoman 1893–1897*. Doc. no. 6., pp. 10–13 (1897).
2. For details of the rise of these schisms and cleavages see Louise Nalbandian, *The Armenian Revolutionary Movement. The Development of Armenian Political Parties through the Nineteenth Century* (Berkeley and Los Angeles: Univer-

sity of California Press, 1963); Sarkis Atamian, *The Armenian Community. The Historical Development of a Social and Ideological Conflict* (New York: Philosophical Library, 1955).

3. For the theocratically determined and politically framed liabilities devolving upon the Armenian *millet* in the Ottoman Empire in this regard see the pertinent comments of two experts in this area, namely, British diplomat and Chief Dragoman G. H. Fitzmaurice and author Bat Ye'or in Vahakn N. Dadrian, *The History of the Armenian Genocide. Ethnic Conflict from the Balkans to Anatolia to the Caucasus,* 4th ed. (Providence/Oxford: Berghahn Books, 1997), p. 147, 168 notes 119 and 120.

4. Foremost among these advocates for Christian Armenians was an erudite and articulate British clergyman, Canon of Ripon. He is Malcolm MacColl. See his *The Sultan and the Powers* (London: Longmans, Green and Co., 1896); idem. *England's Responsibility Towards Armenia,* four editions (London: Longmans, Green and Co. 1895, 1896).

5. Ewald Banse, *Die Länder und Völker der Türkei.* (The lands and peoples of Turkey) (Berlin: Georg von Westermann Publishing House, 1916), p. 76.

6. Jean-Pierre Alem, *L'Arménie* (Paris, 1962), p.47, quoted in Tessa Hofmann and Gerayer Koutcharian, "The History of Armenian-Kurdish Relations in the Ottoman Empire" *Armenian Review* 39, no. 4 (Winter 1986), p. 35.

7. E. Banse, *Der arische Orient* (The Arian Orient) (Leipzig: B. G. Teubner, 1910), p. 60.

8. Freiherrn von Schweiger-Lerchenfeld, "Das neue vilayet Van" (The new province Van), *Österreichische Monatsschrift für den Orient* (1877), p. 42.

9. Paul Rohrbach, *In Turan und Armenien* (Berlin: Georg Stilke, 1898), p. 231.

10. Edson L. Clark, *Turkey* (New York: Collier, 1902), pp. 527–8.

11. *Zhamanag* (Armenian daily in Istanbul) 1(14) July 1914.

12. *Stamboul* (French daily), 10 December 1913, quoted in Feroz Ahmad, *The Young Turks* (Oxford: Clarendon Press, 1969), p. 144.

13. His initiative in redrawing provincial boundaries is mentioned in Ercümend Kuran, "Küçük Said Paşa (1840–1914) as a Turkish Modernist," *International Journal of Middle East Studies* I (1970), p. 127. For some revelations in his memoirs see *Said Paşanın Hatıratı* (Memoirs of Said Paşa), vol. I, (Istanbul, 1328 old style or 1912 new style), pp. 30ff., 201–5.

14. Baron Wladimir Giesl, *Zwei Jahrzehnte im Nahen Osten* (Two decades in the Near East), General Major R.V. Steinitz, ed. (Berlin: Verlag für Kulturpolitik, 1927), p. 120.

15. Benoit-Brunswick, *La verité sur Midhat Pacha* (Paris: E. Leroux, 1877), p. 4.

16. Khoren Kapigian, *Haigagan Hartzu Arevelyan Hartzi Metch* (The Armenian Question within the Eastern Question), (Beirut: n.p., 1962), pp. 150–1.

17. One side of the dispute favoring Turkish arguments and by and large defending Turkish statistical data on this issue is presented in Justin McCarthy, *Muslims and Minorities: The Population of Ottoman Anatolia and the End of the Empire* (New York: New York University Press, 1983). For a critique of McCarthy's methodology see Vahakn N. Dadrian, "Ottoman Archives and Denial of the Armenian Genocide" in *The Armenian Genocide: History, Politics, Ethics,* R.G. Hovanissian, ed. (New York: St. Martin's Press, 1992), pp. 294–7, and Marashlian in n. 18.

18. Levon Marashlian, *Politics and Demography: Armenians, Turks, and Kurds in the Ottoman Empire* (Cambridge, MA: Zoryan Institute, 1991), pp. 1–37.

19. For the common usage of the term Greater Armenia at that time see British Ambassador (to Turkey) Earl of Dufferin's 23 August 1881, no. 723 report to

the British foreign minister, Earl Granville. FO 424/123, no. 75, p. 119 where the term Greater Armenia is used.

20. "Die Verbreitung der Armenier in der asiatischen Türkei und in Transkaukasien" (The distribution of the Armenians in Asiatic Turkey and Transcaucasia), A. Supan, ed. (based on the compilations of Lieutenant General G. L. Selenoy and N. ven Seidlitz) in *Petermann's Geographische Mitteilungen* 42 (1896), pp. 1–10. See especially pp. 5–7. These figures on the numerical superiority of the Armenians in certain districts and counties of Van, Bitlis, and Diyarbekir provinces are confirmed in Major Trotter's 7 September 1880 report to the British ambassador to Turkey, Sir W.E. Goschen. FO 424/107. No. 104/1. Registry no. 37, p. 174.

21. Vahakn N. Dadrian, *The History of the Armenian Genocide*. [n. 3], pp. 151–7.

22. Stanford J. Shaw and Ezel Kural Shaw, *History of the Ottoman Empire and Modern Turkey* vol. 2 (Cambridge: Cambridge University Press, 1977), p. 294.

23. *Memoirs of Halide Edib* (New York: Century, 1926), p. 334.

24. Galip Vardar, *Ittihad ve Terakki İçinde Dönenler* (The inside story of Ittihad ve Terakki), S.N. Tansu, ed. (Istanbul: Inkilâp, 1960), p. 150.

25. Fridjof Nansen, *L'Arménie et le Proche Orient* (Paris: Librairie Orientaliste, 1928), pp. 330–1.

26. FO 195/2450-45/5. 28 August 1913, 45/6 and folio 40.

27. Arnold J. Toynbee, *The Western Question in Greece and Turkey* (Boston: Houghton Mifflin Co., 1922), p. 139.

28. The Shaws, *History of the Ottoman Empire* [n.22], p. 306. The Law had entered into force on 15 March 1913.

29. *The Orange Book*, doc. no. 92, dated 16 (29)September 1913.

30. FO 195/2450, 45/5, folios 59, 62.

31. Ambassador's 18 November 1915 "Private and Confidential" letter to Secretary of State Lansing. *U.S. National Archives*. R.G. 59.867.00/798½, p.7.

32. Vardar, *Ittihad ve Terakki* [n.24], p. 255.

33. Suat Parlar, *Osmanlıdan Günümüze Gizli Devlet* (The secretive state: From Ottoman days to the present). (Istanbul: Spartakus Publications, 1996), p. 91.

34. Taner Akçam, *Siyasi Kültürümüzde Zulüm ve İşkence* (Atrocity and torture in our political culture) (Istanbul, Iletişim, 1992), p. 239.

35. *Die armenische Frage und der türkische Standpunkt* (The Armenian question and the Turkish standpoint) (Berlin: Türk Yurdu, 1919), p. 13.

36. FO 881/5168, folio 23, Vice Consul Eyres, 15 September 1883 report.

37. *Papers Relating to Foreign Relations of the United States*, 1864, IV, pp. 377–8; see also the same Minister's 22 May 1866 report titled, "The Evils of the System"

38. FO [n.36], folio 17.

39. Général Izzet-Fuad, *Autres Occasions Perdues...Critique Stratégique de la Campagne d'Asie Mineure 1877–1878* (Paris: R. Chapelot, 1908), see préface, pp. xi–xii.

40. Henry Morgenthau, *Ambassador Morgenthau's Story* (Garden City, NY: Doubleday, Page and Co., 1918), p. 51.

41. C. Max Kortepeter, *Ottoman Imperialism during the Reformation: Europe and the Caucasus* (New York: New York University Press, 1972), pp. viii and ix.

42. See chapter 7, note 18.

43. Fethi Okyar, *Uç Devirde Bir Adam* (A man of three eras), C. Kutay, ed. (Istanbul: Tercüman, 1980), pp. 108–22. The quotations are from pp. 121–3.

44. Ibid., pp. 104–5; C. Kutay, "Talât Paşanın Gurbet Hatıraları" (Talât Paşa's memoirs in exile), *Tercüman* (Turkish newspaper in Istanbul), installments 10 and 20, December 18 and 22, 1982, respectively.

45. Yakup Kadri Karaosmanoğlu, *Hüküm Gecesi* (The night of decision) 2d ed., A. Özkırımlı, ed. (Istanbul, Iletişim, 1987), pp. 300–7.
46. Christopher J. Walker, *Armenia: The Survival of a Nation*, 2d rev. ed., (New York: St. Martin's, 1990), p. 13.
47. *T.B.M.M. Gizli Celse Zabıtları* (The transcripts of the secret sessions of the Grand National Assembly of Turkey), vol. 1 (Ankara, 1985), p. 179. 17 October 1920 sitting.
48. Kâzım Karabekir, *Istiklâl Harbimiz* (Our War of Independence), 2d ed. (Istanbul: Türkiye Publishing House, 1969), p. 844.
49. A.J. Grant and Howard Temperly, *Europe in the Nineteenth and Twentieth Centuries (1789–1950)*, 6th ed. (London: Longmans, 1962), p. 450.
50. Dadrian, History of the Armenian Genocide [n.21], pp. 360–61.
51. Paul C. Helmreich, *From Paris to Sèvres: The Partition of the Ottoman Empire at the Peace Conference of 1919–1920* (Columbus, OH: Ohio State University Press, 1974), pp. 295–96.

13

Conclusion

The main hypothesis of this volume was the view that genocide in any form and at any level presupposes a conflict between perpetrator and victim-group and that the enactment of genocide itself is a lethal undertaking for the purpose of resolving that conflict radically. In other words, genocide appears here as a means to an end rather than an end unto itself. In order to understand however the circumstances under which such an end germinates, matures, and crystallizes itself, one has to understand the circumstances of the genesis and growth of the conflict itself. In other words, one has to examine the history of the conflict. The task of understanding the Armenian genocide is in this sense inextricably interwoven with the task of dissecting the Turko-Armenian conflict in terms of its origin and its evolutionary stages. In an effort to encapsulate the arch determinants of this conflict certain substantive problems relating to theocracy, demography, and the factor of power relations were singled out in the summary discussion in chapter 12. In order to emphasize the determinants' primary significance for this study, their intrinsic relationship to the formative stages of the Turko-Armenian conflict may be restated briefly.

Theocracy is a type of state organization that is predicated upon religious creeds and dogmas. In such a system a high premium is placed upon a citizenry that incorporates uniform religious affiliations. Ideally, therefore, theocracies are more suitable for societies possessing an optimum degree of homogeneity. Multiethnic societies, on the other hand are, more often than not, heterogeneous. The Ottoman Empire had such a multiethnic, heterogeneous complexion that was not only inimical to, but was in conflict with its theocratic ethos and the collateral state organization embodying that ethos. The troubles that consequently arose and beset the empire were particularly compounded by a special feature of Ottoman theocracy, namely, Islam. Islam and its canon laws were not merely different from the belief systems of the non-

Muslim ethnic groups. Rather they were antithetical, despite repeated professions to the contrary. At the strictly theological and doctrinal level, these belief systems were indeed anathema to Islam and to the Ottoman protagonists of Islam. The coexistence within a single state system of such contrary religious blocs was bound to generate cleavages in the respective communities. In other words, the Ottoman social system from its very inception was pregnant with a multitude of vexing and troublesome problems. In due time, these problems crystallized into acute nationality conflicts which proved themselves as the Achilles' heel of the Ottoman Empire. The Turko-Armenian conflict was an integral part of this syndrome of nationality conflicts.

But conflicts between national groupings need not lead to a resolve by one of the parties to destroy the other. Even after undergoing a process of intensification, a conflict of this type can be amenable to a settlement through either mutual accommodation or, in the absence of it, to a resolution by one of the parties' recourse to lethal violence, the scale of which need not be massive and genocidal. The genocidal outcome of the Turko-Armenian conflict was largely expressive of the ominously portentous manner in which the Ottoman-Turkish authorities defined, interpreted, and reacted to that conflict. Here, the repressive and sanguinary aspects of Ottoman culture came repeatedly into play. Broadly speaking, culture is a frame of mind which is more or less taken for granted by the people sharing in the ways of life of a society identified with a given culture. The dominant element in Ottoman political culture was a spirit of belligerence that in principle could not tolerate conflict with subordinate subject minorities. That belligerence issued from a confluence in that culture of the forces of Islamic dogmas and the ballast of martial traditions. Being somehow interdependent, these twin factors mutually reinforced each other throughout the military campaigns the Ottoman imperial armies waged and in the process conquered and subjugated a host of non-Muslim nationalities. The rudiments of the Turko-Armenian conflict can be traced to this dual phenomenon of conquest and subjugation. And it was the condition of this very phenomenon that provided the mechanism through which the Ottoman Turks evinced zero tolerance to conflict with the Armenians. Rejecting all other options, the Turks decided to escalate and radicalize the conflict with the Armenians with a view to eventually resolving it through organized mass murder.

As stated above, the Turko-Armenian conflict was part of a larger conflict pitting the Ottoman Turks against a host of other subject nationalities. The question arises as to why only the Turko-Armenian conflict ended with genocide. A full answer will have to consider several factors foremost among which are geography, demography, and the politics of power relations. These are factors which functioned as critical constraints severely handicapping the Armenians, constraints which were inoperative, or the least operative, in the case of the other non-Muslim nationalities. These constrains not only impeded the struggle of the Armenians to end their afflictions in the provinces but even facilitated the flow of events through which the afflictions progressively worsened only to end in genocide. Unlike nearly all other nationalities, the Armenians, despite their dispersal elsewhere in the Ottoman Empire, continued to maintain in the eastern parts of the empire compact clusters of indigenous populations with a relatively high degree of density. This fact was implicitly acknowledged by the six Great Powers when they inserted in Article 61 of the Berlin Treaty of 1878 the words "the provinces inhabited by the Armenians." In fact in the ratified March 1878 San Stefano Treaty which, the Berlin Treaty later supplanted, these provinces were explicitly described as "Armenia," despite the admitted numerical superiority of the combined populations of various Muslim groupings. In commenting on the demographic aspect of this problem, British historian and statesman James Bryce made the following observation:

> Of [Turkey's] inhabitants nearly two million are Armenian Christians. A possibly larger, but quite uncertain, number are Mohammedans, but as these Mohammedans belong to different races, speaking different tongues, and as nearly half of them are savage nomads, the Armenians constitute the most important element in the population. *They are more numerous than any single section of the Moslem inhabitants* [italics added].[1]

As to the "six provinces," the reference was, of course, to the provinces of Sivas, Diyarbekir, Harput, Erzurum, Bitlis, and Van; it was for the benefit of these provinces that the Powers were pursuing "Armenian Reforms," not only in 1894–96, but also in 1912–14. Ever since then, the Ottoman authorities, directed by Sultan Abdul Hamit, considered the Armenian populations of these provinces a major liability for Turkey. In fact, given the presumed affinity for Russia of the bulk of these populations, that liability was magnified in the eyes of many Ottoman rulers who became alarmed in consideration of the respective implications of the factors of geography, demography, and international politics.

As a result, there emerged, in the thinking of Young Turk leaders the magnified specter of a lurking, imperialist Russia, the historical nemesis of Turkey, and the ancillary prospect of the formation of a satellite Armenia in eastern Turkish territories. Moreover, the consequences of such a development were deemed by the Turks to be far more grave than all the territorial and related losses in the Balkans and elsewhere. In fact Abdul Hamit is reported to have declared metaphorically that the progressive shrinkage of the size of the empire elsewhere were mere amputations of the arms and legs of the body of the empire, adding that this may cripple but not end life. However, the sultan reportedly further added, that the loss of the eastern provinces would be tantamount to losing the body's digestive organs which would mean: death. In other words, the territorial implications of the pursuit of Armenian Reforms had alarmed the Turks to such a degree that they envisaged in these reforms a peril of existential magnitude.

This territorial aspect of the problem was further accentuated in the case of the Ittihadist Young Turks by the impetus of the aims of the pan-Turkish and pan-Turanist ideology. Having discarded all pretenses of multiethnic Ottomanism, the more omnipotent leaders of the Ittihad party, led by their high priest of ideology, Ziya Gökalp, openly expressed their desiderata for the dreamland of Turan. The road to that dreamland passed, however, through adversarial Armenia. The need to surmount and obliterate once and for all this geographic-territorial obstacle served as an ancillary animus in the Ittihadist proneness to opt for genocide against the Armenians.

This represents a juncture of developments at which demography begins to assume a critical significance. Armenian reforms were anathema as far as vital Turkish national interests were concerned and, therefore, draconian measures were needed to render them inapplicable. The adoption of these measures was carried out by stages. The initial stage, perhaps the most consequential, involved the procedures of artful redistricting through which Armenians were steadily and methodically reduced to numerical minorities in all of the newly recast six provinces. Moreover, through such gerrymandering the contiguity of large Armenian population clusters was disrupted, thereby creating separated and disconnected Armenian population blocs. The second stage is associated with the handling of the hundreds of thousands of *muhacirs*, the Muslim migrants and refugees from the Russian Caucasus and the Balkans primarily, large masses of whom were settled in and around areas densely populated by Armenians. The third stage pertained to the eras of the massacres which in part were the result of the failure of the above-mentioned two other undertakings. These could not stem the tide of the Armenian reform movement which at the time of the initiation of the massacres had gained a new impetus and even a transformation through the advent of the Armenian revolutionary movement; in fact the latter eventually supplanted the former.

The successful execution of the massacres proceeded without any significant resistance on the part of the victim population and without the slightest attempt at intervention on the part of the Powers. It demonstrated the decisive importance of the factor of power relations or, more precisely, of the substantial disparity of power relations, in the final consummation of the Turko-Armenian conflict. That disparity issued more than anything else from (1) the preordained vulnerability of the Armenians, whose inferior sociopolitical status within the Ottoman state system made them quite impotent vis-à-vis the dominant Turks, and (2) the associated twin vulnerability that resulted from the postures of the Powers whose anticipated inaction provided the warrant for the emergence of that vulnerability; the reference is to the absence of external deterrence, or the absence of a credible threat of counteractive, retaliatory measures.

Thus, not only the direction and escalation but, even more important, the outcome of the Turko-Armenian conflict is seen here being contingent on the exertions of more than just the two factors of theocracy and demography. Indeed, even more relevant in terms of contingency is the factor of power relations favoring the dominant group with almost a monopolistic access to the resources of power in the body politic. The significance of this factor of power was dramatically demonstrated in the episode of the 1895–96 Zeitoun insurrection. Unlike the rest of their compatriots in the Ottoman Empire, the Armenian highlanders of Zeitoun were armed, they knew how to utilize the advantages of their natural fortress, and consequently were able to inflict a series of defeats on a numerically much superior Turkish army unit, the Fifth Army Corps, reinforced by their large appendage of irregulars. The Zeitounlis not only prevented the anticipated massacre of the inhabitants of Zeitoun but are believed to have forestalled similar massacre at nearby Adana—at a time when the rest of the provincial Armenian population was engulfed in the inferno of the 1894–96 Abdul Hamit era massacres. Something similar happened in the April-May 1915 defensive uprising of Van. In both cases the combative Armenians were afforded the opportunity to remain, temporality at least, victorious—through the intercession (in Zeitoun) and intervention (in Van) of the Powers. In the latter case it was the Russians who intervened alone as part of their military campaign against the Turkish Third Army that earlier had launched an abortive offensive in the area. In both cases large clusters of Armenian populations were protected from the destructive clutches of the Turkish civilian and military assault groups, thereby averting the genocidal massacres to which most of the rest of the targeted unarmed Armenian population fell victim.

Given the decisive role Armenian vulnerability, internal as well as external, played in facilitating the conception, organization and implementation of the Armenian genocide, it may be appropriate to conclude this study with this major assertion: in genocidal decision making and the allied act of perpetration, power relations are of critical import; the greater the disparity in the power positions of the contestant groups, the greater the chances of resort to optimum violence by the significantly more powerful group. Ultimately, therefore, one may argue that the arch determinant in the enactment of genocide is the factor of critically disparate power relations separating the substantially more powerful group from the substantially weak and vulnerable target group. At issue here is an intense conflict in the escalation of which the internal vulnerability of the targeted victim-group is gravely amplified by the more or less transparent absence of any credible external deterrence aimed at the potential perpetrator-group.

Note

1. James Bryce, "The Future of Asiatic Turkey," *Fortnightly Review*, vol. 138, New Series (1 June 1878), p. 931.

Appendix
The Questionable Features of the
Ottoman Calculus of the Demography
of the Armenians

The issue of the numerical strength or weakness of the Ottoman Armenian population in relation to the dominant Turks and Muslims of the empire in several respects was central to the unfolding of the Turko-Armenian conflict. As the Armenian reform movement developed, its success to a large extent hinged on the outcome of the statistical numbers game the Ottoman authorities launched with a view to undermining, and ultimately invalidating, the rationale of the scheme of "Armenian Reforms." That scheme acquired particular significance for the Ottoman Turks when the six Great Powers in July 1878, through Article 61 of the Berlin Treaty, sought to impel the former to restructure its administration in those provinces which were "inhabited by the Armenians." Through this stipulation the Turks had incurred an international obligation and the Armenians had acquired an international right. The Turko-Armenian conflict essentially reflected the tension existing between these two conditions. The intensification of that conflict is intimately connected with the Turkish effort to oppose the Armenian reform scheme with an opposing scheme to nullify the need for Armenian reforms by resort to a variety of preemptive measures. Before initiating a series of massacres as a last resort, the Ottoman authorities undertook measures to manipulate the arrangement of the boundaries of the provinces containing large clusters of Armenian populations with a view to altering the respective demographic landscape. The details of this undertaking have been provided in chapter 12, "The Expedient of Redistricting and Rearranging the Provincial Boundaries." This Appendix expands the framework of that discussion by providing additional details. At the same time it seeks to spotlight some of the flaws of the methodology on the basis of which those statistical computations, which underlie the demographic landscape the authorities have purposively recast, are presently being vouchsafed and defended by certain demographers.

Some Examples of Mishandling
of Armenian Population Statistics

There are two aspects to the disputes surrounding the issue of the numerical strength or weakness of Ottoman Armenians. Being quite germane to the developmental phases of the Turko-Armenian conflict they may be addressed here briefly. In their attempt to bolster the credibility of official Ottoman-Turkish statistics on population figures, many demographers continue to dismiss Armenian, especially Armenian patriarchate, figures as inflated and unreliable. Justin McCarthy, of whom later, is but one of them. In his detailed monograph on this subject Kemal Karpat does not hesitate to issue blanket deprecations in this respect. According to him, British military consuls in the provinces "regularly challenged" the figures submitted by the Armenian patriarch of whom these consuls were "constantly critical."[1] The patriarch, as many others, including a host of Ottoman officials, certainly did err in a number of cases and the patriarch was indeed challenged on occasion by these consuls whose standards were such as to level that challenge even more acutely against Ottoman official figures. But statements in statistical demography, in order to have any value, must hinge on optimum accuracy. The figures of the patriarch were not only not challenged "regularly" but were at times even credited with reliability by these consuls functioning in the period covered by Karpat. In his 11 July 1881 report to British Ambassador Dufferin, for example, Major Henry Trotter, "Consul of Turkish Armenia and Kurdistan," whom Karpat describes as a valuable expert "trained in statistics and cartography," declared the patriarch's statistical Tables on the Armenian populations of Erzurum, Bitlis, Van, and Harput to be reliable, or to use his words, "not far from the truth."

> I have carefully examined the papers recently submitted by the Patriarch, and have not found anything therein to make me alter my opinion as to the relative number of Christians and Moslems. The Tables show signs of having been carefully got up, and are probably nearer the truth than any statistics hitherto supplied from the Patriarchate; in fact, the numbers given for the purely Armenian population are more detailed and probably more correct than any we have.[2]

Moreover, Karpat selectively uses one portion of Trotter's report to prove that "the official lists" of Ottoman authorities in the districts of

Harput, Erzurum, and Bayburt "to be comparatively accurate."[3] However, Trotter at the end of the same report complained that "the Christian element in Diyarbekir and Harput, especially in the latter, is considerably underestimated in the official estimate."[4] These estimates "are the official figures that have been supplied by the local authorities...with the sanction of the Turkish authorities."[5] Karpat in the same work places the onus for "the dishonest use of population statistics" and "the manipulation of population statistics for political purposes" at the doorsteps of "various ethnic and religious groups" and he implies that conversely the Ottoman-Turkish authorities are exempt from any such onus.[6]

Given the dominant role Karpat continues to play in contemporary Turkish historiography in general and Ottoman-Turkish demography in particular, this stance deserves some scrutiny. It might be less convincing to juxtapose and contrast his charge of dishonesty with the views of a host of European experts; they are often treated as natural suspects in terms of anti-Turkish bias. Instead, reference may be made to a Turkish author whose credentials can be gauged by the history of his distinguished career in the administration of the Ottoman state—in both the Hamidian and Ittihadist regimes. Even an ardent Turkish nationalist and popular chronicler Cemal Kutay described this author's work, which is being referenced here, as "an earnest and unbiased source" (*ciddi ve tarafsız kaynak*).[7] In his analysis of the various aspects of the Armenian Question and the attendant Turko-Armenian conflict, author Hüseyin Kâzım Kadri explicitly states that there was deliberate dishonesty in compiling official Armenian population figures.[8] Here are some of his pertinent statements:

> During the reign of Abdul Hamit we lowered the population figures of the Armenians (*nüfusunu azalttık*)[9].... By the order of Abdul Hamit the number of the Armenians deliberately had been put in low figures.[10]

In fact, on this score Abdul Hamit is on record for denouncing his own census officials. In an undated memorandum, believed to have been prepared in the spring of 1895 and directed to then Grand Vizier Ahmed Cevad, the sultan rejected the 900,000 figure as "very exaggerated" when told that the figure represented the number of Armenians residing in the Ottoman Empire.[11] (Since the topic explored by the sultan involved the Ottoman Armenians in general, rather than those of a specific region of the empire, it is to be inferred that the 900,000 figure submitted to the sultan represented the Turkish version of the totality of the Ottoman Armenian population of the time). Following this tradition of depicting the Armenians as a numerically quite inferior minority, Cevdet Küçük, another contemporary Turkish author, came up with a new yardstick to measure the size of the Armenian population of the empire. The fashioning and introduction of that yardstick is traced to Sultan Abdul Hamit who "pointed out that even in the most densely populated areas the Armenians constituted only 3 percent of the total population." Accordingly, the sultan allegedly maintained that in the Ottoman Empire "the total Armenian population never exceeded 450,000."[12] The evidence is clear and revealing. The supreme and autocratic ruler of Turkey imperiously involved himself in statistics and demography, thereby exerting irresistible pressure and influencing the outcomes sought.

The following case illustrates the point. Chronicling the history of Muş (which later was made part of the newly created Bitlis province), an Armenian author relates an occurrence of falsification through a deliberate undercutting of minority statistics. It appears that the local Turkish government prevailed upon an Armenian member of that local government to lower the number of Armenians in the area by more than 100,000. By the same token, the Armenian was prevailed upon to raise the number of Muslims by about 45 percent. The whole idea was to avoid complications with the central authorities who insisted on low figures for the Armenians and by the same token high figures for the Muslims. This was in connection with the 1880 census of Patriarch Nercess, who upon learning of the willful misrepresentation issued a malediction that was solemnly read in church and which resulted in the Armenian and his family being ostracized for a number of years by the Armenian community.[13]

The work of Justin McCarthy is replete with similar errors and fallacies and which presently is being treated in detail for a projected separate essay. When dealing with this specific case of Muş, for example, without providing specific data, he declared the statistics on Muş to be "fairly accurate," as far as the district's Armenian population was concerned, and that "Armenian and Ottoman population figures" for the entire vilayet "differed less than for other provinces." The question may be posed: how accurate, and therefore, reliable is McCarthy himself when he makes certain assertions and then offers his conclusions in this area of inquiry? The following account involving a strictly methodological procedure is but one example of the problematic character of these twin issues of accuracy and reliability. In analyzing the Armenian population province by province McCarthy uses as a principal yardstick the 1330 *hicri*, i.e., 1911–12, Ottoman statistical data which were published in *mali* (fiscal year) 1330, or 1913–14. "The year was chosen because [among other reasons] the 1330 [data] was the best...." Moreover, McCarthy inaccurately claims that "Most of the population records on eastern Anatolia listed in the 1330 [statistics] were collected in 1330 *hicri* year, [i.e.,] 1911–12."[14] This assertion is flatly contradicted by several sources. One of them is Meir Zamir who states that "the last census...had taken place in 1905." (As McCarthy rightly points out the Ottoman censuses essentially involved a reliance on registration records.) The Ottoman authorities modified each year the data of the 1905 census based on reports sent every three months to the Census Department in Istanbul. "The Census Department continually updated its statistics in accordance with the new figures and at the end of each year new tables were prepared." This "most comprehensive" census of 1905 (1321 *mali* or fiscal year) was the last of its kind and all other subsequent compilations were based on it and not "on an overall survey."[15] This fact is officially confirmed by Refet, the director of the General Bureau of the Registrar in the Ottoman capital. In a signed statement, attached to the official statistical Tables for 1914, which were published on 14 April 1919, Refet explicitly states that all Ottoman population statistics since 1905 are exclusively based on 1905 census data—with annual modifications (*la statistique de l'état de population de l'Empire Ottoman est dressée à la fin de chaque année*).[16] In the statement cited above, there is not even a hint by McCarthy that the 1905 census data formed the common and uniform basis of all subsequent statistical data which were but modifications and adjustments of that of 1905. In his Appendix 2 McCarthy indicates that he has seen the original Ottoman-Turkish version of the above-mentioned French language official statistical tables in the Istanbul Archeological Museum Library. He either didn't read and study it, or didn't do so carefully. Refet, the director of the General Bureau of the Registrar (*Sicili Nüfus Idarei Umumiyesi Müdüriyeti*) of the Interior Ministry, in the preface rather meticulously sets forth the legal and statistical conditions under which "the census" (*récensement*) in question and subsequent "censuses" had been compiled.[17]

In his overall assessment Karpat maintains that "Ottoman official statistics issued after 1881/82 had so improved in consistency and reliability that the British came to rely on them and they were accepted by most of the foreigners with only minor reservations." This statement is made in order to contrast it with "the subjective and utterly false information concerning the Armenian population [that was used] by various 'experts.'"[18] A decade later, the very same British authorities felt constrained, however, to complain that the official Ottoman statistics, purporting to portray the Proportional Population of Moslems and Christians in the Six Anatolian Provinces, were in disagreement with those "in the possession of this Embassy." In fact British Ambassador Philip Currie was complaining to his prime minister, the Marquis of Salisbury, that "considerable discrepancies exist between the two." Currie was referring to the 1890 statistical tables prepared by Britain's Erzurum consul, Clifford Lloyd, whose tables were juxtaposed and compared with those prepared by Ottoman authorities.[19] Moreover, fifteen years later, in 1905, the Ottoman authorities produced yet another set of tables, which were mentioned above and which once more were found to be in disagreement with those prepared by the Geographical Section of the Foreign Office. Adjusted by 1914, but produced only in 1919, the Ottoman statistics were compared with a new set of data including Turkish data for 1917. The actual basis for this comparison, however, was a report on "Population of Asiatic Turkey at the Outbreak of the War" prepared by an American professor, D. Magie; Magie was a member of the American delegation to the Peace Conference in Paris. The British considered him as "strictly impartial" and, therefore, relied mainly on his figures. After evaluating the results of this comparison the above-mentioned author Zamir concluded that "the Ottoman statistics from 1914 [represented] a continuous understatement of the non-Moslem population throughout the Empire." He discerned a significant "disparity" for the Armenians in the eastern provinces, especially for "the provinces of Van, Bitlis, Mamuretal-Aziz (Harput), Diyarbekir, Erzurum, and the independent district of Maraş, where the British figures are 62 percent higher (847,000) compared with 523, 065." Even though he makes allowance for the possibility that "many non-Moslems avoided registration for fear of conscription and taxation" thus somewhat contributing to the deficiency, Zamir nevertheless allows that "The understatement of the non-Moslem figures appears to be intentional."[20]

Furthermore, as far as Karpat is concerned, all the intricate patterns of redistricting in the provinces of eastern Turkey had only one purpose, namely, "more efficient administration." As to the losses the Armenian population incurred up to 1914. "A sizeable portion had either migrated to Russia or had been detached from the Ottoman state."[21] The 1894–96 Abdul Hamit era massacres and the 1909 twin Adana massacres entailing large-scale decimations and dislocations in the major Armenian population centers are treated as nonexistent occurrences and, therefore, irrelevant to any discussion on significant changes in the size of the Ottoman Armenian population, i.e., a significant reduction of that size through empire-wide massacres.[22] A more or less similar stance is evinced in McCarthy's treatment of the Armenian losses sustained in the World War I genocide. As far as he is concerned, the victims simply "died or migrated."[23]

The Methodological Fallacy of Confounding All Ottoman Muslims with the Turks and Using Religion as a Statistical Yardstick

From its very inception the Turko-Armenian conflict was essentially a conflict between the Armenians and the Turks. The conflict with the Kurds, Circassians, Lazes, and any other ethnic group, subsumed under the category of Muslims, was but a by-product of that principal and quintessential conflict. In fact it may even be argued that in the various stages of the growth, intensification, and consummation of that conflict elements of these ethnic groups in appreciable numbers were co-opted by Ottoman-Turkish authorities to serve as allies and surrogates, often in the role of functionally efficient proxies, that is, killer bands in search of loot and spoils. In this sense one is prompted to wonder as to the probable difference in the course and outcome of the Turko-Armenian conflict absent the co-opted assistance of these support groups. The importance of demography emerges here as a critical factor in assessing the problem posed by this question. What could have the Turks done to solve the so-called Armenian Question in their own way without the active help of these confederate groups? The question implies the existence of a definable population entity distinct from all these other confederate groups, namely, so called Turks proper. In terms of ethnography, if not a vaguely perceived notion of race, such an entity would be most difficult, if not impossible, to discern. The reasons lie in the circumstances in which the Turkish nation originated and subsequently underwent formative stages that eventually produced a most composite ethnic entity broadly described as Turks.

Almost two centuries before the Ottoman tribal leader Ertuğrul in the thirteenth century ushered in the rudimentary conditions for the emergence of an Ottoman nationhood, another branch of Central Asian Turkic peoples, the Seljuks, had already built an empire in Anatolia.

The ensuing episodes of tribal comingling through gradual infiltration of the northwestern regions of Anatolia by the Osmanlıs, who in the process supplanted the rulers of the disintegrating Seljuk empires, hastened the inevitable process of coalescence of several branches of the Turks. Indigenous Turkish peasantry, nomadic tribes drifting in the region, including Mongols, and later Tatars, joined to produce the embryo of an evolving Turkic nation. Actually, the name Turk was first introduced by the Chinese in the sixth century to describe a nomadic people who had founded a vast empire extending from Mongolia to the Black Sea. Moreover, both ethnic groups, the Seljuks and the Ottomans (*Osmanlıs*), belonged to the larger Turkic Oghuz confederation of Mongolian lineage. In any event, this amalgam of ethnic Turks formed the nucleus of an ethnic entity that over the centuries continued to speak Turkish with some dialect-variations and persisted to function as the dominant element in the formation and career of a multiethnic Ottoman Empire. The rise of that empire was primarily due to a proclivity among the leaders of the emerging nation-state for militarism and a companion propensity for officialdom.

As the empire expanded through conquest, however, and with it the overall size of the empire's population grew incrementally, this constitutive Turkish element progressively became inferior in numbers. The result was the incidence of a typical sociological phenomenon. A numerically inferior group, a minority, functioned as a dominant group vis-à-vis a host of subsidiary ethnic groups whose combined populations represented an overwhelming majority in numbers. British sources estimate that at the outbreak of the Young Turk Ittihadist revolution in 1908 the size of this core Turkish element ranged between 6 and 8 million people[24] controlling a population whose size was estimated to have ranged between 25 and 30 million people. On the other hand, Tekin Alp, the pro-Ittihadist exponent of modern Turkish nationalism, maintained in an article on "Thoughts on the Nature and Plan of a Greater Turkey" that the Turks proper constituted only "a tenth of the whole Turkish nation."[25] One of the British military consuls who were sent to Turkey in the aftermath of the 1878 Berlin Treaty, whose Article 61 stipulated effective reforms in eastern Turkey, was Colonel C.W. Wilson; he was appointed "consul general in Anatolia." According to Abidin Paşa, a veteran Ottoman statesman, who served as governor-general in the several provinces of the empire, was granted the title of vizier, and in 1879 became foreign minister, the colonel was "truth personified, absolutely impartial, and thoroughly trusted by the Turks."[26] In a 16

June 1880 comprehensive memorandum, marked "Confidential" Wilson stated that in Anatolia "The *Turks Proper* are always numerically small, are chiefly found in the towns...form the greater portion of the official class."[27]

The ultimate value of all the statistical compilations and tables depicting the Armenians in eastern Turkey as a numerical minority must be assessed against the background of this paramount historical and demographic reality, particularly in view of the fact that the framework of analysis here is the Turko-Armenian conflict. In that conflict, as underscored above, the Armenians were pitted primarily against the Turks and not against the other elements who were Muslims but were not necessarily Turks. The issues of religion and creed were incidental rather than central to that conflict. And yet with a degree of factitiousness that defies simple logic, Ottoman authorities continuously used religion as a yardstick to gather and quantify population data through which the Armenians were almost uniformly depicted as numerical minorities in their ancestral territories. The complex picture of a highly heterogeneous society was reduced to the simple equation of "Muslims versus non-Muslims." Everyone, but above all the Ottoman authorities, knew that the Armenian *millet* was only in part a religious community, despite the nominal denotations of the term. Its social and cultural institutions transcended the boundaries of religion, imparting to that community a distinct ethnic identity that should not have been confounded with or reduced to mere religious belongingness. In Ottoman statistics that standard of ethnicity was completely overlooked and ignored as the Armenians were counterposed to the Muslims as an encompassing general category, thereby asserting the paramountcy of the principles of religion and creed. However difficult it might have been, the strict canons of demography required that in the statistical compilations the Armenians be juxtaposed and numerically compared with those population groups that might be identified as Turks, i.e., the core and dominant elements in the multiethnic landscape of the empire. This did not happen because it was neither practical nor profitable for the dominant Turks, and the reliance on a disparity of criteria of counting, and computation entailed results which were tantamount to "comparing apples and oranges."

The extent of this disparity, existing at the time when the disputes on numbers arose, may be gauged by focusing on the array of ethnic groupings the above-mentioned Colonel Wilson depicts and describes as far as his jurisdiction in Anatolia was concerned: they are portrayed as diverse people of distinct stocks, and as such are differentiated from "the Turks proper." When initiating the modern Republic of Turkey, Mustafa Kemal (Atatürk), the founder of that republic, was quite cognizant of the fact that in the Turkey that he was envisaging "the Muslim elements did not constitute a single nation only (*yalnız bir cins millet*)." One had to reckon with "Kurds, Circassians, Lazes." He stressed that Turkey comprised "different Muslim elements" (*muhteif anasırı islamiyeden mürekkeptir*).[28] A contemporary study, on the other hand, lists forty-seven such ethnic groups in Turkey today.[29] Moreover, the disparity at issue here has a dual character. On the one hand it concerns the yardstick of numbers, involving a juxtaposition of the population figures of Muslims (only religion) versus Armenians (religion *and* nationality). On the other hand, and perhaps equally important, the disparity concerns the expedient of subsuming under the uniform category of Muslims all these ethnically heterogeneous rather than homogenous Muslim groupings. Thus, there is a major methodological fallacy on both accounts of demographic statistics, i.e., quantitatively and qualitatively. This is particularly the case with the Kurds about whom it is said that they "are only Muslims skin-deep."[30] In commenting on this issue Colonel Wilson in his above-cited memorandum reported as follows:

> The Shiite Kurds have on more than one occasion complained to me of the unjust manner in which they are treated by the Turkish officials, and have even expressed a wish to become Christians...[31]

The persistence of this type of discordant heterogeneity within modern Turkey is abundantly evinced in several pieces of scholarly output.[32] In fact the discords have transformed themselves into acute conflicts that have plagued the successive regimes of the Ottoman Empire and of the Turkish Republic.[33] These conflicts have presently assumed such an intense character[34] that the method of forcible and massive dislocations, which led to the destruction of the Ottoman Armenian population, is being applied, with comparable severity, against large segments of the Kurdish population in eastern Turkey.[35] It is as if the Turko-Armenian conflict of the past at many levels has been supplanted by the Turko-Kurdish conflict of the present, raising the specter of Turkish initiatives aiming at a kind of resolution that is akin to that which was applied to the Armenians.

It is clear that in the overall picture of demography the Armenians are seen being reduced in stages to a numerical minority in their own ancestral lands—especially against the combined population of Muslim Turks and Kurds. It is equally clear that this demographic change was engineered by the empire's central authorities as it was brought about through the latter's deliberate initiatives involving gerrymandering and a continuous influx of Muslim settlers from several parts of the Caucasus and the Transcaucasus as well as from the Balkan peninsula. Even Henry Finnis Blosse Lynch, one of the most careful researchers and versatile nineteenth-century British geographer-ethnographers,[36] recognized the particular impact of the factor of gerrymandering when he wrote: "in estimating the population of the Armenian provinces, vast outlying districts were included...."[37]

The progressive and sustained character of the process of redistricting in the provinces of eastern Turkey is chronologically described in a recent study of the ethnography of the Armenians of Turkey as it existed prior to the genocide by Raymond Kevorkian and Paul Paboudjian.[38] The long time political expert on nationality issues of the British Embassy at Istanbul, M. Fitzmaurice, who, in a private letter to W.G. Tyrell, Foreign Minister E. Grey's secretary, had referred to the "anti-Christian gerrymandering" of previous Ottoman governments[39] stated in a 12 August 1913 memorandum prepared for his superiors in the Foreign Office, that:

> The Armenian provinces were in 1878 designedly broken up into exceptionally small units to enable the Ottoman Government to deal more effectually with the Armenian population by process of elimination.[40]

André Mandelstam, an expert in international law and at the same time an expert regarding the problems associated with the Turko-Armenian conflict, explained that the Ittihadist Young Turks tried the same stratagem during the 1912–13 negotiations on a new Armenian Reform Act, that was finally agreed upon and signed by Turkey and the Powers on 8 February 1914. He mentions Turkey's promulgation of a new Turkish law, through which the manner of the distribution of the Armenian population of the two projected new provincial sectors was so arranged as to create in both sectors a Muslim majority.[41] Counterposed to these Ottoman-Turkish efforts was the remedy the six Powers had proposed in their 8 September 1880 Collective Note. In it these Powers had proposed that in rearranging the demography and administrative set-up of the provinces "inhabited by the Armenians," the principle of "optimum homogeneity of the ethnic elements should be adhered to (*à réunir le plus d'elements homogènes possible*). An effort should be made to group the Armenians together" (...*devrait tendre à grouper les Arméniens*).[42] Despite these aggregate governmental measures, which gained impetus through the negative impact Article 61 of the 1878 Berlin Treaty had upon Ottoman-Turkish authorities, in most regions of historical Armenia the Armenians constituted a clear majority. Indeed, when juxtaposed and compared with those population segments that were neither Kurds, nor Circassians, could not be identified with any other ethnic grouping and were recognized as Turks proper, the Armenians in most areas had the advantage of numerical superiority. Major Henry Trotter who, according to Karpat, was "apparently trained in statistics and cartography"[43] and as such deserved credence, in 1881 declared that "In the provinces of Erzurum, Van and Bitlis...the Armenians...considerably outnumber the Turks...."[44] Almost fifteen years later Lynch argued that there were certain districts in these provinces in which "the Armenians were in a majority" against the combined population of all Muslims[45]—despite all the measures of redistricting and Muslim refugee resettlement in these areas.[46] Furthermore, Lynch injects a caveat about the statistical meaning of the category of "Muslim," suggesting that multitudes of Christians who voluntarily or forcibly converted to Islam retained their loyalty to their ethnic origin. Here is his observation on this point:

> To express these results in general language, we may say that the seat of the Turkish population is the country on the north of Erzerum, while the Kurds inhabit the more southerly districts of the tableland, extending to the southern peripheral mountains. But what is the meaning of the name Turkish which has been used to distinguish the one from the other element? We must certainly guard ourselves from the danger of attributing to a convenient political designation an ethnological sense. We are justified in declaring that the Mussulman inhabitants of the northern districts of the Government of Erzerum are not of Kurdish origin; on the other hand, the ground is less tenable if we suppose that they belong to the Turkish race. How large an admixture of Turkish blood may flow within their veins, is a question which it is impossible to determine; it was rather the fertile country on the west of the Euphrates that presented the most attractive settling ground to the invading hordes of Turks. I am given to believe that a considerable number derive from the widely spread Georgian family; but that family has here mixed with other race elements, of which the Turkish is one. In what pertains to national solidarity, in the possession of common interests and common sentiments, these Mussulman inhabitants of the northern districts may justly be classed as Turks. But even this statement is subject to exception and cannot be universally applied. Just as in the northern zone of peripheral mountains there still exist whole districts of which the inhabitants have adopted the Mohammedan religion, but retain their essential affinity to the Greek race to which they belong, so within the statistical area of the table and among the ranks of the Mussulmans may be found considerable aggregates of people who, although of Armenian origin, profess the dominant creed. In the northern province an important instance of this change in

religion rather than in nationality is found in the district of Tortum between Erzerum and the town of Olti; the Mussulman inhabitants of that district are said to be the descendants of the ancient Armenian families who are known to have lived there within historical times.[47]

A similar assessment is made by the French author S. Zarzecki in his analysis of the Armeno-Kurdish question. As he relates:

When the Kurds converted to Islam, many Armenian mountaineers followed their example, embraced Muhammed's faith and by comingling with the Kurds augmented their numbers. One may assume that Armenian blood flows in the veins of a great number these fierce (*farouches*) Kurds who inflicted upon the Armenians such terrible sufferings in the last twenty years of Abdut Hamit's reign. When one inquires into their origin, the Kurds themselves are quite embarrassed and give evasive answers.[48]

Summary and Conclusion

As has been expounded in chapter 12, three key factors configure in the evolution of the Turko-Armenian conflict, namely, theocracy, power relations, and demography. Any analysis of one of these factors must, therefore, take into account the exertions of the other two. In assessing the significance of demography, both theocracy and power relations are seen as co-determinants in the origin, direction, and outcome of that conflict. Theocracy not only set the stage for the emergence of the rudiments of the Turko-Armenian conflict by imposing a fixed system of inequities that unalterably favored the Muslims, but also predetermined the outcome of all statistical computations through a system in which all Muslims of the empire were lumped together as a single, unified population category. The contemporary phases of the emergent Turko-Kurdish conflict attest to the fundamental fallacy of this method of computing. That fallacy is even more patent historically when one considers the last stages of the disintegration of the Ottoman Empire when a host of Muslim population groups, e.g., Albanians, Lebanese (half of them Muslims), Syrians, Irakis, Saudis, Egyptians, Yemenis severed their ties to the Ottoman-Turks. These emancipatory enterprises demonstrated once more that religious categories are not always coterminous with ethnic-national categories and that the two should not, therefore, be confounded, especially in statistical compilations.

There is another level at which one may consider the extent of the linkage between theocracy and demography. Unlike many other Muslim nation-states the Ottoman system was ethnically and religiously heterogeneous to a very significant degree. The coexistence of Islam with such numerically large non-Muslim communities placed uncommon strains on Islam not only as a religious belief system but also as a decisive political force. The result was that one was not facing here simply a theocracy, not even simply an Islamic theocracy, but an Ottoman-Turkish brand of Islamic theocracy that stretched and strained all the bounds of militancy intrinsic to the many dogmas of Islam. As a result, there developed a belligerence vis-à-vis these non-Muslim nationalities that was as lethal as implacable. The Annual Report for Turkey 1908, prepared by the British Foreign Office, provides some explanation in this respect. After describing the problems associated with the acceptance of the principle of equality for non-Muslims by the Muslim population, the report offers a comment on the unusual identification with Islam by the Ottoman Turks:

> The idea of equality with Christians was abhorrent to them, and there were strong evidences in the provinces that these Moslem tendencies were coming to the fore...The stubborn and unyielding principle of the Moslem religion...is more fixed and unrelenting in Turkey than in any other Mahommedan [sic]country.[49]

Among a number of Turkish authors arguing along the same lines one particular author attributes this condition to "the propagation of a kind of Islamism that was unprecedented and that gripped the entire empire" (*Görülmemiş bir müslümanlık propagandası tüm imparatorluğu kaplamıştır*). He wrote this when discussing the oppression of the Armenians in that empire.[50]

The relationship of power to demography in the present context is no less significant. Even though the Turks were numerically a minority, they had an almost complete monopoly on power and the resources of power. Accordingly, they were able to reduce all other nationality groups to the status of a minority. In this constellation of a number of subordinate groups, being pitted against a superordinate group, the freedom for initiative and, when necessary, coercion, in the handling of dominant group-minority relations, primarily, if not exclusively, belonged to the latter. The interminable depredations in the distant, eastern provinces of the empire had not only created a pervasive atmosphere of general insecurity but also rampant poverty among many strata of the provincial Armenian population. The waves of internal and external migration were largely due to the inability and/or unwillingness of the central authorities to protect the Armenian citizens of the state. As if to compound this condition, religious dogma reinforced governmental authority in this instance in that the vulnerable Armenians were prohibited, by the proscriptions of the Koran, to carry arms to defend themselves in an environment where practically everybody else among the Muslims was armed to the teeth. Consequently, Armenians, hostage to their impotency through migration, suffered a major setback, demographically speaking. Their numbers attenuated in those provinces which were identified with "historic Armenia" in eastern Turkey. It needs to be emphasized here, nevertheless, that despite this dispersion the density of the residual Armenian population in some provinces in the east such as Van, Bitlis, Eruzurm, and Harput was significant enough to provide weight to Armenian efforts for basic reforms in these provinces which, as far as the Turks were concerned portended, of course, eventual autonomy.

To forestall such an eventuality, the Ottoman rulers, using their authority, as explained in detail in chapter 12, undertook the task of revamping the system of provincial boundaries by reshaping these provinces through redistricting. This process involved the redistribution in the newly arranged boundaries of provinces of both Armenian and Muslim populations in such a way that the number of the Armenians nearly everywhere was drastically reduced. Parallel to this undertaking, the same authorities encouraged the settlement in those areas of multitudes of Muslim refugees from the Caucasus and the Balkans. In brief, through sheer reliance on governmental authority and power the demographic landscape of the Armenians was recast to render Armenian clamors for reform meaningless—meaningless eventually was to become perilous for the Armenians.

The relationship between power and demography is most dramatically and consequentially illustrated by the resort of the Ottoman authorities to the ultimate weapon needed to alter with finality the landscape of the demography of the Armenians of the Ottoman Empire. The Armenian Reforms issue had become the kernel of the Armenian Question that was agitating, vexing, and unsettling the rulers of a decaying empire. Previous measures to deal with that issue proved to be only half-hearted measures as the Armenians, and to some extent the Powers, continued to press on. Even when drastically reduced, existing Armenian population clusters remained a taxing obstacle for the rulers of the Ottoman Empire. The transition from a drastic to a radical alteration meant the undertaking of a surgical operation whereby the problematic population size could be reduced to zero, or near zero. The massacres of the Abdul Hamit era were a test case, a crucible; violent and lethal means could be employed unhampered and with relative ease.

As the noted late Harvard historian William Langer concluded: "It was perfectly obvious that the Sultan was determined to end the Armenian question by exterminating the Armenians."[51] The success of the Sultan's determination in fact foreshadowed the much greater success of the Young Turk Ittihadists who brought the goal of zero population size to fruition through the enactment of genocide thereby intending to resolve with apparent finality the lingering Turko-Armenian conflict.

Notes

1. Kemal H. Karpat, *Ottoman Population 1830–1914: Demographic and Social Characteristics* (Madiscon, WI: University of Wisconsin Press, 1985) p. 52, right hand column; p. 53, left hand column.
2. FO 424/123, Reg. no. 583 p. 39. No. 27/1.
3. Karpat, *Ottoman Population* [n. 1], p. 54, left hand column.
4. 7 September 1880 report in FO 424/107, Reg. no. 37, p. 173.
5. Ibid., p. 174.
6. Karpat, *Ottoman Population* [n. 1], p. 4, right hand column.
7. Cemal Kutay, *Talât Paşanın Gurbet Hatıraları* (The Memoirs of Talât Paşa in Exile) vol. 1, 2d ed. (Istanbul: Private Publication, 1983), p. 280.
8. Hüseyin Kâzım Kadri, *Balkanlardan Hicaza: Imparatorluğun Tasfiyesi. 10 Temmuz Inkilâbı ve Netayici* (From the Balkans to Hejaz: The liquidation of the Empire. The July 10/23 Revolution and its outcome). (Istanbul: Pınar, 1992). The book originally appeared in Ottoman Turkish under the title: *10 Temmuz Inkilâbı ve Netayici. Türkiye Inkirazının Saikleri: Makedonya, Ermenistan ve Suriye Meseleleri* (The July 10/23 Revolution and its outcome. The reasons for the demise of Turkey: The problems of Macedonia, Armenia and Syria) (Istanbul: Islam and Askeri Publishers, 1920, or 1336 old style). Kadri at that time used his pen-name, Şeyh Muhsin Fani. Here is a brief biography of Kadri. During the Abdul Hamit regime he was a fiscal official. After the 1908 Ittihadist revolution he was a co-founder of the party's mouthpiece, the *Tanin* newspaper. Subsequently he occupied several official posts, including District governor of Samsun, governor-general of Aleppo province, prefect of Istanbul, twice governor-general of Saloniki, deputy in the Ottoman Parliament. After the war, during the Armistice he became vice president of the Ottoman Chamber of Deputies, deputy from Aydın and minister of commerce and agriculture. In 1921 he became minister of public works and was member of the sultan's government's Delegation which proceeded to Ankara to negotiate with the Kemalists. He knew English, French, Persian, Italian, and classic Greek. Himself the son of a governor-general, he attended an English school in Izmir and subsequently went to Europe to study agriculture. He enjoyed a general high esteem for his "honesty" (*dürüst*). Ibrahim A. Gövsa, *Türk Meşhurları Ansiklopedisi* (The Encylopedia of famous Turks) (n.p., 1946), p. 211, and "with a respectable administrative career...he has a reputation as an honest man." (FO 406/44, p. 201).
9. Kadri, *Balkanlardan* [n. 8], p. 126; in the original Ottoman version, p. 116.
10. *Ibid.*, p. 133; in the original Ottoman version, p. 123.
11. Sultan II. Abdülhamid Han, *Devlet ve Memleket Görüşlerim* (My Views on the State and the Country) A. Alaeddin Çetin and Ramazan Yıldız, eds. (Istanbul: Çığır, 1976), p. 158. See also Mehmet Hocaoğlu, *Abdülhamit Hanın Muhtıraları*

(The Memoranda of Abdülhamit) (Istanbul: Türkiyat, 1989), p. 55. Hocaoğlu, appears to be erring about the date of this memorandum which he reckons to be around 1896. But, if it was directed to Grand Vizier Cevad towards the end of his term it has to be spring or early summer 1895.

12. Cevdet Küçük, "The Armenian Population in Anatolia in the Nineteenth Century," trans. from Turkish by H. Umune, in *The Eastern Question: Imperialism and the Armenian Community* (Ankara: Institute for the Study of Turkish Culture, 1987), p. 79. The original source is A P. *Yıldız Tasnifi*, Kısım (file) 36, Evrak (dossier) 139/2, Zarf (envelope) 139, Karton 18.

13. 'Sarkis Pteyani Hushere' [The Memoirs of Sarkis Pteyan], in *Harazat Patmutiun Tarono* [The Authentic History of Taron] (Cairo: Sahag-Mesrob, 1962), p. 22. The Armenian governmental official in charge of the census was Garabed Potigian, whose original, real figures for the Armenians of Muş district (*sancak*) comprising the inhabotants of Muş Plain, Sassoun, and the counties of Muş, Bulanık, and Manazgerd districts were reported as 225,000, against 55,000 Turks; upon the insistence of his Turkish superiors the first figure was reduced to 105,000, the second raised to 95,000. British author H.F.G. Lynch relates a similar incident of bullying a terrified Armenian and forcing him to lower a real figure in order to portray the Armenian presence in Muş as puny as possible. "Pursuing our way, we meet an Armenian priest—a young, broad-shouldered, open-faced man. He seems inclined to speak, so we ask him how many churches there may be in Mush (Muş). He answers, seven; but the commissary had said four. A soldier addresses him in Kurdish; the poor fellow turns pale, and remarks that he was mistaken in saying seven; there cannot be more than four...Such are a few of our experiences during our short sojourn at Mush. We were not merely shadowed by the police, but prevented from enjoying any of the profit and pleasure which a traveller seeks in return for all his trouble and expense. To protest to the Mutesarrif would have been worse than useless; and the policy of the British Foreign Office is so weak in these countries that we lose the advantages of our Consular system...Terror, the most abject terror, was in the air. We drank it in from the very atmosphere about us—a consuming passion, like that of jealousy—a haunting, exhausting spectre, which sits like a blight upon life." H.F.B. Lynch, *Armenia. Travels and Studies*, vol. 2 (Beirut, Khayats, 1965), p. 171.

14. Justin McCarthy, *Muslims and Minorities: The Population of Ottoman Anatolia and the End of the Empire* (New York: New York University Press, 1983), pp. 65, 72.

15. Meir Zamir, "Population Statistics of the Ottoman Empire in 1914 and 1919," *Middle Eastern Studies* 17 (1981), p. 86.

16. *Tableaux indiquant le nombre des divers éléments de la population dans l'Empire Ottoman au 1er Mars 1330 (14 Mars 1914).* (Istanbul: Zellitch Brothers, 1919). Foreword by Refet. FO 371/4229/86552. May 1919.

17. McCarthy, *Muslims and Minorities* [n. 14], pp. 166, 186 n. 14, also pp. 40, 56. Karpat, however, duly recorded in a footnote the relationship of the 1905 (1321) data to subsequent statistical figures. *Ottoman Population* 1830–1914 [n. 1], p. 189, left hand column.

18. Ibid., p. 54, right hand column.

19. *British Blue Book Series.* Turkey no. 8 (1896). Doc. no. 109. 19 March 1986 report. enclosure no. 2, p. 99, no. 3, p. 100.

20. Zamir, "Population Statistics" [n. 16], pp. 86–7. In disputing such intentions on the part of Ottoman authorities, namely, to deliberately understate the non-Muslim population figures, McCarthy with reference to the Armenians attributes these "mistakes" to "errors of underregistration and inadequate system," to de-

clare rather categorically that "Ottoman statistics did not selectively discriminate against Armenians." McCarthy, *Muslims and Minorities* [n.14], p. 81. Discerning an intrusion of partisanship in McCarthy's demographic tracts on the Ottoman state , an Ottomanist recently took him to task for being "inconsistent in assigning blame." In his latest work on *Death and Exile: The Ethnic Cleansing of Ottoman Muslims, 1821–1922*, McCarthy again explained away the depredations of Armenians at the hands of Kurds and Circassians" by arguing that the Ottoman state's failure "to control these depredations...was due to lack of resources and authority." However, "when Russian, Bulgarian, and Greek soldiers declined to stop similar events against Muslim peasants, it was done deliberately." In a review of *Death and Exile* by Michael Robert Hickok, *MESA Bulletin* 30 (1996), p. 214.

21. Karpat, *Ottoman Population* [n. 1], p. 54, right hand column.

22. See Vahakn N. Dadrian, *The History of the Armenian Genocide. Ethnic Conflict from the Balkans to Anatolia to the Caucasus.* 4th ed. (Providence/Oxford: Berghahn, 1997), ch. 8, pp. 113–63.

23. McCarthy, *Muslims and Minorities* [n. 14], p. 139. For additional comments on the fallacies intruding in the work of McCarthy, see Vahakn N. Dadrian "Ottoman Archives and Denial of the Armenian Genocide" in *The Armenian Genocide: History, Politics, Ethics*, Richard G. Hovanissian, ed., (New York: St. Martin's Press, 1992), pp. 284, 291, 293–7.

24. *Turkey. Annual Report for 1910*, FO 424/250. April 1911, p. 4; The Ottoman Dominion (A "Round Table" pamphlet) (London: Fisher Unwin, 1917), pp. 14–5.

25. Quoted in *Turkey. A Past and a Future* (A "Round Table" pamphlet) (London: Hodder and Stoughton, 1917), p. 7. Speaking of the notion of "Turks proper," Cemal Paşa, a member of the Ittihadist triumvirate, in his memoirs clearly acknowledges the existence in the general Ottoman Muslim population of such Turks (*Türk unsuru*) which "constituted the foundation stone of the Ottoman Empire," adding, "I can never forget that I myself am such a Turk." Cemal Paşa, *Hatıralar* (Memoirs), Behçet Cemal, ed. (Istanbul: Çağdaş, 1977), p. 418.

26. British Ambassador George Goshen's 22 June 1880 and no. 70 report to Foreign Minister Earl Granville. FO 424/106, no. 246, p. 497.

27. Ibid., enclosure no. 15, pp. 499–500.

28. The quotations stem from his speeches of 24 April, 31 May, and 27 July. See Kâzım Öztürk, *Türkiye Cumhuriyeti Hükümetleri ve Programları* (The governments of the Turkish Republic and their programs), (Istanbul: AK Publications, 1968), pp. 127,130, 196.

29. Peter A. Andrews, "Catalogue of Ethnic Groups," *Ethnic Groups in the Republic of Turkey*, P.A. Andrews, ed. (Wiesbaden, Germany: L. Reichert, 1989), pp. 53–178.

30. *Turkey. A Past and a Future* (A "Round Table" pamphlet) (London: Hodder and Stoughton, 1917), p. 7.

31. See note 26, p. 501.

32. Servet Mutlu, "Ethnic Kurds in Turkey: A Demographic Study" *International Journal of Middle East Studies*, vol. 28, no. 4 (1996), pp. 517–41; Mark Levene, "Yesterday's Victims, Today's Perpetrators?: Considerations on Peoples and Territories of the Former Ottoman Empire" *Terrorism and Political Violence* 6, 4 (Winter 1994), pp. 446–8.

33. See Rafet Ballı "Türkiye," in *Kürt Dosyası*, Rafet Ballı, ed. (Istanbul: Cem Yayınevi, 1991). pp. 50, 82; Alpay Kabacalı, *Tarihimizde Kürtler ve Ayaklanmaları* (Istanbul: Cem Yayınevi, 1991); Celile Celil, 19. *Yüzyıl Osmanlı*

Imparatorluğu'nda Kürtler, (trans. from Russian) M. Demir (Ankara: Özge Yayınları, 1991); Vecihi Timuroğlu, *Dersim Tarihi* (Ankara: Yurt Kitap-Yayın, 1991); İsmet G. İmset, *PKK: Ayrılıkçi Şiddetin 20 Yılı (1973–1992)* (Ankara: Türkish Daily News Yayınları, 1993), p. 373; Michael Gunter, *The Kurds, in Turkey: A Political Dilemma* (Boulder, CO: Westview Press, 1990); Martin van Bruinessen, *Ağa Şeyh ve Devlet* (Ağa Şeyh and the State) (first published in Dutch in 1978) (Ankara: Özge, 1992).

34. *The Kurdish Nationalist Movement in the 1990s: Its Impact on Turkey and the Middle East*, Robert Olson, ed. (Lexington, KY: The University Press of Kentucky, 1996).

35. *Forced Evictions and Destruction of Villages in Dersim (Tunceli) and the Western Part of Bingöl, Turkish Kurdistan, September-November 1994* (Amsterdam: SNK, Netherlands Kurdistan Society, 1995).

36. He was educated at Eaton, and Trinity College at Cambridge University, as well as at Germany's Heidelberg University; he subsequently studied law. He presented a paper to the British Royal Geographical Society on his first (1893) trip to Armenia. In all his surveys he was helped by Dr. Oswald with whom he prepared a map on Turkish Armenia and adjacent territories.

37. Lynch, *Armenia* [n. 13], p. 411.

38. Raymond Kevorkian and Paul Paboudjian, *Les Armeniens dans l'Empire Ottoman à la vielle du Génocide* (Paris: Arhis, 1992), pp. 53–4.

39. *British Documents on the Origins of the War 1898–1914, vol. V: The Near East*, G.P. Gooch and H.V. Temperley, eds. (London; H.M. Stationary Office, 1928), no. 211, p. 271. The same view is expressed in E. Doumergue, *L'Arménie, les massacres et la question d'Orient* (Paris: Foi et Vie, 1916), p. 70.

40. FO 40170/19208/13/44 (*British Documents on the Origins of the War* [n. 39], vol. 21, no. 567).

41. André Mandelstam, *Das armenische Problem im Lichte des Völker-und Menschenrechts* (The Armenian problem in light of national and human rights), (Kiel: University of Kiel Institute for International Law, 1931), p. 125.

42. FO 195/2450, p. 14 of the report.

43. Karpat, *Ottoman Population 1830–1914* [n. 1], p. 53, left column.

44. British Ambassador Earl of Dufferin's 18 July 1881 and no. 583 report to Foreign Minister Earl Granville, enclosure no. 81. 11 July 1881, p. 38.

45. Lynch, *Armenia* [n. 13], p. 411.

46. "Die Verbreitung der Armenier in der asiatischen Türkei und in Transkaukasien" (The distribution of the Armenians in Asiatic Turkey and Transcaucasia), A. Supan, ed., (based on the compilations of Lieutenant General G.L. Selenoy and N. ven Seidlitz) in *Petermann's Geographische Mitteilungen* 42 (1896), pp. 1–10. See especially pp. 5–7. These figures on the numerical superiority of the Armenians in certain districts and counties of Van, Bitlis, and Diyarbekir provinces are confirmed in Major Trotter's 7 September 1880 report to British ambassador to Turkey, Sir W.E. Goschen. FO 424/107. No. 104/1. Registry no. 37, p. 174.

47. Lynch, *Armenia* [n. 13], p. 417.

48. S. Zarzecki, "La question Kurdo-arménienne." *Revue de Paris* (15 April 1914), p. 881.

49. *British Documents* [n. 39], p. 258.

50. Suat Parlar, *Osmanlı'dan Günümüze Gizli Devlet* (The Secret State: From Ottoman days to the present). (Istanbul: Spartakus Publications, 1996), p. 53. For Abdul Hamit's "reinterpretation and perversion of Ottoman Islamic political theory" see Kemal H. Karpat, "The Transformation of the Ottoman State, 1789–

1908" *International Journal of Middle East Studies*" 3 (1972), p. 271. For the view that "Up to its very last years, the Ottoman Empire used religion as a leverage to control state affairs through the medium of *fetvas*." See Yusuf H. Bayur, *Türk Inkilâbı Tarihi* (History of the Turkish Revolution) vol. 3, part 3 (Ankara: Türk Tarih Kurumu, 1957), p. 481. For a view akin to Parlar, the main reference here, see note 14 of chapter 1 describing England's Erzurum Consul J.G. Taylor's analysis of "the decadence" of the Ottoman Empire in the year 1868 which he attributes to the Ottomanization of Islam through "oppression, persecution and exclusion."

51. William L. Langer, *The Diplomacy of Imperialism 1890–1902*. vol. 1 (New York: A. Knopf, 1935), p. 203.

Bibliography

Primary Sources. State and National Archives. Official Documents

Austria

Austrian Foreign Ministry Archives (Vienna), *Politisches Archive (PA)*, Abteilung 37: Konsulate: 1896, Karton 303, reports no. 74, March 5; no. 77, March 12; and no. 90, 26 March 1896.

Germany

German Foreign Ministry Archives, 1871–1914. *Akten des Auswärtigen Amtes, 1871–1914, vol. 10. Das türkische Problem 1895.* Berlin, 1923, Report no. 162/2444, 26 October 1895, pp. 84–5.
German Foreign Ministry Archives, Türkei 159, no. 2, band 12, A18643, no. 69 secret, 14 October 1910 report.
German Foreign Ministry Archives. Many of the volumes in the Türkei 183 series.

French

Archives du Ministère des Affaires Étrangères: N.S. 1, Turquie, Politique Intérieure. Jeuns Turcs. Paris, 11 Feb. 1897.
French Foreign Ministry Archives (Paris), N. S. Turquie: Jeuns Turcs, vol. 7, pp. 92–7.
France. Ministère des Affaires Etrangères, Commission de Publication des Documents Rélatifs aux Origines de la Guerre de 1914. *Documents diplomatiques français (1871–1914)*, 1er série, *(1871–1900)*, vol. 11. Paris, Imprimerie Nationale, 1947.

Great Britain

Blue Book, Turkey, no. 1, 1890.
Blue Book, Turkey, no. 4, 1880.
Blue Book, Turkey, no. 6, 1881.
Blue Book, Turkey, no. 8, 1896.
Blue Book, Turkey, no. 16, 1877.
British Foreign Office Archives. Kew, London.

Turkey. Annual Report for 1910.

British Documents on the Origins of the War 1898–1914, 2 vols. G. P. Gooch and Harold Temperley, eds. London, 1926.

British Documents on the Origins of the War 1898–1914. Vol. 5: *The Near East.* G.P. Gooch and Harold Temperley, eds. London, 1928.

Reports from Her Majesty's Consuls Relating to the Condition of the Christians in Turkey, 1867 volume.

The Treatment of the Armenians in the Ottoman Empire, 1915–1916. British Foreign Office. Miscellaneous Doc. no. 31. London, 1916.

Turkey

Tableaux indiquant le nombre des divers éléments de la population dans l'Empire Ottoman au 1er Mars 1330 (14 Mars 1914). Istanbul, Zellitch Bros., 1919.

Takvimi Vekâyi issues (the official gazette of the Ottoman government covering the trials of the Turkish Military Tribunal prosecuting the authors of the Armenian genocide).

T.B.B.M. Gizli Celse Zabıtları (The transcripts of the secret sessions of the Grand National Assembly of Turkey), vol. 1. Ankara, 1985.

T.C. Başbakanlık Devlet Arşiveleri Genel Müdürlüğü. Osmanlı Arşivi Daire Başkanlığı, *Osmanlı Belgelerinde Ermeniler, 1915–1920* (The Armenians in Ottoman Documents, 1915–1920). Ankara, 1994.

United States

Congressional Record, 54th Congress, 1st sess., vol. 28, part 1.

Papers Relating to Foreign Relations of the United States, 1864, IV.

U.S. National Archives. R.G. (Record Group) Series 59.

Israel

Armenian Patriarchate Archive. Series H. 17.

Secondary Sources. Published in Books
Turkish

Akçam, Taner. *Islam'da Hoşgörü ve Sınırı* (Tolerance and its limits in Islam). Ankara, Başak, 1994.

———. *Siyasi Kültürümüzde Zulüm ve Işkence* (Atrocity and torture in our political culture). Istanbul, Yletişim Publications, 1992.

Avcıoğlu, Doğan. *Milli Kurtuluş Tarihi* (History of the National Liberation) vol. 3. Istanbul, Istanbul Publishers, 1974.

Han Abdülhamid, Sultan II. *Devlet ve Memleket Görüşlerim* (My views on state and country), A. Alaeddin Çetin ve Ramazan Yıldız, eds. Istanbul, Çığır Publications, 1976.

Akşin, Sina. *100 Soruda Jön Turkler ve Ittihad ve Terakki* (The Young Turks and Ittihad in the context of 100 questions). Istanbul, Gerçek, 1980.

Bayur, Y. H. *Türk Inkilâbı Tarihi*, vol. 2, part 2, Ankara, 1983; vol. 2, part 4. Ankara, Turkish Historical Society, 1952.

Beşikci, Ismail. *Doğu Anadolunun Düzeni: Sosyo-Ekonomik ve Etnik Temeller* (Eastern Anatolian policies: ethnic and socioeconomic foundations). Erzurum, Sumer, 1969.

van Bruinessen, Martin. *Ağa Şeyh ve Devlet* (Ağa Şeyh and the State). Ankara, Özge, 1992.

Celil, Celile. *Yüzyıl Osmanlı Imparatorluğu'nda Kürtler* (The Kurds in a century of Ottoman rule), trans. From Russian by M. Demir. Ankara, Özge Publications, 1991.

Cemal Paşa, *Hatıralar* (Memoirs), completed and edited by Behçet Cemal, his son. Istanbul, Çağdaş, 1977.

Çavdar, Tevfik. *Talât Paşa*. Ankara, Dost, 1984.

Cevdet Paşa, A. *Tezâkir* (Memoirs), vol. 1, C. Baysun, ed. Ankara, Turkish Historical Society, 1953.

Cinlioglu, H. T. *Osmanlılar Zamanında Tokat* (Tokat in the Ottoman era). Part 3. Tokat, 1951.

Danişmend, Ismail Hami. *Izahlı Osmanlı Tarihi Kronolojisi* (Annotated chronology of Ottoman history), vol. 4. Istanbul, Türkiye Publications, 1961.

Demirel, Muammer. *Birinci Dünya Harbinde Erzurum ve Çevresinde Ermeni Harektleri* (Armenian actions in and around Erzurum in World War I). Ankara, General Staff Publication, 1996.

Falih Rıfkı Atay, *Çankaya*. Istanbul, Sena, 1980.

———. *Zeytindağı* (Mt. Olive). Istanbul, Ayyıldız, 1981.

Gazigiray, A. Alper. *Osmanlılardan Günümüze Kadar Vesikalarla Ermeni Terrörürün Kaynakları* (Documentary sources of Armenian terror from Ottoman times to the present). Istanbul, Gözen, 1982.

Gövsa, Ibrahim A. *Türk Meşhurları Ansiklopedisi* (The encyclopedia of famous Turks). n.p., 1946.

Halil Paşa. *Bitmeyen Savaş* (A fight without end). M.T. Sorgun, ed. Istanbul, Yedigün, 1972.

Hocaoğlu, Mehmed. *Abdülhamit Hanın Muhtıraları* (The memoranda of Abdülhamit). Istanbul, Türkiyat, 1989.

———. *Arşiv Vesikaları ile Tarihte Ermeni Mezâlimi ve Ermeniler* (Documents on Armenian atrocities in the course of history and the Armenians). Istanbul, Anda, 1976.

Ismet, G. Imset. *PKK: Ayrılıkçi Şiddetin 20 Yılı (1973–1992)*. (The severity of twenty years of separatism). Ankara, Turkish Daily News Publications, 1993.

Kabacalı, Alpay. *Tarihimizde Kürtler ve Ayaklanmaları.* (The Kurds and their uprising in our history). Istanbul, Cem Press, 1991.

Kadri, Hüseyin Kâzım. *Balkanlardan Hicaza. Imparatorluğun Tasfiyesi. 10 Temmuz Inkilâbı ve Netayici.* (The liquidation of the Empire. From the Balkans to Hicaz. The July 10 revolution and its outcome). Istanbul, Pınar, 1992.

Karaosmanoğlu, Yakup Kadri, *Hüküm Gecesi* (The night of decision), 2d ed. A. Özkırımlı, ed. Istanbul, Iletişim, 1987.

Karabekir, Kâzım, *Istiklâl Harbimız* (Our War of Independence), 2d ed. Istanbul, Türkiye Publishing House, 1969.

Kuran, Ahmed Bedevi. *Inkilâb Tarihimiz ve Ittihad ve Terakki* (The history of our revolution and union and progress). Istanbul, Tan, 1948.

Kutay, Cemal. *Talât Paşanin Gurbet. Hatıraları* (The memoirs of Talât Paşa in exile). 3 vols. Istanbul, Düzgü Press, 1983.

———. *Türkiye Istiklâl ve Hürriyet Mücadeleleri Tarihi* (The history of Turkey's struggles for independence and freedom), vol. 13. Istanbul, Tarih, 1960.

Okyar, Fethi. *Uç Devirde Bir Adam* (A man of three eras), C. Kutay, ed. Istanbul, Tercüman, 1980.

Öztürk, Kâzım. *Türkiye Cumhuriyeti Hükümetleri ve Programları* (The governments of the Turkish Republic and their programs). Istanbul, AK Publications, 1968, pp. 127, 130, 196.

Parlar, Suat *Osmanlı'dan Günümüze Gizli Devlet* (The secret State. From Ottoman days to the present). Istanbul, Spatakus, 1996.

Sabis, Ali Ihsan. *Harp Hatıralarım* (My war memoirs) vol. 2. Ankara, Güneş, 1951.

Said Paşanın Hatıratı (Memoirs of Said Paşa), vol. 1. Istanbul, 1328 (old style).

Talat Paşanın Hatıraları (Talat Paşa's memoirs). Enver Bolayir, ed. Istanbul, Güven, 1946.

Timuroğlu, Vecihi. *Dersim Tarihi.* Ankara, Yurt Kitap-Yayın, 1991.

Tunaya, Tarık Zafer. *Türkiyede Siyasal Partiler 1859–1952* (Political parties in Turkey 1859–1952). Istabul, Doğan Bros., 1952.

Vardar, Galib. *Ittihad ve Terakki Içinde Dönenler,* S.N. Tansu, ed. Istanbul, Inkilâp, 1960.

Yaman, Abdullah. *Ermeni Meselesi ve Türkiye* (The Armenian question and Turkey). Istanbul, Otag, 1973.

Yıldırım, Ali. *Osmanlı Engizisyonu* (The Ottoman Inquisition). Ankara, Emel, 1996.

English

The Eastern Question and the Armenians (pamphlet) London, 1878.

Forced Evictions and Destruction of Villages in Dersim (Tunceli) and the Western Part of Bingöl, Turkish Kurdistan, September-November 1994. Amsterdam, SNK (Netherlands Kurdistan Society), 1995.

The Kurdish Nationalist Movement in the 1990s: Its Impact on Turkey and the Middle East, Robert Olson, ed. Lexington, The University Press of Kentucky, 1996.

The Life of Midhat Pasha. A Record of His Services, Political Reforms, Banishment, and Judicial Murder, Derived from Private Documents and Reminiscences by His Son Ali Haydar Bey. London, John Murray, 1903.

Turkey: A Past and a Future. London, Hodder and Stoughton, 1917.

Aflalo, F. G. *Regilding the Crescent.* Philadelphia, Lippincott, 1911.

Atamian, Sarkis. *The Armenian Community. The Historical Development of a Social and Ideological Conflict.* New York, Philosophical Library, 1955.

Berkes, Niyazi. *The Development of Secularism in Turkey.* Montreal, McGill University Press, 1964.

Bryce, James. *Transcaucasia and Ararat.* London, Macmillan, 1896.

Bryce, Viscount (and Arnold J. Toynbee). *The Treatment of the Armenians in the Ottoman Empire 1915–16.* (Official publication of the British Foreign Office), miscellaneous doc. no. 31, London, 1916.

Childs, W. J. *Across Asia Minor on Foot*, 3d ed. Edinburgh and London, W. Blackwood, 1918.

Clark, Edson L. *Turkey.* New York, Collier, 1902.

Creagh, James. *Armenians, Koords, and Turks*, vol. 2. London, S. Tinsley, 1880.

Curzon, Robert. *Armenia: A Year at Erzeroum, and on the Frontiers of Russia, Turkey and Persia.* London, John Murray, 1854.

Dadrian, Vahakn N. *The History of the Armenian Genocide: Ethnic Conflict from the Balkans to Anatolia to the Caucasus.* 4th enlarged ed. Oxford and Providence, Berghahn Books, 1997.

Davis, William S. *A Short History of the Near East.* New York, Macmillan, 1923.

Edib, Halide, *Memoirs.* New York, Century, 1926

Emin, Ahmed. *Turkey in the First World War.* New Haven, Yale University Press, 1930.

Fenwich, Charles G. *International Law*, 2d ed. New York, D. Appleton-Century, 1934.

Gallenga, A. *Two Years of the Eastern Question*, vol. 1. London, Samuel Tinsley, 1877.

Gibb, H. A. R. and Harold Bowen. *Islamic Society and the West*, I, part 2. New York, Oxford University Press, 1962.

Gunter, Michael. *The Kurds in Turkey: A Political Dilemma.* Colorado, Westview Press, 1990.

Helmreich, Paul C. *From Paris to Sèvres: The Partition of the Ottoman Em-*

pire at the Peace Conference, 1919–1920. Columbus, Ohio State University Press, 1974.

Hepworth, George H. *Through Armenia on Horseback*. New York, Dutton, 1898.

Karpat, Kemal H. *Ottoman Population 1830–1914 Demographic and Social Characteristics*. Madison, University of Wisconsin Press, 1985.

Kemal Bey. *The Memoirs of Kemal Bey*. Summerville Story, ed. London, Constable and Co., 1920.

Kortepeter, C. Max. *Ottoman Imperialism During the Reformation: Europe and the Caucasus*. New York, New York University Press, 1972.

Langer, William L. *The Diplomacy of Imperialism 1890–1902*. vol. 1. New York, A. Knopf, 1935.

Lewis, Bernard. *The Emergence of Modern Turkey*, 2d ed. London, Oxford, New York, 1968.

Lynch, H. F. B. *Armenia: Travels and Studies*, 2 vols. Beirut, Khayats, [1901]1965.

MacColl, Malcolm. *The Sultan and the Powers*. London, Longmans, Green and Co., 1896.

———. *England's Responsibility Towards Armenia*. London, Longmans, Green, and Co., 1895, 1896.

Marashlian, Levon. *Politics and Demography: Armenians, Turks, and Kurds in the Ottoman Empire*. Cambridge, MA, Zoryan Institute, 1991.

Mardin, Şerif. *The Genesis of Young Ottoman Thought*. Princeton, NJ, Princeton University Press, 1962.

McCarthy, Justin. *Muslims and Minorities. The Population of Ottoman Anatolia and the End of the Empire*. New York, New York University Press, 1983.

Melson, Robert. *Revolution and Genocide: On the Origins of the Armenian Genocide and the Holocaust*. Chicago, University of Chicago Press,1993.

Morgenthau, Henry. *Ambassador Morgenthau's Story*. Garden City, NY, Doubleday, Page, 1918.

Mundy, Talbot. *The Eye of Zeitoun*. New York, McKinley, Stone, and Mackenzie, 1920.

Nalbandian, Louise. *The Armenian Revolutionary Movement. The Development of Armenian Political Parties through the Nineteenth Century*. Berkeley and Los Angeles, University of California Press, 1963.

Nansen, Fridjof. *Armenia and the Near East*. London, George Allen and Unwin, 1928.

De Nogales, Rafael. *Four Years Beneath the Crescent*. Muna Lee, trans. New York, Scribner's, 1926.

Olson, Robert, ed. *The Kurdish Nationalist Movement in the 1990s: Its Impact on Turkey and the Middle East*. Lexington, The University Press of Kentucky, 1996.

Ramsay, W. M. *Impressions of Turkey during Twelve Years' Wanderings*. New York, London, Hodder and Staughton, 1897.

Rolin-Jaquemeyns, M. G. *Armenia, the Armenians, and the Treaties*. London, John Heywood, 1891.

Servier, André. *Islam and the Psychology of the Musulman*. A. S. Moss-Blundell, trans. London, Chapman and Hall, 1924.

Shaw, S. J. and E. K. Shaw. *History of the Ottoman Empire and Modern Turkey*, vol. 2. New York, Cambridge University Press, 1977.

Temperley, Harold. *Europe in the Nineteenth and Twentieth Centuries (1879–1950)*. 6th ed. London, Longmans, 1962.

Thomas, Lewis and Richard Frye. *The United States and Turkey and Iran*. Cambridge, MA, Harvard University Press, 1951.

Townsend, A. E. *A Military Consul in Turkey*. Philadelphia, London, Lippincott, Seeley, 1910.

Toynbee, Arnold J. *A Study of History* (abridgement of vols. 7–10). New York, 1957.

———. *The Western Question in Greece and Turkey*. Boston, Houghton Mifflin Co., 1922.

———. *Turkey: A Past and a Future*. London, Hodder and Stoughton, 1917.

Walker, Christopher J. *Armenia: The Survival of a Nation*. 2d rev. ed. New York, St. Martin's, 1990.

Whitman, Sidney. *Turkish Memories*. London, Scribner's, 1914.

Young, George. *Contstantinople*. New York, Barnes and Noble, [1926]1992.

German

Alp, Tekin. *Türkismus und Pantürkismus* (Turkism and panturkism). Weimar, Kiepenheuer, 1915.

Banse, Ewald, *Die Länder and Völker der Türkei* (The lands and peoples of Turkey). Berlin, George von Westermann, 1916.

———. *Der arische Orient* (The Arian Orient). Leipzig, B.G. Teubner, 1910.

Christoffel, Ernst. *Zwischen Saat und Ernte* (Between sowing and harvest). Berlin-Friedenau, Verlag der Christlichen Blindemission im Orient, 1933.

Giesl, Baron Wladimir. *Zwei Jahrzehnte im Nahen Osten* (Two decades in the Near East), General-Major R. V. Steinitz, ed. Berlin, Verlag für Kulturpolitik, 1927.

Lepsius, Johannes. *Der Todesgang des armenischen Volkes*. Berlin-Potsdam, Missions Verlag, 1930.

Mandelstam, André. *Das armenische Problem im Lichte des Völker-und Menschenrechts* (The Armenian problem in light of national and human rights). Kiel, University of Kiel Institute for International Law, 1931.

Moltke, Helmuth von. *Briefe über Zustände und Begebenheiten in der Türkei aus den Jahren 1835 bis 1839* (Letters on conditions and events in Turkey in the years 1835–1839), 4th ed. Berlin, E.S. Mittler and Sohn, 1882.

Muhtar Pascha, Mahmud. *Meine Führung im Balkankriege* (My leadership in the 1912 Balkan War), Imhoff Pascha, trans., 5th ed. Berlin, E.S. Mittler and Sohn, 1913.

Pomiankowski, Joseph. *Der Zusammenbruch des Ottomanischen Reiches.* Vienna, Amalthea, [1928]1969.

Rohrbach, Paul. *In Turan und Armenien.* Berlin, Georg1 Stilke, 1898.

Schweiger-Lerchenfeld, Amand Freiherrn von. *Armenien.* Jena, H. Constenoble, 1878.

Wagner, Moritz. *Reise nach Persien und dem Lande der Kurds* (Travel in Persia and the land of the Kurds), vol. 2. Leipzig, Arnoldische, 1852.

Ziemke, Kurt. *Die neue Türkei. Politische Entwicklung* (The new Turkey: Political development). Stuttgart, Berlin, Leipzig, Deutsche Verlags-Anstalt, 1930.

French

Documents Diplomatiques (Livre Jaune). Affaires Arméniennes. Projets de Réformes, 1893–1894. Paris, Impremerie Nationale, 1897.

(Documents Diplomatiques) Livre Jaune. Affaires Arméniennes. Supplément, 1895–1896. Paris, Impremerie Nationale, 1897.

Russes et Turcs: La guerre d'Orient (Russians and Turks: The war in the east), vol. 1. Paris, Librarie de la Société Anonyme, 1878.

Alem, Jean-Pierre. *L'Armènie.* Paris, 1962.

Benoit-Brunswick. *La verité sur Midhat Pacha.* Paris, E. Leroux, 1877.

Bérard, Victor. *La Politique du Sultan.* 3d ed. Paris, Michel Lévy Frères, 1897.

De Chalet, Comte. *Arménie Kurdistan et Mésopotamie.* Paris, Plon, Nourrit and Co., 1892.

de Contenson, Ludovic. *Chrétiens et Musulmans: Voyages et Études* (Christians and Muslims: Travels and studies). Paris, Plon, Nourrit and Co., 1901.

Cuinet, Vital. *La Turquie d'Asie* (Asiatic Turkey), I. Paris, Leroux, 1891.

Doumergue, E. *L'Arménie, les massacres et la question d'Orient.* 2d ed. Paris, Librarie de Foi et Vie, 1916.

Du Velay, *Essai sur l'histoire Financière de la Turquie* (Essay on the fiscal history of Turkey). Paris, Rousseau, 1903.

Engelhardt, E. *La Turquie et le Tanzimat, histoire des réformes dans l'Empire Ottoman depuis 1826 jusqu'à nos jours* (Turkey and the Tanzimat, history of reforms from 1826 up to our time), vol. 1. Paris, Cotillon and Co., 1882; vol. 2. Paris, Cotillon and Co., 1884.

Izzet-Fuad, Général. *Autres Occasions Perdues...Critique Stratégique de la Campagne d'Asie Mineure 1877–1878.* Paris, R. Chapelot, 1908.

de la Jonquière, Le Viscomte. *Histoire de l'Empire Ottoman.* New and rev. ed., vol. 2. Paris, Librarie Hachette, 1914.

Kévorkian, Raymond and Paul Paboudjian. *Les Arméniens dans l'Empire Ottoman à la veille du Génocide.* Paris, Arhis, 1992.

Langlois, Victor. *Les Arméniens de la Turquie et les Massacres du Taurus* (The Armenians of Turkey and the Taurus massacres). Paris, Claye, 1863.

——. *Voyage de la Cilicie et dans les montagnes du Taurus éxecuté pendant les années 1852–3* (Travel in Cilicia and the Taurus Mountains undertaken in the years 1852–3). Paris, Duprat, 1861.

Mandelstam, André. *Le Sort de l'Empire Ottoman* (The fate of the Ottoman Empire). Paris, Payot, 1917.

Nansen, Fridjoy. *L'Arménie et le Proche Orient.* Paris, Librarie Orientaliste, 1928.

Özkaya, Inayetullah Cemal. *Le Peuple Arménien et les Tentatives de rendre en servitude le peuple Turk* (The Armenian people and the attempts to reduce the Turkish people to servitude). Istanbul, Ankara, Institut pour l'étude de la Turquie, 1971.

Vandal, Albert. *Les Arméniens et la Réforme de la Turquie.* Paris, Plon, 1897.

Armenian

Aghayan, Dzadour. *Antranik. Tarashrtchan. Tebker* (Antranik. An Epoch. Events. Figures). Yerevan, Armenia, IHFA Publication, 1994.

Haygashen (Almanac), 1922.

Aghassee (Garabed Tour-Sarkissian), *Zeitoun yev eer Shurtchanagneru* (Zeitoun and its environs). Rev. ed. Beirut, Sheerag, [1897]1968.

Boghossian, S.G. *Kurderu yev Haigagan Hartzu,* (The Kurds and the Armenian Question). Yerevan, Hayasdan, 1991.

Garibdjanian, Kevork. *Zhovourtagan Heros Antranik* (Popular hero Antranik). Yerevan, Armenia, Hayasdan, 1990.

Harazat Patmutiun Tarono (The authentic history of Taron). Cairo, Sahag-Mesrob, 1962.

Kapigian, Garabed. *Yeğernabadoum Sepasdio* (The holocaust of Sıvas). Boston, Hairenik, 1924.

Kapigian, Khoren. *Haigagan Hartzu Arevelyan Hartzee Metch 1860–1880* (The Armenian Question within the Eastern Question 1860–1880). Beirut, n.p., 1962.

Khazarian, H. *Tzeghasban Turku* (The genocidal Turk). Beirut, Hamazkayeen, 1968.

Kossian, Father Hagop. *Partzur Haik* (Upper Armenia), I. Vienna, Mechitarian Press, 1925.

Leo [A. Babakhanian], *Tourkahay Heghapochoutian Kagaparapanoutiunu* (The ideology of the Turkish-Armenian revolution), vol. 1. Paris, Bahree, 1934.

Marmarian, Arsen (pen-name of Vahan Totoventz) *Zoravar Antranig yev eer Baderazmneru* (General Antranik and his wars). Istanbul, 1920.

Meliksetian, Vaspour. *Zeitounee Herosamarderu* (The heroic battles of Zeitoun). Yerevan, 1960.

A.N. Munatzaganian and H.G. Hagopian, *Zoravar Antranik* (General Antranik), vol. 1, Moscow, 1991.

Nourikhan, Father Minas. *Badmoutiun Zhamanagagitz 1847–1867*, (Contemporary history, 1847–1867), vol. 2. Venice, St. Lazare, 1896.

————. *Zhamanagagitz Badmoutiun 1868–1878* (Contemporary history, 1868–1878), vol. 3. Venice, St. Lazare, 1907.

Panper Hayasdanee Archivneree (Bulletin of Armenia's archives). Vol. 1, no. 10, 1965.

Sabah-Kulian, *Badaskhanadouneru* (The responsible ones). Beirut, Donikian, [1916]1974.

Sasouni, Garo. *Kurd Azkayeen Zharjoumneru yev Hai-Kurdagan Haraperoutiunneru* (The Kurdish national movements and the Armeno-Kurd relations). Beirut, Hamazkayeen, 1976.

Suni, Armen. *Haigagan Vashdu Antranigee Aratchnortutiamp 1912–1913 Tuaganneroun Balkanian Baderazmoun* (The Armenian company in the 1912–13 Balkan War under the leadership of Antranik). Baku, 1914.

Tchelebian, Antranik. *Zoravar Antranik* (General Antranik). Yerevan, Arevig, 1990.

Varantian, Mikayel. *Haigagan Sharzhman Nakhabadmoutiunu* (The history of the origins of the Armenian Revolutionary Movement), vol. 2. Geneva, Armenian Revolutionary Federation Press, 1914.

Yeramian, Hampartzoum. *Houshartzan Van-Vaspourakanee* (Memorial for Van-Vaspourakan). Alexandria, Egypt, n.p., 1929.

Zaven Arkyebiskobos, *Badriarkayan Housherus, Vaverakirner gev Vugayoutiunner* (My Patriarchal memoirs. Documents and Testimonies). Cairo, Nor Asdgh, 1947.

Zoravar Antranynigee Govgasian Djagadee Badmagan Orakrotiunu. 1914–1917. (General Antranik's historical diary about the Caucasian front 1914–1917). Boston, 1924.

Italian

Latino, Anatolio. (pseudonym of Enrico Vitto), *Gli Armeni e Zeitoun*, vol. 2, 2d ed. Firenze, Bernardo, 1899.

Articles

Turkish

Ballı, Rafet. "Türkiye" in *Kürt Dosyası*. Istanbul, 1991.

Beydilli, Kemal. "1828–1829 Osmanlı -Rus Savaşında Doğu Anadolu'dan Rusya'ya Göçürülen Ermeniler" (On the Armenians who were resettled in

Russia during the 1828–1829 Russo-Turkish War), *Belgeler* (Documents), vol. 13, no. 17. Ankara, 1988.

Küçük, Cevdet. "The Armenian Population in Anatolia in the Nineteenth Century" trans. from Turkish by H. Umune, in *The Eastern Question: Imperialism and the Armenian Community.* Ankara, 1987, p. 79.

Sertoğlu, Mithat. "Türkiyede Ermeni Meselesi" (The Armenian question in Turkey), *Belgelerle Türk Tarih Dergisi* 2 (November 1967), p. 48.

Suphi, Hamdullah, "Ermeniler ve Biz" (The Armenians and Us) *Ikdam.* 17 December 1912.

English

Andrews, Peter A. "Catalogue of Ethnic Groups," *In Ethnic Groups in the Republic of Turkey.* Wiesbaden, Germany, 1989, pp. 53–178.

Bryce, James. "The Future of Asiatic Turkey," *Fortnightly Review* 138, new series (1 June 1878), p. 931.

Dadrian, Vahakn N. "The Armenian Genocide in Official Turkish Records: Collected Essays," special issue of *Journal of Political and Military Sociology,* vol. 22, no. 1. (Summer 1994), 208 pp.

———. "Documentation of the Armenian Genocide in German and Austrian Sources," in Israel W. Charny, ed., *The Widening Circle of Genocide: A Critical Bibliographic Review,* vol. 3. New Brunswick, NJ, 1994, pp. 77–125. Expanded and published as a separate unit, 125pp.

———. "Documentation of the Armenian Genocide in Turkish Sources," in Israel W. Charny, ed., *Genocide: A Critical Bibliographic Review,* vol. 2. London, New York, 1991, pp. 86–138.

———. "The Documentation of the World War I Armenian Massacres in the Proceedings of the Turkish Military Tribunal," *International Journal for Middle East Studies* 23, no. 4 (1991), pp. 549–576.

———. "Factors of Anger and Aggression in Genocide," *Journal of Human Relations* 19, no. 3 (1971), pp. 394–417.

———. "The Naim-Andonian Documents on the World War I Destruction of the Ottoman Armenians: The Anatomy of a Genocide," *International Journal for Middle East Studies* 18, no. 3 (1986), pp. 311–60.

———. "Ottoman Archives and Denial of the Armenian Genocide," *The Armenian Genocide: History, Politics, Ethics.* R. Hovannisian, ed. New York, 1992, pp. 294–7.

———. "The Secret Young-Turk Ittihadist Conference and the Decision for the World War I Genocide of the Armenians," *Holocaust and Genocide Studies* 7, no. 2. (Fall 1993), pp. 173–201.

Davison, Roderic H. "The Armenian Crisis: 1912–1914," *American Historical Review* 43, no. 3 (April 1948), pp. 481–505.

———. "Turkish Attitudes Concerning Christian-Muslim Equality in the Nineteenth Century," *American Historical Review* 59 (July 1954), pp. 844–64.

Dillon, Emile J. "The Fiasco in Armenia," *Fortnightly Review* 59 (March 1896), pp. 341–58.

An Eastern Statesman. "Contemporary Life and Thought in Turkey." *Contemporary Review* 37 (Feb. 1880), pp. 334–56.

Etmekjian, Lilian. "The Armenian National Assembly of Turkey," *Armenian Review* 29, no. 1–113. (Spring 1976), pp. 38–52.

Hoffman, Tessa and Gerayer Koutcharian. "The History of Armenian-Kurdish Relations in the Ottoman Empire," *The Armenian Review* vol. 39, no. 4. (Winter, 1986).

Karpat, Kemal H. "Ottoman Population Records and the Census of 1881/2–1893," *International Journal of Middle Eastern Studies* 9 (May 1978), pp. 227–74.

———. "The Transformation of the Ottoman State, 1789–1908," *International Journal of Middle East Studies* 3 (1972).

Kuran, Ercümend. "Küçük Said Paşa (1840–1914) as a Turkish Modernist," *International Journal of Middle East Studies* 1 (1970).

Levene, Mark. "Yesterday's Victims, Today's Perpetrators?: Considerations on Peoples and Territories of the Former Ottoman Empire," *Terrorism and Political Violence* vol. 6, no.4 (Winter 1994), pp. 446–8.

Melson, Robert. "A Theoretical Inquiry into the Armenian Massacres of 1894–1896," *Comparative Studies in History and Society* 24, no. 3 (July 1982), pp. 481–509.

Mutlu, Servet. "Ethnic Kurds in Turkey: A Demographic Study" *International Journal of Middle East Studies* 28, 4 (1996), pp. 517–41.

Nalbandian, Vartouhie. "The Armenian Revolutionary Movement," *Armenian Review* 2, nos. 4–8 (Winter 1949–50).

Pears, Sir Edwin. "Christians and Islam in Turkey," *Century* 63 (February 1913).

Sarkissian, Arshag O. "Concert Diplomacy and the Armenians 1890–1897," in Arshag O. Sarkissian, *Studies in Diplomatic History and Historiography*, London, Longmans, Green, 1961, pp. 48–75.

———. "History of the Armenian Question to 1885," *University of Illinois Bulletin* 35, no. 80 (3 June 1938), pp. 1–151.

Zamir, Meir. "Population Statistics of the Ottoman Empire in 1914 and 1919," *Middle Eastern Studies* 17 (1981), p. 86.

German

La Barbe, "Die Steuern im türkischen Armenien und die Ursachen der armenischen Bewegung" (Taxes in Turkish Armenia and the causes of the Armenian movement), *Neue Zeit* 16 (1897).

Jäckh, Ernst, "Vorderaien nach dem Balkankrieg" *Asiatisches Jahrbuch* (1913).

Schweiger-Lerchenfeld, Freiherrn von. "Das neue vilayet Van" (The new

province Van), *Österreichische Monatsschrift für den Orient* (1877).
Supan, A. "Die Verbreitung der Armenier in der asiatischen Türkei und in Transkaukasien" (The distribution of the Armenians in Asiatic Turkey and Transcaucasia), A. Supan, ed., (based on the compilations of Lieutenant-General G. L. Selenoy and N. ven Seidlitz) in *Petermann's Geographische Mitteilungen* 42 (1896), pp. 1–10.

French

Pinon, René. "La Liquidation de L'Empire Ottoman," *Revue des Deux Mondes* 53 (September 1919).
Zarzecki, S. "La question Kurdo-arménienne," *Revue du Paris* (April 1914).

Armenian

Anoushavan. "Zeitounee Antzialeetz yev Nergayeetz," (On the past and present of Zeitoun), in *Araks* (St. Petersburg, Russia) I (November 1887), pp. 105–29.
Bozadjian, Püzant. "Tebee Ayash. Heen u Nor Housher" (To Ayash: Old and New Memories) in *Houshartzan April Dasnoumegee* (Memories for April 11[24]). Istanbul, 1919.
Der Ghevontian, A. N. "Hai Zhoghovourtee Vidjagu Khalifayutian Deerabedoutyan Nerko" (The condition of the Armenian people under the domination of the caliphate), *Lraper* (publication of the State University of Yerevan) 4 (April 1975), pp. 74–88.
Colonel A.H. Haroutunian, "Antraniku Vorbes Mardig yer Zoravar" (Antranik as a fighter and a general). *Badmapanasiragan Hantes*, vol. 28, no. 1 (1965).
'Sarkis Pteyani Hushere' [The Memoirs of Sarkis Pteyan] in *Harazat Patmutiun Tarono*. Aghan Daronetzee ed., Cairo, 1962.

Newspapers

Turkish

Dunya; Milliyet; Tercüman; Tercümanı Hakikat, Ikdam.

British

Times.

Armenian

Dzagadamard; Hairenik; Huntchak; Jogovourtee Tzain; Massis; Nor Giank; Pountch; Püzantion;Tashink; Zhamanag.

French

La Liberté; Renaissance; Stamboul.

German

Neue Zeit
Osmanischer Lloyd.

Russian

Kievskaya Misl
Kolos Moskoy.

Name Index

Subject Index